DISTRIBUTED AND PARALLEL SYSTEMS
CLUSTER AND
GRID COMPUTING

THE KLUWER INTERNATIONAL SERIES IN ENGINEERING AND COMPUTER SCIENCE

DISTRIBUTED AND PARALLEL SYSTEMS
CLUSTER AND
GRID COMPUTING

edited by

Zoltán Juhász
University of Veszprém, Veszprém, Hungary
Péter Kacsuk
MTA SZTAKI, Budapest, Hungary
Dieter Kranzlmüller
Johannes Kepler University, Linz, Austria

 Springer

EDITORS:

Zoltán Juhász
University of Veszprém
Veszprém, Hungary
juhasz@irt.vein.hu

Péter Kacsuk
MTA SZTAKI
Budapest Hungary
kacsuk@sztaki.hu

Dieter Kranzlmüller
Johannes Kepler Univeristy
Linz Austria
dk@gup.jku.at

DISTRIBUTED AND PARALLEL SYSTEMS: CLUSTER AND GRID COMPUTING
edited by Zoltán Juhász, Péter Kacsuk, Dieter Kranzlmüller
Kluwer International Series in Engineering and Computer Science Volume 777

A C.I.P. Catalogue record for this book is available from the Library of Congress.

ISBN 0-387-23094-7   e-ISBN 0-387-23096-3
Printed on acid-free paper.

Printed in the United States of America.

9 8 7 6 5 4 3 2 1   SPIN 11055273, 11321613

springeronline.com

Contents

Preface   ix

Part I Grid Systems

glogin - Interactive Connectivity for the Grid   3
Herbert Rosmanith and Jens Volkert

Parallel Program Execution Support in the JGrid System   13
Szabolcs Pota, Gergely Sipos, Zoltan Juhasz and Peter Kacsuk

VL-E: Approaches to Design a Grid-Based Virtual Laboratory   21
Vladimir Korkhov, Adam Belloum and L.O. Hertzberger

Scheduling and Resource Brokering within the Grid Visualization Kernel 29
Paul Heinzlreiter, Jens Volkert

Part II Cluster Technology

Message Passing vs. Virtual Shared Memory, a Performance Comparison   39
Wilfried N. Gansterer and Joachim Zottl

MPI-I/O with a Shared File Pointer Using a Parallel Virtual File System 47
Yuichi Tsujita

An Approach Toward MPI Applications in Wireless Networks   55
Elsa M. Macías, Alvaro Suárez, and Vaidy Sunderam

Deploying Applications in Multi-SAN SMP Clusters   63
Albano Alves, António Pina, José Exposto and José Rufino

Part III Programming Tools

Monitoring and Program Analysis Activities with DeWiz   73
Rene Kobler, Christian Schaubschläger, Bernhard Aichinger,
Dieter Kranzlmüller, and Jens Volkert

Integration of Formal Verification and Debugging Methods in
P-GRADE Environment   83
Róbert Lovas, Bertalan Vécsei

Tools for Scalable Parallel Program Analysis - Vampir NG and DeWiz   93
Holger Brunst, Dieter Kranzlmüller, Wolfgang E. Nagel

Process Migration In Clusters and Cluster Grids   103
József Kovács

Part IV P-GRADE

Graphical Design of Parallel Programs With Control Based on Global
Application States Using an Extended P-GRADE Systems   113
M. Tudruj, J. Borkowski and D. Kopanski

Parallelization of a Quantum Scattering Code using P-GRADE 121
Ákos Bencsura and György Lendvay

Traffic Simulation in P-Grade as a Grid Service   129
T. Delaitre, A. Goyeneche, T. Kiss, G. Terstyanszky, N. Weingarten,
P. Maselino, A. Gourgoulis, and S.C. Winter.

Development of a Grid Enabled Chemistry Application   137
István Lagzi, Róbert Lovas, Tamás Turányi

Part V Applications

Supporting Native Applications in WebCom-G   147
John P. Morrison, Sunil John and David A. Power

Grid Solution for E-Marketplaces Integrated with Logistics 155
L. Bruckner and T. Kiss

Incremental Placement of Nodes in a Large-Scale Adaptive Distributed   165
Multimedia Server
Tibor Szkaliczki, Laszlo Boszormenyi

Component Based Flight Simulation in DIS Systems   173
Krzysztof Mieloszyk, Bogdan Wiszniewski

Part VI Algorithms

Management of Communication Environments for Minimally Synchronous
Parallel ML   185
Frédéric Loulergue

Analysis of the Multi-Phase Copying Garbage Collection Algorithm   193
Norbert Podhorszki

A Concurrent Implementation of Simulated Annealing and Its Application
to the VRPTW Optimization Problem   201
Agnieszka Debudaj-Grabysz and Zbigniew J. Czech

Author Index   211

Preface

DAPSYS (Austrian-Hungarian Workshop on Distributed and Parallel Systems) is an international conference series with biannual events dedicated to all aspects of distributed and parallel computing. DAPSYS started under a different name in 1992 (Sopron, Hungary) as a regional meeting of Austrian and Hungarian researchers focusing on transputer-related parallel computing; a hot research topic of that time. A second workshop followed in 1994 (Budapest, Hungary). As transputers became history, the scope of the workshop widened to include parallel and distributed systems in general and the 1st DAPSYS in 1996 (Miskolc, Hungary) reflected the results of these changes. Since then, DAPSYS has become an established international event attracting more and more participants every second year. After the successful DAPSYS'98 (Budapest) and DAPSYS 2000 (Balatonfüred), DAPSYS 2002 finally crossed the border and visited Linz, Austria.

The fifth DAPSYS workshop is organised in Budapest, the capital of Hungary, by the MTA SZTAKI Computer and Automation Research Institute. As in 2000 and 2002, we have the privilege again to organise and host DAPSYS together with the EuroPVM/ MPI conference. While EuroPVM/MPI is dedicated to the latest developments of the PVM and MPI message passing environments, DAPSYS focuses on general aspects of distributed and parallel systems. The participants of the two events will share invited talks, tutorials and social events fostering communication and collaboration among researchers. We hope the beautiful scenery and rich cultural atmosphere of Budapest will make it an even more enjoyable event.

Invited speakers of DAPSYS and EuroPVM/MPI 2004 are Al Geist, Jack Dongarra, Gábor Dózsa, William Gropp, Balázs Kónya, Domenico Laforenza, Rusty Lusk and Jens Volkert. A number of tutorials extend the regular program of the conference providing an opportunity to catch up with latest developments: *Using MPI-2: A Problem-Based Approach* (William Gropp and Ewing Lusk), *Interactive Applications on the Grid - the CrossGrid Tutorial* (Tomasz Szepieniec, Marcin Radecki and Katarzyna Rycerz), *Production Grid systems and their programming* (Péter Kacsuk, Balázs Kónya, Péter Stefán).

The DAPSYS 2004 Call For Papers attracted 35 submissions from 15 countries. On average we had 3.45 reviews per paper. The 23 accepted papers cover a broad range of research topics and appear in six conference sessions: Grid Systems, Cluster Technology, Programming Tools, P-GRADE, Applications and Algorithms.

The organisation of DAPSYS could not be done without the help of many people. We would like to thank the members of the Programme Committee and the additional reviewers for their work in refereeing the submitted papers and ensuring the high quality of DAPSYS 2004. The local organisation was managed by Judit Ajpek from CongressTeam 2000 and Agnes Jancso from MTA SZTAKI. Our thanks is due to the sponsors of the DAPSYS/EuroPVM joint event: IBM (platinum), Intel (gold) and NEC (silver).

Finally, we are grateful to Susan Lagerstrom-Fife and Sharon Palleschi from Kluwer Academic Publishers for their endless patience and valuable support in producing this volume, and David Nicol for providing the WIMPE conference management system for conducting the paper submission and evaluation.

PÉTER KACSUK

ZOLTÁN JUHÁSZ

DIETER KRANZLMÜLLER

Program Committee

I

GRID SYSTEMS

GLOGIN - INTERACTIVE CONNECTIVITY FOR THE GRID*

Herbert Rosmanith and Jens Volkert
GUP, Joh. Kepler University Linz
Altenbergerstr. 69, A-4040 Linz, Austria/Europe
hr@gup.uni-linz.ac.at

Abstract

Todays computational grids are used mostly for batch processing and through-put computing, where jobs are submitted to a queue, processed, and finally de-livered for post-mortem analysis. The *glogin* tool provides a novel approach for grid applications, where interactive connections are required. With the solution implemented in *glogin*, users are able to utilize the grid for interactive applica-tions much in the same way as on standard workstations. This opens a series of new possibilities for next generation grid software.

Keywords: grid computing, interactivity

1.   Introduction

Grid environments are todays most promising computing infrastructures for computational science [FoKe99], which offer batch processing over networked resources. However, even in a grid environment, it may sometimes be neces-sary to log into a grid node. Working on a node with an interactive command-shell is much more comfortable for many tasks. For example, one might want to check the log files of a job. Without an interactive shell, it would be neces-sary to submit another job for the same result. This is much more impractical than interactive access to the system.

Today, the administrators of such grid nodes accommodate this by giving their users UNIX accounts. This has some disadvantages. Firstly, user ad-ministration also has to be done on the UNIX level. This is an unnecessary additional expense, since – from the grid point of view – we are already able to identify the users by examining their certificates. Secondly, access to shell

*This work is partially supported by the EU CrossGrid project, "Development of Grid Environment for Interactive Applications", under contract IST-2001-32243.

functionality like telnet or even secure shell [Ylon96], may be blocked by fire-wall administrators. This leads to configurations where users are given accounts on multiple machines (one without the administrative restrictions of a prohibitive network configuration) only to be able to bounce off to the final grid node. No need to say, that this is a very uncomfortable situation for both the users and the administrators.

The above mentioned problem is addressed in this paper by focusing on the following question: Is there a way to somehow connect to the grid node? The resulting solution as described below is based on the following idea: in order to submit jobs, one has to be able to at least contact the gatekeeper. Why don't we use this connection for the interactive command-shell we desire? The way to do this is described in this paper and has been implemented as the prototype tool *glogin*[1].

As we work with our shell, we will recognise that we have got "true interactivity" in the grid. Keystrokes are sent to the grid-node only limited by the speed of the network. Based on this approach, we might now ask how we can control any interactive grid-application, not just shells.

This paper is organised as follows: Section 2 provides an overview of the approach: it shows how to overcome the limitations of the Globus-gatekeeper and get interactive connections. In Section 3, the details of how to establish a secure interactive connection and how to run interactive commands (such as shells and others) are shown. Section 4 compares related work in this area, before an outlook on future work concludes this paper.

2.   Overview of Approach

Limitations of Globus-Gatekeeper

As of today, various implementations of grid-middleware exist. However, *glogin* has been developed for the Globus-Toolkit [GTK], an open source software toolkit used for building grids. GT2 is the basic system used in several grid-projects, including the EU CrossGrid project [Cros01].

A central part of GT is the Globus-gatekeeper which was designed for a batch-job-entry system. As such, it does not allow for bidirectional communication as required by an interactive shell. Looking at the Globus programming API, we have to understand that the connection to the Globus-gatekeeper allows transportation of data in one direction only. This is done by the Globus GASS server, a https-listener (Globus transfers all data by means of http/s), which is set up as part of the application, reads data from the gatekeeper and delivers it to the standard output file descriptor. A possibility for transporting data in the opposite direction using the currently established gatekeeper–GASS server connection is not available.

In addition, there is another batch-job-attribute of the Globus-gatekeeper which turns out to be preventing the implementation of an interactive shell. It has been observed that data sent from the grid is stored into the so called "GASS cache". There seem to be two different polling intervals at which it is emptied: If a program terminates fast enough, the GASS cache is emptied at program termination time, otherwise, the GASS cache is emptied every 10 seconds, which means that the data in the cache will be stored past program termination for 10 seconds at worst. As of Globus-2.4, there is no API call to force emptying the cache. Thus, if one needs an interactive shell, a different approach has to be used.

An example demonstrates this situation. Assuming we have a shell script named "count.sh", which outputs an incremented number every second:

```
i=0
while : ; do
  echo $i
  let i=i+1
  sleep 1
done
```

If we start this job via the Globus-gatekeeper, we will see nothing for the first 10 seconds, then, all at once, the numbers from 0 to 9 will be displayed, followed by a another 10 second pause, after which the numbers from 10 to 19 will be displayed and so on until we terminate the job.

Getting Interactive Connections

The solution is as follows: since the connection between the GASS server and Globus-gatekeeper can only be used for job-submission, a separate connection has to be created. Once the remote program has been started on the grid-node, it has to take care of communication itself[2]. Figure 1 shows the steps performed when creating a separate connection.

(1) the requesting client contacts the gatekeeper
(2) the gatekeeper starts the requested service on the same node via `fork()`
(3) the requested service creates a listener socket
(4) the requesting client directly contacts the requested service

A direct connection without the Globus-gatekeeper's interference between the client and the service has now been established. Interactive data exchange between the peers can now take place. Since both peers make use of the Globus-software, they can establish a secure connection easily.

We have to be aware that this approach only works with the fork at the gatekeeper machine. At the moment, the requested service is required to run

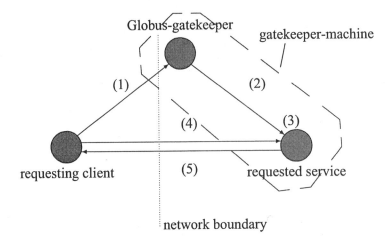

Figure 1.   Setting up a separate connection

on the same machine the gatekeeper is on. It is currently not possible that the requested service is started at some node "behind" the gatekeeper. Since the "worker nodes" can be located in a private network [Rekh96], connection establishment procedure would have to be reversed. However, if we limit ourselves to passing traffic from the (private) worker-nodes to the requesting client via the gatekeeper, we could use traffic forwarding as described below.

3.   Details of the Implementation

Connection Establishment

Figure 1 above is only a general sketch. Below we provide details on implementation. On the whole, it boils down to two questions:

> We talk of a "client" and a "service". What does this mean with respect to "glogin"? What is the "service" if we want a login-shell?

For ease of implementation and for ease of use, *glogin* is both the client and the service. In (1), *glogin* contacts the Globus-gatekeeper by using the Globus job submission API and requests that a copy of itself is started in (2) on the grid-node. *glogin* has an option to differentiate between client and service mode. By specifying -r, *glogin* is instructed to act as the remote part of the connection.

> How does the client know where to contact the service?

With "contact", we mean a TCP-connection. In (3), the service creates a TCP-listener and waits for a connection coming from the client in (4). Therefore it has to somehow communicate its own port-number where it can be reached to the client. At this point in time, the only connection to the client is the Globus-gatekeeper. So the service could just send the port-number to that connection. But as we have learned earlier, all information passed back over this connection is stuck in the GASS cache until either the program terminates, the cache overflows or 10 seconds have elapsed. Since the size of the cache is unknown to us (and we do not want to wait 10 seconds each time we use *glogin*), the method of program-termination has been chosen. So, after *glogin* has acquired a port-number, it returns it via the gatekeeper connection and exits. But just before it exits, it forks a child-process, which will inherit the listener. The listener of course has the same properties as its parent, which means that it can be reached at the same TCP-port address. Therefore, on the other side of the connection, the client is now able to contact the remote *glogin*-process at the given address.

The mechanism of dynamic port selection also honours the contents of the GLOBUS_TCP_PORT_RANGE environment variable, if it is set. In this case, *glogin* will take care of obtaining a port-address itself by randomly probing for a free port within the specified range. If the environment variable is not set, it generously lets the operating system choose one.

Another option is not to use dynamic port probing at all, but a fixed address instead. This can be specified by using the -p parameter. However, this is not good practise, since one can never be sure if this port is already in use. At worst, another instance of *glogin* run by a different user could use the same port, which would result in swapped sessions. *glogin* has code which detects this situation and terminates with an error in this case. Note that this problem is also present when dynamic port selection is used, although it is less likely to occur. In fact, with dynamic port selection, such a situation probably is triggered by an intentional, malicious attempt to hijack a session.

Secure Connection Establishment

The mechanism above demonstrates how a connection can be established. At this point, all we have is plain TCP/IP. If we were to start exchanging data now, it would be easy to eavesdrop on the communication. Therefore, a secure communication can be established by using the same security mechanism that Globus already provides.

The GSS-API [Linn00] is our tool of choice: the client calls "gss_init_sec_context", the service calls the opposite "gss_accept_sec_context". Now we can easily check for hijacked sessions: the "Subject" entry from the certificate is the key to the gridmap-file, which determines the user-id. This user-id has to match the user-id currently in use. If it does not, then the session was hijacked and we have to terminate instantly.

Otherwise, we have a bidirectional connection ready for interactive use. All we have to do now is to actually *instruct* glogin *what* to do.

Getting shells and other commands

glogin is responsible for (secure) communication. Following the UNIX philosophy it does not take care of providing shell-functionality itself, rather, it executes other programs which offer the required functionality. Therefore, why not just execute those programs instead of calling *glogin*? The answer is included in the description above: due to the batch-job-nature of the system, we need a helper-program for interactivity. It is not possible to perform the following command:

```
globusrun -w -r <grid-node> '&(executable=/bin/bash)'
```

and hope to get an interactive shell from the Globus-gatekeeper.

If we want to execute interactive commands on the grid node, there is a second requirement we have to fulfill. There are several ways of exchanging data between programs, even if they are executed on the same machine. For our purpose, we need a data pipe, which is the usual way of exchanging data in UNIX. Commands usually read from standard input and write to standard output, so if we want *glogin* to execute a particular command and pass its information to the client side, we have to intercept these file descriptors. In order to do this, we definitely need what is called a "pipe" in UNIX. But still, if we have *glogin* execute a shell (e.g. bash), we will not see any response. Why is this?

Traffic forwarding

The answer to this last question above is as follow: we have to use what is called a "pseudo-terminal". A pseudo terminal [Stev93] is a bidirectional pipe between two programs, with the operating system performing some special tasks. One of this special task is the conversion of VT100 control characters such as CR (carriage return) or LF (line feed). This is the reason why the command shell did not work: the keyboard generates a CR, but the system library expects to see a LF to indicate the end of a line, EOL.

Now that we are using pseudo terminals (or PTYs), we can exploit an interesting feature: we can place the PTY in "network mode" and assign IP-addresses to it. This is pretty straight forward, because instead of adding network aware code, all we need to do is to connect the "point to point protocol daemon" [Perk90], "pppd" to *glogin*. This turns our gatekeeper-node into a "GSS router". Once the network is properly configured, we can reach all worked nodes by means of IP routing, even though the may be located in a private network.

The downside of this approach is the administrative cost: it requires system administrator privileges to edit the ppp configuration files. It also requires that the pppd is executing with root privileges. This means that, although this solution is very "complete" since it forwards *any* IP traffic, it is probably not very feasible for the standard user.

Another method of forwarding traffic implemented in *glogin* is "port forwarding". Instead of routing complete IP networks, port forwarding allocates specific TCP ports and forwards the traffic it receives to the other side of the tunnel. One port forwarded connection is specified by a 3-tuple consisting of (bind-port, target-host, target-port), it is possible to specify multiple forwarders on both sides of the tunnel. The worker nodes in a private network behind the gatekeeper can connect to the *glogin* process running on the gatekeeper machine, which will send the traffic to the other *glogin* process on the workstation. From there, traffic will be sent to "target-host" at "target-port". Since the target host can also be the address of the workstation, traffic will be sent to some application listening to the target port on the workstation.

As an additional bonus, forwarding of X11 traffic has also been implemented. It differs from port forwarding in that we have to take care of authentication (the X-Server may only accept clients with the matching "cookie"). While port forwarding requires that each new remote connection results in a new local connection, multiple X11 clients are sent to one X11 server only.

4.   Related Work

The importance of an approach as provided by *glogin* is demonstrated by the number of approaches that address a comparable situation or provide a similar solution: NCSA offers a patch [Chas02] to OpenSSH [OSSH] which adds support for grid-authentication. Installation of OpenSSH on grid-nodes usually requires system administrator privileges, so this option might not be available to all users. *gsh/glogin* can be installed everywhere on the grid-node, even in the users home-directory. In contrast to OpenSSH, *glogin* is a very small tool (27 kilobytes at the time of the writing), while sshd2 is about 960 kilobytes in size. Unlike OpenSSH, *glogin* is a single program and provides all its functionality in one file. It does not require helper-programs and configuration-files. This means that *glogin* doesn't even need to be installed - it can be submitted to the Globus-gatekeeper along with the interactive application. OpenSSH requires some installation effort - *glogin* requires none.

Interactive sessions on the grid are also addressed in [Basu03]. This solution is based on using VNC [Rich98], and can be compared to X11-forwarding with *gsh/glogin*. In practise, it has turned out that VNC is a useful but sometimes slow protocol with unreliable graphic operations. With *glogin*, we have a local visualisation frontend and a remote grid-application, which can communicate over a UNIX pipe or TCP sockets. This architecture is not possible when using VNC, since the visualisation frontend will also run remotely. Since this solution doesn't require pseudo-terminals, VPNs with Globus cannot be built.

In [Cros04], a method for redirecting data from the standard input, output and error filedescriptors is shown. This functionality is similar to *glogin's* feature of tunneling data from unnamed UNIX pipes over the grid. However, there is no possibility for redirecting traffic from TCP-sockets. This solution also seems to require the "Migrating Desktop" [KuMi02], a piece of software available for CrossGrid [Cros01]. Therefore, its usage is restricted to the CrossGrid environment. Like the solution presented by HP, building VPNs is not possible since pseudo-terminals are not used.

5.   Conclusions and Future Work

The *glogin* tool described in this paper provides a novel approach to interactive connections on the grid. *glogin* itself has been implemented using the traditional UNIX approach "keep it simple". By using functionality available in the Globus toolkit and the UNIX operating system, interactive shells are made available for grid environments. With *glogin*, users can thus perform interactive commands in the grid just as on their local workstations.

The *glogin* tool is part of the Grid Visualisation Kernel [Kran03], which attempts to provide visualisation services as a kind of grid middleware extension. However, due to successful installation of *glogin* and the many requests received by the grid community, *glogin* has been extracted and packaged as a stand-alone tool.

Besides the basic functionality described in this paper, *glogin* has been extended towards forwarding arbitrary TCP-traffic the same way ssh does: this includes securely tunneling X11-connections over the grid as well as building VPNs and supporting multiple local and remote TCP-port-forwarders. The usability of these features with respect to interactive applications has to be investigated. Further research will explore the cooperation of *glogin* with GT3/OGSA and the PBS jobmanager.

Acknowledgments

The work described in this paper is part of our research on the Grid Visualization Kernel GVK, and we would like to thank the GVK team for their support. More information on GVK can be found at

http://www.gup.uni-linz.ac.at/gvk

Notes

1. More information about *glogin* and executables can be downloaded at
http://www.gup.uni-linz.ac.at/glogin

2. This solution has already been shown at the CrossGrid-Conference in Poznan in summer 2003, but at that time, secure communication between the client and the remote program had not been implemented.

References

[Basu03] Sujoy Basu; Vanish Talwar; Bikash Agarwalla; Raj Kumar: *Interactive Grid Architecture for Application Service Providers*, Technical Report, available on the internet from http://www.hpl.hp.com/techreports/2003/HPL-2003-84R1.pdf
July 2003

[Chas02] Philips, Chase; Von Welch; Wilkinson, Simon: *GSI-Enabled OpenSSH*
available on the internet from http://grid.ncsa.uiuc.edu/ssh/
January 2002

[Cros01] *The EU-CrossGrid Project*, http://www.crossgrid.org

[Cros04] Various Authors: *CrossGrid Deliverable D3.5: Report on the Result of the WP3 2nd and 3rd Prototype* pp 52-57, available on the internet from
http://www.eu-crossgrid.org/Deliverables/M24pdf/CG3.0-D3.5-v1.2-PSNC010-Proto2Status.pdf
February 2004

[FoKe99] Foster, Ian; Kesselmann, Carl: *The Grid, Blueprint for a New Computing Infrastructure*, Morgan Kaufmann Publishers, 1999

[GTK] *The Globus Toolkit*, http://www.globus.org/toolkit

[KuMi02] M. Kupczyk, R. Lichwała, N. Meyer, B. Palak, M. Płóciennik, P. Wolniewicz: *Roaming Access and Migrating Desktop*, Crossgrid Workshop Cracow, 2002

[Kran03] Kranzlmüller, Dieter; Heinzlreiter, Paul; Rosmanith, Herbert; Volkert, Jens: *Grid-Enabled Visualisation with GVK*, Proceedings First European Across Grids Conference, Santiago de Compostela, Spain, pp. 139-146, February 2003

[Linn00] Linn, J.: *Generic Security Service Application Program Interface*, RFC 2743, Internet Engineering Task Force, January 2000

[OSSH] *The OpenSSH Project*, http://www.openssh.org

[Perk90] Perkins; Drew D.: *Point-to-Point Protocol for the transmission of multi-protocol datagrams over Point-to-Point links*, RFC 1171, Internet Engineering Task Force, July 1990

[Rekh96] Rekhter, Yakov; Moskowitz, Robert G.; Karrenberg, Daniel; de Groot, Geert Jan; Lear, Eliot: Address Allocation for Private Internets, RFC 1918, Internet Engineering Task Force, February 1996

[Rich98] T. Richardson, Q. Stafford-Fraser, K. Wood and A. Hopper: *Virtual Network Computing*, IEEE Internet Computing, 2(1):33-38, Jan/Feb 1998

[Stev93] W. Richard Stevens *Advanced Programming in the UNIX Environment*, Addison-Wesley Publishing Company, 1993

[Ylon96] Ylönen, Tatu. *SSH Secure Login Connections over the Internet*, Sixth USENIX Security Symposium, Pp. 37 - 42 of the Proceedings, SSH Communications Security Ltd. 1996
http://www.usenix.org/publications/library/proceedings/sec96/full_papers/ylonen/

PARALLEL PROGRAM EXECUTION SUPPORT IN THE JGRID SYSTEM*

Szabolcs Pota[1], Gergely Sipos[2], Zoltan Juhasz[1,3] and Peter Kacsuk[2]

[1]*Department of Information Systems, University of Veszprem, Hungary*

[2]*Laboratory of Parallel and Distributed Systems, MTA-SZTAKI, Budapest, Hungary*

[3]*Department of Computer Science, University of Exeter, United Kingdom*
pota@irt.vein.hu, sipos@sztaki.hu, juhasz@irt.vein.hu, kacsuk@sztaki.hu

Abstract   Service-oriented grid systems will need to support a wide variety of sequential and parallel applications relying on interactive or batch execution in a dynamic environment. In this paper we describe the execution support that the JGrid system, a Jini-based grid infrastructure, provides for parallel programs.

Keywords: service-oriented grid, Java, Jini, parallel execution, JGrid

1.   Introduction

Future grid systems, in which users access application and system services via well-defined interfaces, will need to support a more diverse set of execution modes than those found in traditional batch execution systems. As the use of the grid spreads to various application domains, some services will rely on immediate and interactive program execution, some will need to reserve resources for a period of time, while some others will need a varying set of processors. In addition to the various ways of executing programs, service-oriented grids will need to adequately address several non-computational issues such as programming language support, legacy system integration, service-oriented vs. traditional execution, security, etc.

In this paper, we show how the JGrid [1] system – a Java/Jini [2] based service-oriented grid system – meets these requirements and provides support for various program execution modes. In Section 2 of the paper, we discuss the most important requirements and constraints for grid systems. Section 3 is the core of the paper; it provides an overview of the Batch execution service

*This work has been supported by the Hungarian IKTA programme under grant no. 089/2002.

that facilitates batch-oriented program execution, and describes the Compute Service that can execute Java tasks. In Section 4 we summarise our results, then close the paper with conclusions and discussion on future work.

2.   Execution Support for the Grid

Service-orientation provides a higher level of abstraction than resource- oriented grid models; consequently, the range of applications and uses of service-oriented grids are wider than that of computational grids. During the design of the JGrid system, our aim was to create a dynamic, Java and Jini based service-oriented grid environment that is flexible enough to cater for the various requirements of future grid applications.

Even if one restricts the treatment to computational grids only, there is a set of conflicting requirements to be aware of. Users would like to use various *programming language*s that suit their needs and personal preferences while enjoying platform independence and reliable execution. Interactive as well as batch *execution mode*s should be available for *sequential* and *parallel programs*. In addition to the execution mode, a set of inter-process communication models need to be supported (shared memory, message passing, client-server). Also, there are large differences in users' and service providers' *attitude to grid development*; some are willing to develop new programs and services, others want to use their existing, non-grid systems and applications with no or little modification. Therefore, *integration* support for legacy systems and user programs is inevitable.

3.   Parallel execution support in JGrid

In this section we describe how the JGrid system provides parallel execution support and at the same time meets the aforementioned requirements concentrating on (*i*) language, (*ii*) interprocess communication, (*iii*) programming model and (*iv*) execution mode.

During the design of the JGrid system, our aim was to provide as much flexibility in the system as possible and not to prescribe the use of a particular programming language, execution mode, and the like. To achieve this aim, we have decided to create two different types of computational services. The Batch Execution and Compute services complement each other in providing the users of JGrid with a range of choices in programming languages, execution modes, interprocess communication modes.

As we describe in the remaining part of this section in detail, the Batch Service is a Jini front end service that integrates available job execution environments into the JGrid system. This service allows one to discover legacy batch execution environments and use them to run sequential or parallel legacy user programs written in any programming language.

Table 1. Support in JGrid

Category	Compute Service	Batch Service
Programming language	Java	any
Execution Mode	interactive, batch	primarily batch
Communication	shared mem, msg passing, client/server, tuple space	runtime dependent (shared mem, msg passing)
Legacy user programs	no	yes
Legacy service integration	no	yes
Application domain	any	mainly HPC

Batch execution is not a solution to all problems however. Interactive execution, co-allocation, interaction with the grid are areas where batch systems have shortcomings. The Compute Service thus is special runtime system developed for executing Java tasks with maximum support for grid execution, including parallel program execution, co-allocation, cooperation with grid schedulers. Table 1 illustrates the properties of the two services.

The Batch Execution Service

The Batch Execution Service provides a JGrid service interface to traditional job execution environments, such as LSF, Condor, Sun Grid Engine. This interface allows us to integrate legacy batch systems into the service-oriented grid and users to execute legacy programs in a uniform, runtime-independent manner.

Due to the modular design of the wrapper service, various batch systems can be integrated. The advantage of this approach is that neither providers nor clients have to develop new software from scratch, they can use well-tested legacy resource managers and user programs. The use of this wrapper service also has the advantage that new grid functionality (e.g. resource reservation, monitoring, connection to other grid services), normally not available in the native runtime environments, can be added to the system.

In the rest of Section 3.1, the structure and operation of one particular implementation of the Batch Execution Service, an interface to the Condor [3] environment is described.

Internal Structure.   As shown in Figure 1, the overall batch service consists of the native job runtime system and the front end JGrid wrapper service. The batch runtime includes the Condor job manager and N cluster nodes. In addition, each node also runs a local Mercury monitor [4] that receives execution information from instrumented user programs. The local monitors are connected to a master monitor service that in turn combines local monitoring

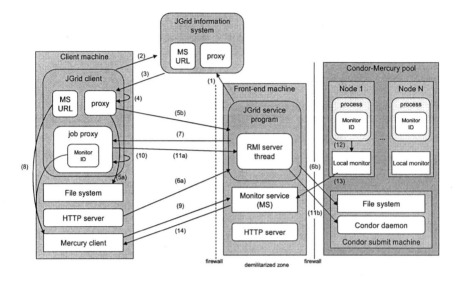

Figure 1.   Structure and operation of the Batch Execution Service.

information and exports it to the client on request. Figure 1 also shows a JGrid information service entity and a client, indicating the other required components for proper operation.

The resulting infrastructure allows a client to dynamically discover the available Condor [3] clusters in the network, submit jobs into these resource pools, remotely manage the execution of the submitted jobs, as well as monitor the running applications on-line.

Service operation.   The responsibilities of the components of the service are as follows. The JGrid service wrapper performs registration within the JGrid environment, exports the proxy object that is used by a client to access the service and forwards requests to the Condor job manager. Once a job is received, the Condor job manager starts its normal tasks of locating idle resources from within the pool, managing these resources and the execution of the job. If application monitoring is required, the Mercury monitoring system is used to perform job monitoring. The detailed flow of execution is as follows:

1 Upon start-up, the Batch Execution Service discovers the JGrid information system and registers a proxy along with important service attributes describing e.g. the performance, number of processors, supported message passing environments, etc.

2 The client can discover the service by sending an appropriate service template containing the Batch service interface and required attribute values to the information system. The Batch Executor's resource prop-

erties are described by Jini attributes that can be matched against the service template.

3 The result of a successful lookup operation results in the client receiving the proxy-attribute pair of the service.

4 The client submits the job by calling appropriate methods on the service proxy. It specifies as method arguments the directory of the job in the local file system, a URL through which this directory can be accessed, and every necessary piece of information required to execute the job (command line parameters, input files, name of the executable, etc.).

5 The proxy archives the job into a Java archive (JAR) file (5a), then sends the URL of this file to the front end service (5b).

6 The front end service downloads the JAR file through the client HTTP server (6a), then extracts it into the file system of a submitter node of the Condor pool (6b).

7 As a result of the submit request, the client receives a proxy object representing the submitted job. This proxy is in effect a handle to the job, it can be used to suspend or cancel the job referenced by it. The proxy also carries the job ID the Mercury monitoring subsystem uses for job identification.

8 The client obtains the monitor ID then passes it - together with the MS URL it obtained from the information system earlier - to the Mercury client.

9 The Mercury client subscribes for receiving the trace information of the job.

10 After the successful subscription, the remote job can be physically started with a method call on the job proxy.

11 The proxy instructs the remote front end service to start the job, which then submits it to the Condor subsystem via a secure native call. Depending on the required message passing mode, the parallel program will execute under the PVM or MPI universe. Sequential jobs can run under the Vanilla, Condor or Java universe.

12 The local monitors start receiving trace events from the running processes.

13 The local monitor forwards the monitoring data to the master monitor service

14 The master monitor service sends the global monitoring data to the interested client.

Once the job execution is finished, the client can download the result files via the job proxy using other method calls either automatically or when required. The files then will be extracted to the location in the local filesystem as specified by the client.

It is important to note that the Java front end hides all internal implementation details, thus clients can use a uniform service interface to execute, manage and monitor jobs in various environments. In addition, the wrapper service can provide further grid-related functionalities not available in traditional batch execution systems.

The Compute Service

Our aim with the Compute Service is to develop a dynamic Grid execution runtime system that enables one to create and execute dynamic grid applications. This requires the ability to execute sequential and parallel interactive and batch applications, support reliable execution using checkpointing and migration, as well as enable the execution of evolving and malleable [5] programs in a wide area grid environment.

Malleable applications are naturally suited to Grid execution as they can adapt to a dynamically changing grid resource pool. The execution of these applications, however, requires strong interaction between the application and the grid; thus, suitable grid middleware and application programming models are required.

Task Execution. Java is a natural choice for this type of execution due to its platform independence, mobile code support and security, hence the Compute Service, effectively, is a remote JVM exported out as a Jini service. Tasks sent for execution to the service are executed within threads that are controlled by an internal thread pool. Tasks are executed in isolation, thus one task cannot interfere with another task from a different client or application.

Clients have several choices for executing tasks on the compute service. The simplest form is remote evaluation, in which the client sends the executable object to the service in a synchronous or asynchronous `execute()` method call. If the task is sequential, it will execute in one thread of the pool. If it uses several threads, on single CPU machines it will run concurrently, on shared memory parallel computers it will run in parallel.

A more complex form of execution is remote process creation, in which case the object sent by the client will be spawned as a remote object and a dynamic proxy created via reflection, implementing the `TaskControl` and other client-specified interfaces, is returned to the client. This mechanism allows clients e.g. to upload the code to the Compute Service only once and call various methods on this object successively. The `TaskControl` proxy will have a major role in parallel execution as shown later in this section.

A single instance of the Compute Service cannot handle a distributed memory parallel computer and export it into the grid. To solve this problem we created a ClusterManager service that implements the same interface as the Compute Service, hence appears to clients as another Compute Service instance, but upon receiving tasks, it forwards them to particular nodes of the cluster. It is also possible to create a hierarchy of managers e.g. for connecting and controlling a set of clusters of an institution.

The major building blocks of the Compute Service are the task manager, the executing thread pool and the scheduler. The service was designed in a service-oriented manner, thus interchangeable scheduling modules implementing different policies can be configured to be used by the service.

Executing Parallel Applications. There are several approaches to executing parallel programs using Compute Services. If a client discovers a multi-processor Compute Service, it can run a multi-threaded application in parallel. Depending on whether the client looks up a number of single-processor Compute Services (several JVMs) or one multi-processor service (single JVM), it will need to use different communication mechanisms. Our system at the time of writing can support communication based on (*i*) MPI-like message passing primitives and (*ii*) high-level remote method calls. A third approach using JavaSpaces (a Linda-like tuple space implementation) is currently being integrated into the system.

Programmers familiar with MPI can use Java MPI method calls for communication. They are similar to mpiJava [6] and provided by the Compute Service as system calls. The Compute Service provides the implementation via system classes. Once the subtasks are allocated, processes are connected by logical channels. The Compute Service provides transparent mapping of task rank numbers to physical addresses and logical channels to physical connections to route messages. The design allows one to create a wide-area parallel system.

For some applications, MPI message passing is too low-level. Hence, we also designed a high level object-oriented communication mechanism that allows application programmers to develop tasks that communicate via remote method calls. As mentioned earlier, as the result of remote process creation, the client receives a task control proxy. This proxy is a reference to the spawned task/process and can be passed to other tasks. Consequently, a set of remote tasks can be configured to store references to each other in an arbitrary way. Tasks then can call remote methods on other tasks to implement the communication method of their choice. This design results in a truly distributed object programming model.

4.   Results

Both the Batch Execution Service and the Compute Service have been implemented and tests on an international testbed have been performed. The trial runs demonstrated (*i*) the ease with which our services can be discovered dynamically with JGrid, (*ii*) the simplicity of job submission to native batch environments via the Batch Execution Service, and the (*iii*) ability of the Compute Service to run tasks of wide-area parallel programs that use either MPI or remote method call based communication.

Further tests and evaluations are being conducted continuously to determine the reliability of our implementations and to determine the performance and overheads of the system, respectively.

5.   Conclusions and Future Work

This paper described our approach to support computational application in dynamic, wide-area grid systems. The JGrid system is a dynamic, service-oriented grid infrastructure. The Batch Execution Service and the Compute Service are two core computational services in JGrid; the former provides access to legacy batch execution environments to run sequential and parallel programs without language restrictions, while the latter represents a special runtime environment that allows the execution of Java tasks using various interprocess communication mechanisms if necessary.

The system has demonstrated that with these facilities application programmers can create highly adaptable, dynamic, service-oriented applications. We continue our work with incorporating high-level grid scheduling, service brokers, migration and fault tolerance into the system.

References

[1]   The JGrid project: http://pds.irt.vein.hu/jgrid

[2]   Sun Microsystems, *Jini Technology Core Platform Specification*, http://www.sun.com/jini/specs.

[3]   M. J. Litzkow, M. Livny and M. W. Mutka, "Condor : A Hunter of Idle Workstations" *8th International Conference on Distributed Computing Systems (ICDCS '88)*, pp. 104-111, IEEE Computer Society Press, June 1988.

[4]   Z. Balaton, G. Gombás, "Resource and Job Monitoring in the Grid", *Proc. of the Euro-Par 2003 International Conference*, Klagenfurt, 2003.

[5]   D. G. Feitelson and L. Rudolph, "Parallel Job Scheduling: Issues and Approaches" *Lecture Notes in Computer Science*, Vol. 949, p. 1-??, 1995.

[6]   M. Baker, B. Carpenter, G. Fox and Sung Hoon Koo, "mpiJava: An Object-Oriented Java Interface to MPI", *Lecture Notes in Computer Science*, Vol. 1586, p. 748-??, 1999.

VL-E: APPROACHES TO DESIGN A GRID-BASED VIRTUAL LABORATORY

Vladimir Korkhov, Adam Belloum and L.O. Hertzberger
FNWI,
University of Amsterdam,
Kruislaan 403, 1098 SJ, Amsterdam, The Netherlands
vkorkhov@science.uva.nl
adam@science.uva.nl
bob@science.uva.nl

Abstract   This paper addresses the issues of building Virtual Laboratory environments and presents architecture of VL-E - a Grid-enabled virtual laboratory being developed at University of Amsterdam. The Virtual Laboratory concepts are usually described as having the objective to bridge the gap between the application layer and lower layers that compose the infrastructure needed to support these applications. In the Grid environment the core layer of middleware is usually provided by toolkits like Globus ([Foster and Kesselman, 1998]) that enable low-level functionality and encourage building higher level toolkits that would offer new facilities, such as a robust access to different management facilities, adequate fault tolerance in distributed systems, reliable super-scheduling techniques, workflow support, web portal technology, advanced information management techniques and virtual reality visualization. Here we present a structural overview of VL-E and discuss some related issues brought up by nature of Grid environment.

Keywords: Grid, virtual laboratory, process flow, data flow, resource management

Introduction

The concepts of virtual laboratories have been introduced to support e-Science, they address the tools and instruments that are designed to aid scientists in performing experiments by providing high-level interface to Grid environment. Virtual laboratories can spread over multiple organizations enabling usage of resources across different organization domains. Potential e-Science applications manipulate large data sets in distributed environment; this data is to be processed regardless its physical place. It is thus of extreme importance for the virtual laboratories to be able to process and manage the produced data, to store it in a systematic fashion, and to enable a fast access to it. The virtual laboratory concepts encapsulate the simplistic remote access to external devices as well as the management of most of the activities composing the e-Science application and the collaboration among geographically distributed scientists.

In essence the aim of the virtual laboratories is to support the e-Science developers and users in their research, which implies that virtual laboratories should integrate software designed and implemented independently and coordinate any interaction needed between these components. Virtual laboratories architecture thus has to take care of many different aspects, including a structural view, a behavioral view, and a resource usage view.

In this paper we present architecture and some major components of VL-E environment - a virtual laboratory being developed at University of Amsterdam.

1.   The Virtual Laboratory Architecture

The proposed architecture for VL-E environment is composed of two types of components: permanent and transient. The life cycle of the transient components follows the life cycle of common scientific experiment. The transient components are created when a scientist or a group of scientists start an experiment; they are terminated when the experiment is finished.

The core component of VL-E concept is a virtual experiment composed of a number of processing modules which communicate with each other. From the VL-E users point of view these modules are processing elements, users can select them from a library and connect them via pairs of input and output ports to define a data flow graph, referred to as a topology. From a resource management point of view the topology can be regarded as a meta-application. The modules can be considered as sub-tasks of that meta-application which has to be mapped to Grid environment in a most efficient way. One of the aims of our research work is the development of effective resource management and scheduling schemes for Grid environment and VL-E toolkit. The model of the VL scientific experiment we are considering in the work is extensively explained in [Belloum et al., 2003].

The components of the VL-E architecture are presented on figure 1. These components are:

- Session Factory: when contacted by a VL client, it creates an instance of the Session Manager (SM) which controls all the activities within a session.

- Intersession Collaboration Manager: controls and coordinates the interaction of VL end-users cross sessions.

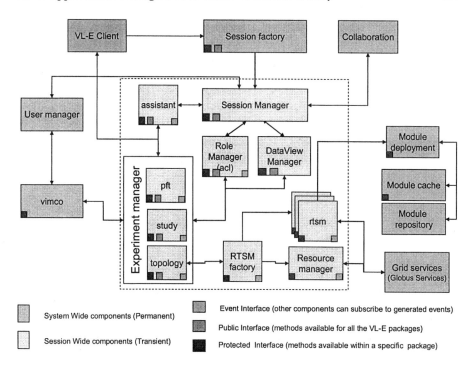

Figure 1. VL-E Architecture

■ Module deployment: when a resource has been selected to execute an end-user task (module), this component takes care of deploying the module on this host and ensures that all the needed libraries are available.

■ Module cache: this component is in charge of optimizing the deployment of the VL module.

■ Module repository: this repository stores all the modules that can be used to compose a virtual experiment.

■ VIMCO: is the information management platform of VL-E, it handles and stores all the information about virtual experiments.

■ Session Manager: controls all the activities within the session

■ RTSM (Run-Time System Manager): performs the distribution of tasks on Grid-enabled resources, starts distributed experiment and monitors its execution.

■ RTSM Factory: creates an instance of Run-Time System Manager (RTSM) for each experiment

- Resource Manager: performs resource discovery, location and selection according to module requirements; maps tasks to resources to optimize experiment performance utilizing a number of algorithms and scheduling techniques.

- Study, PFT and Topology Managers: components that implement the concept of study introduced in section 2.

- Assistant: supports the composition of an experiment by providing templates and information about previously conducted experiments.

2. The concept of study in VL-E

One of the fundamental challenges in e-Science is the extraction of useful information from large data sets. This triggers the need for cooperation of multi-disciplinary teams located at geographically dispersed sites.

To achieve these goals, experiments are embedded in the context of a *study*. A study is about the meaning and the processing of data. It includes descriptions of data elements (meta-data) and process steps for handling the data. A study is defined by a formalized series of steps, also known as process flow, intended to solve a particular problem in a particular application domain. The process steps may generate raw data from instruments, may contain data processing, may retrieve and store either raw or processed data and may contain visualization steps.

A Process Flow Template (PFT) is used to represent such a formalized workflow (Fig. 2). A study is activated by instantiating such a PFT. This instantiation is called a process flow instantiation (PFI). A user is guided through this PFI using context-sensitive interaction. The process steps in the PFT represent the actual data flow in an experiment. This usually entails the data flow stemming from an instrument through the analysis software to data storage facilities. Consequently, an experiment is represented by a data flow graph (DFG). This DFG usually contains experiment specific software entities as well as generic software entities. We will call these self-contained software entities as modules.

3. Resource management in VL-E

One of the focuses of our research is the development of a resource management system for the VL-E environment. In this context, applications are presented by a set of connected by data flow independent modules that perform calculations and data processing, access data storage or control remote devices. Each module is provided with a "module description file" that in particular contains information about module resource requirements (called also quality of service requirements - QoS). Our intention is to build a resource

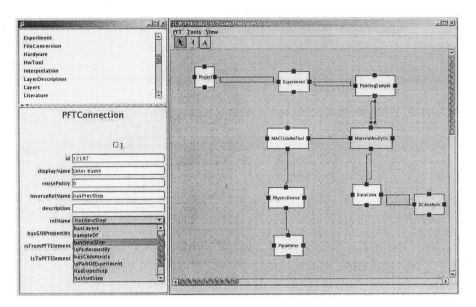

Figure 2.   Process Flow Template (PFT)

management system that performs scheduling decisions based on this information about modules requirements, dynamic resource information from Grid information services (e.g. MDS, [Czajkowski et al., 2001]) and forecasts of resource load (e.g. NWS, [Wolski et al., 1999]).

In the current design of VL-E architecture the Resource Manager (RM) is connected to Run-Time System Manager Factory (RTSMF) which receives a request to run an application (composed of a set of connected modules) from the Front-End and sends the data about the submitted application with module requirements (QoS) to RM, which performs resource discovery, location and selection according to module requirements. RM composes a number of candidate schedules that are estimated using specified cost model and resource state information and predictions, optimal schedule is selected, resources used in the schedule reserved, and the schedule is transmitted back to RTSMF. Then RTSMF translates the schedule to Run-Time System for execution. During the execution RM continues monitoring the resources in case rescheduling will be needed.

The resource manager operates using application information, available resource information, cost and application models (Fig. 3). Application information includes requirements, which define quality of service requested by modules. These requirements contain values such as the amount of memory needed, the approximate number of processing cycles (i.e. processor load),

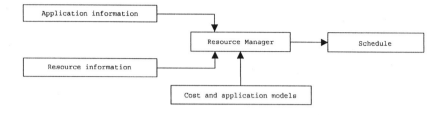

Figure 3.   Resource Manager

the storage and the communication load between modules. We use RSL-like language to specify these requirements (RSL is a resource specification Language used in a the Globus toolkit to specify the job to be submitted to the Grid Resource Allocation Manager, [Czajkowski et al., 1998]). Resource information is obtained from the Grid information service (MDS) which also provides forecasts of resource state from Network Weather Service (NWS). This helps to estimate resource load in specified time frame in the future and model application performance. The cost and application models are used by the resource manager to evaluate the set of candidate schedules for the application. We have conducted a number of experiments using different types of meta-scheduling algorithms (several heuristic algorithms and simulated annealing technique), the results and analysis are presented in [Korkhov et al., 2004].

4.   Related Work

During the last five years, both research and industrial communities have invested a considerable amount of effort in developing new infrastructures that support e-Science. Several research projects worldwide have started with the aim to develop new methods, techniques, and tools to solve the increasing list of challenging problems introduced by E-applications, such as the Virtual Laboratories being developed at Monash University, Australia ([Buyya et al., 2001]), Johns Hopkins University, USA (http://www.jhu.edu/ virtlab/virtlab. html), or at the University of Bochum in Germany ([Rohrig and Jochheim, 1999]). One important common feature in all these Virtual Laboratories projects is the fact that they base their research work on the Grid technology. Furthermore, a number of these projects try to tackle problems related to a specific type of E-application. At Johns Hopkins University researchers are aiming at building a virtual environment for education over the WWW. Their counterparts in Germany are working on a collaborative environment to allow performing experiments in geographically distributed groups. The researchers at Monash University are working on development of an environment where large-scale experimentation in the area of molecular biology can be performed.

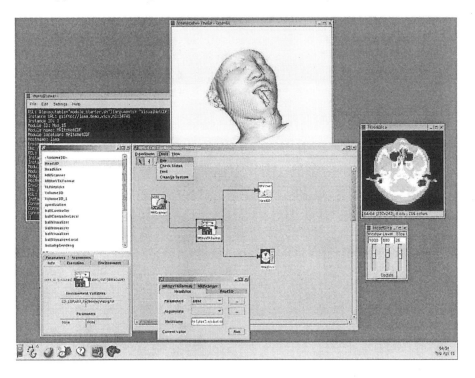

Figure 4. MRI scanner experiment

These are just a few examples of research projects targeting issues related to e-Science. Similar research projects are under development to support computational and data intensive applications such as the iVDGL (International Virtual Data Grid Laboratory, http://www.ivdgl.org/workteams/facilities), DataTAG (Research and Technological development for TransAtlantic Grid) ([D.Bosio et al., 2003]), EU-DataGrid (PetaBytes, across widely distributed scientific communities), PPDG (Particle Physics Data Grid, http://www.ppdg.net/), and many others.

The VL-E approach differs from the other Virtual laboratory initiatives since it took the challenge to address generic aspects of the expected virtual laboratory infrastructure. The aim of the VL-E project is not to provide a solution for a specific E-application; instead, VL-E aims at supporting various classes of applications.

5. Conclusions

In this paper we introduced the architecture of VL-E environment which supports a range of e-Science applications (material analysis experiment MAC-

SLab, medical experiment with MRI scanner and some others). The proposed VL-E architecture hides the low level details of Grid environment from scientists allowing them to focus only on their domain of expertise. The services offered by the VL-E middleware shield users from the complexity of binding different infrastructures together. An example of running VL-E experiment is presented on figure 4. Here the topology editor window is shown along with X output of remote applications used to retrieve and analyse data from MRI scanner.

In this paper we described the core concept of a study that lays in the basis of our virtual experimenting framework, addressed the issues of resource management in Grid environment. Our research on resource management is outlined in this paper, for more details please refer to [Korkhov et al., 2004].

This work has been partially funded by the Dutch BSIK project 03019:Virtual Laboratory for e-science (VL-e).

References

[Belloum et al., 2003] Belloum, A., Groep, D., Hertzberger, L., Korkhov, V., de Laat, C. T., and Vasunin, D. (2003). VLAM-G: A Grid-based Virtual Laboratory. *Future Generation Computer Systems*, 19(2):209–217.

[Buyya et al., 2001] Buyya, R., Branson, K., Giddy, J., and Abramson, D. (2001). The virtual laboratory: Enabling molecular modeling for drug design on the world wide grid. Technical report, Monash University.

[Czajkowski et al., 2001] Czajkowski, K., Fitzgerald, S., Foster, I., and Kesselman, C. (2001). Grid Information Services for Distributed Resource Sharing. In *The Tenth IEEE International Symposium on High-Performance Distributed Computing (HPDC-10)*. IEEE Press.

[Czajkowski et al., 1998] Czajkowski, K., Foster, I., Karonis, N., Kesselman, C., Martin, S., Smith, W., and Tuecke, S. (1998). A Resource Management Architecture for Metacomputing Systems. In *Proceedings of IPPS/SPDP '98 Workshop on Job Scheduling Strategies for Parallel Processing*, pages 62–82.

[D.Bosio et al., 2003] D.Bosio, J.Casey, A.Frohner, and et al, L. (2003). Next generation eu datagrid data management. In *CHEP 2003, La Jolla - CA, USA*.

[Foster and Kesselman, 1998] Foster, I. and Kesselman, C. (1998). The Globus Project: A Status Report. In *IPPS/SPDP '98 Heterogeneous Computing Workshop*, pages 4–18.

[Korkhov et al., 2004] Korkhov, V., Belloum, A., and Hertzberger, L. (2004). Evaluating Meta-scheduling Algorithms in VLAM-G Environment. In *to be published at the Tenth Annual Conference of the Advanced School for Computing and Imaging (ASCI)*.

[Rohrig and Jochheim, 1999] Rohrig, C. and Jochheim, A. (1999). The virtual lab for controlling real experiments via internet. In *IEEE International Symosium on Computer-Aided Control System Design, CACSD'99, Hawaii*.

[Wolski et al., 1999] Wolski, R., Spring, N., and Hayes, J. (1999). The Network Weather Service: Distributed Resource Performance Forecasting Service for Metacomputing. *Journal of Future Generation Computing Systems, Volume 15, Numbers 5-6, pp. 757-768, October, 1999.*, (5-6):757–768.

SCHEDULING AND RESOURCE BROKERING WITHIN THE GRID VISUALIZATION KERNEL*

Paul Heinzlreiter, Jens Volkert
GUP Linz
Johannes Kepler University Linz
Altenbergerstr. 69
A-4040 Linz
Austria/Europe
heinzlreiter@gup.jku.at

Abstract   The role of grid computing as a tool for computational science which has evolved over the past years leads to additional requirements for grid middleware. One of these requirements is visualization support which is provided by the Grid Visualization Kernel (GVK). To enable proper usage of grid resources for visualization purposes sophisticated scheduling and resource brokering mechanisms are required. These mechanisms enable the automatic construction of a visualization pipeline taking into account the requirements specified by the user as well as resource availability.

Keywords: Scheduling, resource brokering, grid computing, visualization

1.   Introduction

During the last years grid computing has evolved into a standard technique for distributed high-performance and high-throughput computing by harnessing the resources of multiple organizations for running computational intensive applications [9]. This is enabled by grid middleware toolkits such as Globus [8], which has became the de facto standard grid middleware solution.

Compared to the rapid evolution of available middleware solutions which currently provides a solid foundation of basic services, more application specific support by means of middleware extensions still offers a wide field for improvements.

One of the key issues within the scientific computing domain is visualization, which provides the scientist with the appropriate tool for result validation.

*The Grid Visualization Kernel (GVK) is partially supported by the Crossgrid Project of the European Commission under contract number IST-2001-32243.

Since typical grid computing applications operate on large datasets, the visualization task itself also can benefit from the computational power available on the grid. With this in mind, the Grid Visualization Kernel (GVK) [13], which is composed of a set of specific visualization modules running on different grid nodes, has been developed. GVK aims at providing the best visualization performance possible given the type of the requested service and the status of the available grid resources. This is enabled by splitting the requested visualization pipeline into various subtasks, each of which is accomplished by a specific visualization module.

Within this paper the main focus is put on the GVK visualization planner (VP) which identifies the required visualization subtasks and acts as a application-specific resource broker by mapping the tasks onto the available grid resources.

The remaining sections are structured as follows: In Section 2 an overview over related work in field of distributed application scheduling is given. In Section 3 an overview of the functionality of the VP is given, while the subsequent sections elaborate the steps of the visualization planning process. Finally an outlook on future work concludes the paper.

2. Related Work

Various approaches have already been studied in the field of scheduling for distributed applications. A good survey of the problems arising is given in [1]. This paper focuses on the scheduling problem for distributed applications communicating over heterogenous networks. The described approach focuses on providing a specific scheduler for each application, thus taking into account the application specific requirements.

In contrast to this method [6] describes a scheduling approach which is decoupled from the application to be executed. This is achieved by using a performance model of the job to be scheduled.

The scheduling within Nimrod/G [3] focuses on running parameter studies on the grid. It aims at providing economy based resource trading and offers different scheduling strategies like time minimization, cost minimization, and no minimization, which means that the task is scheduled for execution within the given cost and time constraints.

In [14] the scheduling approach used within the EU Crossgrid project is presented. The Crossgrid scheduling system consists of a scheduling agent, a resource searcher, and an application launcher. The matchmaking between jobs and resources is done by the resource searcher. It provides the scheduling agent with different possible sets of resources, which selects the most appropriate one.

The scheduling approach chosen for the Condor-G system [10] uses a grid manager process, which is started locally and handles the communication with the remote resource. It also delivers status information on the remote job to the local Condor-G scheduler. An additional task of the grid manager is detection of remote resource failures.

Compared to these methods the scheduling within GVK is focused onto the visualization domain and aims specifically at creating a visualization pipeline possibly spreading multiple grid hosts.

3. The GVK Visualization Planner

The visualization process as performed by GVK can be understood as a series of transformations which lead from the input data to the final image.

The task of the VP is to identify a series of data transformations which have to be applied to the data to generate the desired output. Its input is given by the visualization request, which describes the visualization as requested by the user of GVK. The output of the VP is a execution schedule for a set of grid modules, which form an appropriate visualization pipeline for the requested visualization task. The required modules are subsequently invoked using the Globus GRAM [4] service. To enable this the VP delivers its results in the form of RSL scripts [11].

During the visualization planning process the following informations have to be determined:

- Structure of the pipeline

  - Required modules
  - Interconnections between the modules

- Visualization algorithms to be used

- Execution locations for the modules

The task of the VP can be splitted into the following steps:

1 Task decomposition

2 Resource information gathering

3 Rendering algorithm selection

4 Resource mapping

Several factors are taken into account at different stages within the planning process: The type of the requested visualization, the available software modules and the structure of the input data are evaluated during the first stage of the planning process, the visualization task decomposition. The available grid resources are determined during stage two and are relevant for the rendering algorithm selection and the resource mapping.

In order to cope with this complex scheduling and resource brokering problems, a top-down analysis of the problem is performed. Within the following sections the different phases of the visualization planning process are elaborated following their execution order.

4.   Visualization Task Decomposition

Within the first step of the visualization planning process the transformation of the task described by the visualization request into an ordered set of modules has to be performed.

The main factor which is determining this phase of the planning process is the set of available software modules. At first it is required to check if all required software modules for the pipeline are available. The VP has access to a list of available software modules, which is provided to the VP upon invocation and identifies the modules, which can be started on various grid nodes to be included into the visualization pipeline. It identifies which visualization modules are already available in binary form on the available execution hosts. If that is not the case the executable can be staged to the execution host using the Globus GASS service [2]. The input and output formats of the modules as well as the parallelism approach applied for the algorithm are taken as criteria for evaluating their usability.

The functionality related part of the decision is done based on the data formats which have been defined for the modules input and output interfaces. At first the output format of a module has to match the input format of the subsequent one. Additionally the input format of the first module and the output format of the last have to be selected according to the specification in the visualization request.

After a set of software modules has been identified for each stage of the visualization pipeline, which satisfies the functionality related constraints, the visualization planning process enters the next stage.

5.   Resource Information Gathering

Getting information about the available grid nodes is crucial for the VP. The main source of resource-related information within a Globus-based grid environment is the metadirectory service (MDS) [5, 7]. It delivers information on the static and dynamic aspects of resource availability on the grid.

To enable the selection of appropriate hosts access to aggregate information about all accessible grid hosts is required. This is realized by accessing a Grid Index Information Services (GIIS) server, which represents the aggregate information source. The GVK VP retrieves the available grid hosts as well as information on processing power, available memory and file system usage from the MDS system. For processors the number and speeds are retrieved, considering memory the total and free amount can be checked, and for filesystems the free space and the location is reported. Other informations like network and CPU loads are measured directly using GVK functionality, which enables fast reaction if the network or system load changes significantly. The GVK CPU load sensor has been realized by calling the unix top command and is incorporated into the GVK resource information module which also delivers the relevant parts of the MDS output to the VP. Information about the available network bandwidth is collected by sending test data over the network connections in question. If a specific connection has already been identified as a required datapath payload data can already be transmitted during the bandwidth measurements. The network monitoring then serves as a tool for selecting the appropriate transmission mode such as compressed data transmission [12].

Within this stage of the visualization planning process all available grid hosts are evaluated taking into account their static and dynamic properties.

6. Algorithm Selection and Resource Mapping

During these stages of the visualization planning process the previously selected software modules have to be mapped onto the available resources. The output of stage one identifies a series of required data transformations representing the pipeline. For each data transformation a list of available modules is provided, which offer the appropriate input and output interface. Based on the resource information gathered in step two, the appropriate implementation together with the fitting resource has to be found. The main problem of this selection process is given by the mutual influence of resource and algorithm selection.

In general, one can distinguish sequential algorithms (SQA), shared memory parallel algorithms (SMA), and distributed memory parallel algorithms (DMA). The other criterion identified is the type of hardware. The VP makes a distinction between a single processor system (SPS), a shared memory system (SMS), and a distributed memory system (DMS).

For selecting an appropriate combination of algorithm and hardware the possible combinations are evaluated considering their performance. The following table illustrates the performance gains or losses to be expected if the according hardware-algorithm combination is used. For this comparison it was assumed that each processor offers the same amount of computational power. A plus sign denotes a performance gain, a minus a loss. The appearance of a double plus or minus indicates a significant gain or loss. For a plus minus combination no major performance impact compared to the single processor and sequential algorithm pair is expected.

	SQA	SMA	DMA
SPS	+ -	-	- -
SMS	+ -	+ +	+ +
DMS	+ -	-	+ +

The main criteria for the algorithm and resource selection process in addition to the type of hardware and the programming paradigm used are given by the available number and speed of processors, size of memory, and the bandwidth between the involved hosts.

Considering the size of the input data (IS), network bandwidth (BW), number of processors used (NP), available processor performance (PP), algorithm scalability (AS), problem size (PS), available memory size (MS), and the mapping factor (MF), which expresses the quality of the mapping between algorithm type and resource as shown in the table above, the processing time for one step of the pipeline PT can be calculated as follows:

$$PT = \frac{IS}{BW} + \frac{PS}{NP * PP * AS * MF} * \frac{PS}{MS} \qquad (1)$$

The processing time is the sum of the data transmission time from the previous stage of the pipeline to the stage in question and the processing time on the grid node. These criteria not only include static properties but also highly dynamic ones like network or system load. For the mapping process the status of the dynamic aspects is retrieved during the resource information gathering phase. The algorithm properties relevant for the decision process are provided together with the according software modules and can looked up in the list of available software modules.

Equation 1 only delivers a very rough estimation of the performance of a resource-algorithm combination. Therefore the result can only be interpreted as a relative quality measure and the processing time estimations PT for all possible resource-algorithm combinations have to be compared. Finally the combination yielding the lowest numerical result is selected.

During the selection process the resource mapping for the pipeline stages is done following the expected dataflow direction. But this approach contains a possible drawback: As the network connection bandwidth between two hosts is considered important, a current resource mapping decision can also influence the resource mapping of the stage before if the connecting network is too slow for the expected data amount to be transmitted. For coping with this problem all possible pipeline configurations have to be evaluated.

7. Visualization Pipeline Construction

Using the execution schedule provided by the VP Globus GRAM is invoked to start the required visualization modules on the appropriate grid nodes. To provide the correct input for the GRAM service, the VP generates the RSL specifications for the Globus jobs which have to be submitted.

An important issue to be taken into account is the order of module startup. Considering two neighboring modules within the pipeline one acts as a server, while the other is the client connecting to the server. Therefore its important that the server side module is started before the client side. To ensure this, each module registers itself at a central module, which enables the VP module to check if the server module is already online, before the client is started.

The data exchange between the involved modules is accomplished over Globus IO based connections which can be used in different modes which are further illustrated in [12]. The content of the data transmitted between to modules depends on the communication protocol defined by the modules interfaces.

8. Conclusions and Future Work

Within this paper we have presented an overview of the scheduling and resource selection aspect of the Grid Visualization Kernel. Its purpose is the decomposition of the specified visualization into separate modules, which are arranged into a visualization pipeline and started on appropriate grid nodes, which are selected based on the static and dynamic resource informations retrieved using Globus MDS or measured on the fly.

Future work will mainly focus on further refinements of the algorithm selection and resource mapping strategy, which can be improved in many ways for example taking into account resource sets containing processors with different speeds. Additional plans include improvements of the network load monitoring, such as inclusion of the Network Weather Service [15].

References

[1] F. D. Berman, R. Wolski, S. Figueira, J. Schopf, and G. Shao. *Application-Level Scheduling on Distributed Heterogeneous Networks*, Proceedings Conference on Supercomputing, Pittsburgh, PA, USA, 1996

[2] J. Bester, I. Foster, C. Kesselman, J. Tedesco, and S. Tuecke. *GASS: A Data Movement and Access Service for Wide Area Computing Systems*, Proceedings of the Sixth Workshop on Input/Output in Parallel and Distributed Systems, Atlanta, GA, USA, pp. 78–88, May 1999

[3] R. Buyya, J. Giddy, and D. Abramson. *An Evaluation of Economy-based Resource Trading and Scheduling on Computational Power Grids for Parameter Sweep Applications*, Proceedings Second Workshop on Active Middleware Services, Pittsburgh, PA, USA, 2000

[4] K. Czajkowski, I. Foster, N. Karonis, C. Kesselman, S. Martin, W. Smith, and S. Tuecke. *A Resource Management Architecture for Metacomputing Systems*, Proceedings IPPS/SPDP '98 Workshop on Job Scheduling Strategies for Parallel Processing, pp. 62–82, 1998

[5] K. Czajkowski, S. Fitzgerald, I. Foster and C. Kesselman. *Grid Information Services for Distributed Resource Sharing*, Proceedings of the 10th IEEE International Symposium on High-Performance Distributed Computing, pp. 181–194, August 2001

[6] H. Dail, H. Casanova, and F. Berman. *A Decoupled Scheduling Approach for the GrADS Program Development Environment*, Proceedings Conference on Supercomputing, Baltimore, MD, USA, November 2002

[7] S. Fitzgerald, I. Foster, C. Kesselman, G. von Laszewski, W. Smith, and S. Tuecke. *A Directory Service for Configuring High-performance Distributed Computations*, Proceedings 6th IEEE Symposium on High Performance Distributed Computing, pp. 365–375, August 1997

[8] I. Foster and C. Kesselman. *Globus: A Metacomputing Infrastructure Toolkit*, International Journal of Supercomputing Applications, Vol. 11, No. 2, pp. 4–18, 1997

[9] I. Foster, C. Kesselman, and S. Tuecke. *The Anatomy of the Grid: Enabling Scalable Virtual Organizations*, International Journal of Supercomputer Applications, Vol. 15, No. 3, 2001

[10] J. Frey, T. Tannenbaum, I. Foster, M. Livny, and S. Tuecke. *Condor-G: A Computation Management Agent for Multi-Institutional Grids*, Proceedings of the 10th IEEE Symposium on High Performance Distributed Computing, San Francisco, CA, USA, pp. 55–66, August 2001

[11] The Globus Alliance. *The Globus Resource Specification Language RSL v1.0*, http://www.globus.org/gram/rsl_spec1.html, 2000

[12] P. Heinzlreiter, D. Kranzlmüller, and J. Volkert. *Network Transportation within a Grid-based Visualization Architecture*, Proceedings PDPTA 2003, Las Vegas, NV, USA, pp. 1795-1801, June 2003

[13] P. Heinzlreiter and D. Kranzlmüller. *Visualization Services on the Grid - The Grid Visualization Kernel*, Parallel Processing Letters, Vol. 13, No. 2, pp. 125–148, June 2003

[14] E. Heymann, A. Fernandez, M. A. Senar, and J. Salt. *The EU-CrossGrid Approach for Grid Application Scheduling*, Proceedings of the 1st European Across Grids Conference, Santiago de Compostela, Spain, pp. 17–24, February 2003

[15] R. Wolski, N. Spring, and J. Hayes. *The Network Weather Service: A Distributed Resource Performance Forecasting Service for Metacomputing*, Future Generation Computing Systems, Vol. 15, No. 5-6, pp. 757–768, October 1999

II

CLUSTER TECHNOLOGY

MESSAGE PASSING VS. VIRTUAL SHARED MEMORY A PERFORMANCE COMPARISON

Wilfried N. Gansterer and Joachim Zottl
Department of Computer Science and Business Informatics
University of Vienna
Lenaugasse 2/8, A-1080 Vienna, Austria
{wilfried.gansterer, joachim.zottl}@univie.ac.at

Abstract   This paper presents a performance comparison between important programming paradigms for distributed computing: the classical *Message Passing model* and the *Virtual Shared Memory model*. As benchmarks, three algorithms have been implemented using MPI, UPC and CORSO: (*i*) a classical summation formula for approximating π, (*ii*) a tree-structured sequence of matrix multiplications, and (iii) the basic structure of the eigenvector computation in a recently developed eigensolver. In many cases, especially for inhomogeneous or dynamically changing computational grids, the Virtual Shared Memory implementations lead to performance comparable to MPI implementations.

Keywords: message passing, virtual shared memory, shared object based, grid computing, benchmarks

1.   Introduction

Several paradigms have been developed for distributed and parallel computing, and different programming environments for these paradigms are available. The main emphasis of this article is a performance evaluation and comparison of representatives of two important programming paradigms, the *message passing* (*MP*) model and the *virtual shared memory* (*VSM*) model.

This performance evaluation is based on three benchmarks which are motivated by computationally intensive applications from the Sciences and Engineering. The structure of the benchmarks is chosen to support investigation of advantages and disadvantages of the VSM model in comparison to the MP model and evaluation of the applicability of the VSM model to high performance and scientific computing applications.

The Message Passing Model was one of the first concepts developed for supporting communication and transmission of data between processes and/or processors in a distributed computing environment. Each process can access only its private memory, and explicit send/receive commands are used to transmit messages between processes. Important implementations of this concept are *PVM* (*parallel virtual machine*, [Geist et al., 1994]) and *MPI* (*message passing interface*, www-unix.mcs.anl.gov/mpi). MPI comprises a library of routines for explicit message passing and has been designed for high performance computing. It is the classical choice when the main focus is on achieving high performance, especially for massively parallel computing. However, developing efficient MPI codes requires high implementation effort, and the costs for debugging, adapting and maintaining them can be relatively high.

The Virtual Shared Memory Model (also known as *distributed shared memory* model, *partitioned global address space* model, or *space based* model) is a higher-level abstraction which hides explicit message passing commands from the programmer. Independent processes have access to data items shared across distributed resources and this shared data is used for synchronization and for communication between processes. The advantages over the MP model are obvious: easier implementation and debugging due to high-level abstraction and the reduction of the amount of source code, more flexible and modular code structure, decoupling of processes and data (which supports asynchronous communication), and higher portability of the code. However, the VSM model is usually not associated with classical high performance computing applications, because the comfort and flexibility of a high-level abstraction tends to incur a price in terms of performance.

In this paper, two implementations of the VSM model are considered in order to investigate this performance drawbacks: *UPC* (*Unified Parallel C*, upc.gwu.edu), an extension of the ANSI C standard, and CORSO (Co-ORrdinated Shared Objects, www.tecco.at), an implementation of the shared object based model.

The Shared Object Based (*SOB*) Model is a subtype of the VSM model. In this concept, *objects* are stored in a *space* (virtual shared memory).

A central idea of the space based concept is to have a very small set of commands for managing the objects in the space. This concept has been first formulated in the form of the LINDA tuple space ([Gelernter and Carriero, 1992]), which can be considered the origin of all space based approaches. Modern representatives of the object/space based concept are the freely available JAVASPACES ([Bishop and Warren, 2003]), the GIGASPACES ([GigaSpaces, 2002]), the TSPACES ([Lehman et al., 1999]), and CORSO.

Related Work. Several performance studies comparing different distributed programming paradigms have been described in the literature. Most of them compare UPC and MPI, for example, [El-Ghazawi and Cantonnet, 2002] and are based on different benchmarks than the ones we consider. They use Sobel Edge Detection, the UPC Stream Benchmarks (see also [Cantonnet et al., 2003]), an extension of the STREAM Benchmark ([McCalpin, 1995]), and the NAS parallel benchmarks (NPB, www.nas.nasa.gov/Software/NPB). They show that UPC codes, although in general slower and less scalable, can in some cases achieve performance values comparable to those of MPI codes.

For performance evaluations of UPC, the benchmark suite UPC_Bench has been developed ([El-Ghazawi and Chauvin, 2001]), which comprises synthetic benchmarks (testing memory accesses) and three application benchmarks (Sobel edge detection, *N* Queens problem, and matrix multiplication).

[Husbands et al., 2003], compare the Berkeley UPC compiler with the commercial HP UPC compiler based on several synthetic benchmarks and a few application benchmarks from [El-Ghazawi and Cantonnet, 2002]. They show that the Berkeley compiler overall achieves comparable performance.

Synopsis. In Section 2, we summarize the most important properties of the VSM and SOB models and of their representatives, UPC and CORSO. In Section 3, we discuss our choice of benchmarks. In Section 4, we describe our testbed environment and summarize our experimental results. Section 5 contains conclusions and outlines directions for future work.

2. The Virtual Shared Memory Paradigm

In this section, we give a brief introduction into UPC and CORSO, the two representatives of the VSM model investigated in this paper.

UPC ([El-Ghazawi et al., 2003]) is a parallel extension of the ANSI C standard for distributed shared memory computers. It supports high performance scientific applications. In the UPC programming model, one or more threads are working independently, and the number of threads is fixed either at compile time or at run-time. Memory in UPC is divided into two spaces: (*i*) a private memory space and (*ii*) a shared memory space. Every thread has a private memory that can only be accessed by the owning thread. The shared memory is logically partitioned and can be accessed by every thread.

UPC comprises three methods for synchronization: The *notify* and the *wait* statement, the *barrier* command, which is a combination of notify and wait, and the *lock* and *unlock* commands.

CORSO is a representative of the SOB model. It is a platform independent middleware, originally developed at Vienna University of Technology, now a commercial product, produced by tecco. CORSO supports programming in C, C++, Java, and .NET. In a CORSO run-time environment, each host contains a Coordination Kernel, called CoKe. It communicates with other CoKe's within the network by unicast. If a device does not have enough storage capacity, for example, a mobile device like a PDA, then it can link directly to a known CoKe of another host.

Some important features of CORSO are: (*i*) Processes can be dynamically added to or removed from a distributed job during execution. Such dynamics cannot be implemented either in MPI or in UPC. In MPI, the number of processes is fixed during the run-time, and in UPC it is either a compile-time constant or specified at run-time ([Husbands et al., 2003]). Thus, this feature makes CORSO an attractive platform for dynamically changing grid computing environments. (*ii*) CORSO distinguishes two types of communication objects: *Const* objects can only be written once, whereas *var* objects can be written an arbitrary number of times. (*iii*) For caching, CORSO provides the *eager mode*, where each object replication is updated immediately when the original object was changed, and the *lazy mode*, where each object replication is only updated when it is accessed. (*iv*) CORSO comprises two transaction models, *hard*-commit (in case of failure, the transaction aborts automatically without feedback) and *soft*-commit (the user is informed if a failure occurs).

3.   Benchmarks

The benchmarks used for comparing the three programming paradigms were designed such that they are (*i*) representative for computationally intensive applications from the Sciences and Engineering, (*ii*) increasingly difficult to parallelize, (*iii*) scalable in terms of workload, and (*iv*) highly flexible in terms of the ratio of computation to communication. The following three benchmarks were implemented in MPI, UPC and CORSO: (*i*) two classical summation formulas for approximating π, (*ii*) a tree structured sequence of matrix multiplications, and (*iii*) the basic structure of the eigenvector accumulation in a recently developed block tridiagonal divide-and-conquer eigensolver ([Gansterer et al., 2003]).

Benchmark 1: π Approximation

Computing approximations for π based on finite versions of one of the formulas

$$\pi = \lim_{n \to \infty} \frac{1}{n} \sum_{i=1}^{n} \frac{4}{1 + \left(\frac{i-0.5}{n}\right)^2} = 4\left(1 + \sum_{i=1}^{\infty}(-1)^i\left(\frac{1}{2i+1}\right)\right)$$

is a popular "toy problem" in distributed computing. Because of the simple dependency structure (only two synchronization points) it is easy to parallelize and allows one to evaluate the overhead related with managing shared objects in comparison to explicit message passing.

Implementation. In the parallel implementation for p processors, the problem size n is divided into p parts, and each processor computes its partial sum. Finally, all the partial sums are accumulated on one processor.

Benchmark 2: Tree Structured Matrix Multiplications

The second benchmark is a sequence of matrix multiplications, structured in the form of a binary tree. Given a problem size n, each processor involved generates two random $n \times n$ matrices and multiplies them. Then, for each pair of active neighboring processors in the tree, one of them sends its result to the neighbor and then becomes idle. The recipient multiplies the matrix received with the one computed in the previous stage, and so on. At each stage of this benchmark, about half of the processors become idle, and at the end, the last active processor computes a final matrix multiplication.

Due to the tree structure, this benchmark involves much more communication than Benchmark 1 and is harder to parallelize. The order n of the matrices, which is the same at all levels, determines the workload and, in combination with the number p of processors, the ratio of communication to computation. For $p = 2^k$ ($k \in \mathbb{N}$) the binary tree is balanced, which leads to better utilization of the processors involved than for an unbalanced tree.

Implementation. Benchmark 2 has been implemented in MPI based on a Master-Worker model. In this model, one processor takes the role as a master which organizes and distributes the work over the other processors (the workers). The master does not contribute to the actual computing work, which is a drawback of the MPI implementation in comparison to the UPC and CORSO implementations, where all processors actively contribute computational resources.

In UPC and CORSO, each processor has information about its local task and about the active neighbors in the binary tree. In the current implementation, the right processor in every processor pair becomes inactive after it has transferred its result to the left neighbor.

Benchmark 3: Eigenvector Accumulation

Benchmark 3 is the basic structure of the eigenvector accumulation in a recently developed divide and conquer eigensolver ([Gansterer et al., 2003]). It also has the structure of a binary tree with matrix multiplications at each node. However, in contrast to Benchmark 2, the sizes of the node problems increase at each stage, which leads to a much lower computation per communication ratio. This makes it the hardest problem to parallelize.

Implementation. The implementation of Benchmark 3 is analogous to the implementation of Benchmark 2.

4.   Experimental Results

This section summarizes our performance results for the three benchmarks described in Section 3 implemented in MPI, UPC, and CORSO. Two com-

puting environments were available: (*i*) A *homogeneous* environment, the
Schrödinger II cluster at the University of Vienna, comprising 192 computing nodes. Each node consists of an Intel Pentium 4 (2.53 GHz) with 1 GB
RAM. The nodes are connected by 100 MBit Ethernet. (*ii*) A *heterogeneous*
environment, the PC cluster in our student laboratory, which consists of ten
Intel Pentium 4 nodes connected by 100 MBit Ethernet. The first five nodes
have a clock speed of 2.3 GHz with 1 GB RAM each, and the other five nodes
have a clock speed of 1.7 GHz with 380 MB RAM each.

In terms of software, we used MPICH 1.2.5, the Berkeley UPC compiler
1.1.0, and CORSO version 3.2.

π **Approximation.** Figure 1 shows the speedup values achieved with Benchmark 1. Due to the high degree of parallelism available, the speedup values of

Figure 1.   Speedup values of Benchmark 1 at the Schrödinger and the PC cluster

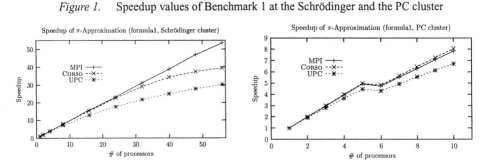

all three implementations are relatively high. The values on the Schrödinger
cluster illustrate the drawbacks of the VSM implementations (overhead associated with virtual shared memory and shared objects, respectivly) in terms of
scalability. The "'stair'" on the PC cluster occurs when the first one of the
slower nodes is used.

Tree Structured Matrix Multiplications. Figure 2 shows the speedup values for Benchmark 2, based on normalizing the execution times to the same
total workload. For a balanced binary tree ($p = 2^k$), the utilization of active

Figure 2.   Speedup values of Benchmark 2 at the Schrödinger and the PC cluster

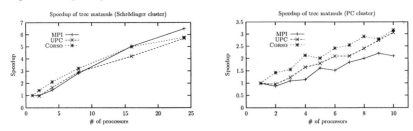

processors is maximal, and therefore the speedup curve shows an oscillating pattern. Due to the master-worker implementation, the speedup value and the execution time for one processor and for two processors are equal.

Eigenvector Accumulation. Table 1 summarizes the execution times for Benchmark 3, and Figure 3 shows the corresponding speedup values. As explained in the previous section, the best results occur for $p = 2^k$ processors. In absolute terms, the speedup values are disappointingly low for all three implementations (in some cases, even a "'slowdown'" occurs). This reflects the difficulty of parallelizing Benchmark 3—in particular, its low computation per communication ratio.

Table 1.   Execution times (in [s]) of Benchmark 3 at the Schrödinger and the PC cluster

	Schrödinger cluster				PC cluster		
p	MPI	UPC	CORSO	p	MPI	UPC	CORSO
1	11.19	10.06	13.68	1	142.5	134.6	159.5
2	11.21	9.64	11.84	2	142.5	121.1	135.5
4	12.45	9.8	11.66	4	164.9	121.3	133.8
8	10.32	10.15	12.05	6	151.9	154	141.4
16	10.25	11.97	32.69	8	146.1	128.2	139.2
24	10.12	13.6	53.74	10	146.4	144.5	155.2

Figure 3.   Speedup values of Benchmark 3 at the Schrödinger and the PC cluster

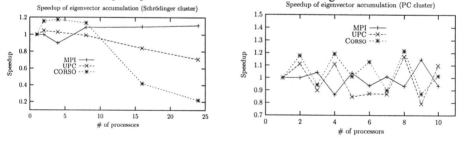

5.   Conclusion and Future Work

We have described performance comparisons between the classical message passing paradigm and the virtual shared memory paradigm, represented by MPI and UPC/CORSO, respectively. As expected, the implementations in the VSM model achieve somewhat lower performance than explicit message passing codes. However, performance loss in the benchmarks we considered is not severe, and in many practical situations it may be outweighed by the greatly reduced coding and debugging effort for UPC and CORSO.

One of our motivations for the performance studies described here is the currently ongoing development of a grid-enabled parallel eigensolver. Therefore, we are refining and improving Benchmark 3, which will be used as building block in this context. For computational grids, we will particularly focus on the design and integration of dynamic load balancing strategies into the benchmarks. The representatives of the VSM model, especially the SOB paradigm, provide excellent infrastructure for this task, and seem to have important advantages over the message passing paradigm. Finally, we will also investigate the combination of task and data parallelism in Benchmark 3, which will significantly improve the parallel performance achieved with this benchmark.

References

[Bishop and Warren, 2003] Bishop, Philip and Warren, Nigel (2003). *JavaSpaces in Practice*. Addison-Wesley.

[Cantonnet et al., 2003] Cantonnet, François, Yao, Yiyi, Annareddy, Smita, Mohamed, Ahmed S., and El-Ghazawi, Tarek A. (2003). Performance monitoring and evaluation of a UPC implementation on a numa architecture. In *International Parallel and Distributed Processing Symposium*. IEEE Press.

[El-Ghazawi and Cantonnet, 2002] El-Ghazawi, Tarek A. and Cantonnet, François (2002). UPC performance and potential: A NPB experimental study. In *Proceedings of the 15th Conference on Supercomputing (SC2002)*. IEEE Press.

[El-Ghazawi et al., 2003] El-Ghazawi, Tarek A., Carlson, William W., and Draper, Jesse M. (2003). *UPC Specification V1.1.1*.

[El-Ghazawi and Chauvin, 2001] El-Ghazawi, Tarek A. and Chauvin, Sébastien (2001). UPC benchmarking issues. In *Proceedings of the 2001 International Conference on Parallel Processing*. IEEE Press.

[Gansterer et al., 2003] Gansterer, Wilfried N., Ward, Robert C., Muller, Richard P., and Goddard, III, William A. (2003). Computing approximate eigenpairs of symmetric block tridiagonal matrices. 25:65–85.

[Geist et al., 1994] Geist, A., Beguelin, A., Dongarra, J. J., Jiang, W., Manchek, R., and Sunderam, V. (1994). *PVM: Parallel Virtual Machine—A Users' Guide and Tutorial for Networked Parallel Computing*. MIT Press, Cambridge, MA.

[Gelernter and Carriero, 1992] Gelernter, David and Carriero, Nicholas (1992). Coordination languages and their significance. *Communications of the ACM*, 35(2):97–107.

[GigaSpaces, 2002] GigaSpaces (2002). GigaSpaces Platform – White Paper. Technical report, GigaSpaces Technologies, Ltd., 532 La Guardia PL 567, New York, NY 10012, USA.

[Husbands et al., 2003] Husbands, Parry, Iancu, Costin, and Yelick, Katherine (2003). A performance analysis of the Berkeley UPC compiler. In *Proceedings of the 17th International Conference on Supercomputing*, pages 63–73. ACM Press.

[Lehman et al., 1999] Lehman, T. J., McLaughry, S. W., and Wycko, P. (1999). T Spaces: The Next Wave. In *32 Annual Hawaii International Conference on System Sciences*, volume 8, page 8037. IEEE Press.

[McCalpin, 1995] McCalpin, John D. (1995). Sustainable memory bandwidth in current high performance computers. Technical report, Silicon Graphics, Inc.

MPI-I/O WITH A SHARED FILE POINTER USING A PARALLEL VIRTUAL FILE SYSTEM IN REMOTE I/O OPERATIONS

Yuichi Tsujita

Department of Electronic Engineering and Computer Science,
Faculty of Engineering, Kinki University
1 Umenobe, Takaya, Higashi-Hiroshima, Hiroshima 739-2116, Japan
tsujita@hiro.kindai.ac.jp

Abstract   A flexible intermediate library named Stampi realizes seamless MPI operations on a heterogeneous computing environment. With this library, dynamic process creation and MPI-I/O in both local and remote I/O operations are available. To realize distributed I/O operations with high performance, a Parallel Virtual File System (PVFS) has been implemented in the MPI-I/O mechanism of Stampi. MPI-I/O functions with a shared file pointer have been evaluated and sufficient performance has been achieved.

Keywords: MPI-I/O, Stampi, shared file pointer, MPI-I/O process, PVFS

1.   Introduction

MPI [1, 2] is the de facto standard in parallel computation, and almost all computer vendors have provided their own MPI libraries. But such libraries do not support MPI communications among different kinds of computers. To realize such mechanism, Stampi [3] has been developed.

Recently, data-intensive scientific applications require a parallel I/O system, and a parallel I/O interface named MPI-I/O was proposed in the MPI-2 standard [2]. Although it has been implemented in several kinds of MPI libraries, MPI-I/O operations to a remote computer which has a different MPI library (remote MPI-I/O) have not been supported. Stampi-I/O [4] has been developed as a part of the Stampi library to realize this mechanism. Users can execute remote MPI-I/O operations using a vendor-supplied MPI-I/O library with the help of its MPI-I/O process which is dynamically invoked on a remote computer. When the vendor-supplied one is not available, UNIX I/O functions are used instead of the library (pseudo MPI-I/O method).

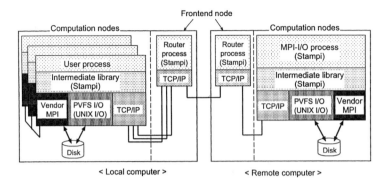

Figure 1.   Architecture of an MPI-I/O mechanism in Stampi.

Recently, PVFS [5] has been developed and available on a Linux PC cluster. It realizes distributed data management and gives users a virtual single file system. Although one of the non-commercial MPI-I/O implementations named ROMIO [6] supports the PVFS system as an underlying I/O device, it does not support remote MPI-I/O operations. To realize effective distributed data management in remote MPI-I/O operations by Stampi, the UNIX I/O functions in the pseudo MPI-I/O method have been replaced with native PVFS I/O functions. Primitive MPI-I/O functions using a shared file pointer were evaluated on interconnected PC clusters.

In the following sections, outline, architecture, and preliminary performance results of the MPI-I/O mechanism are described.

2.   Implementation of PVFS in Stampi

Architectural view of the MPI-I/O mechanism in Stampi is depicted in Figure 1. In the interface layer to user processes, intermediate interfaces which have MPI APIs (a Stampi library) were implemented to relay messages between user processes and underlying communication and I/O systems. Users can execute MPI communication functions including MPI-I/O functions among computers without awareness of differences in underlying communication and I/O systems. To realize distributed I/O on a PVFS file system with high performance, PVFS I/O functions have been introduced in the MPI-I/O mechanism.

As an example, mechanisms of split collective read operations with begin and end statements using a shared file pointer are illustrated in Figures 2 (a) and (b), respectively. When user processes call the function with a begin statement, several parameters including an I/O request are packed in a user buffer using MPI_Pack(). Then it is transfered to an MPI-I/O process using MPI_Send() and MPI_Recv() of the Stampi library. Inside them, Stampi-supplied underlying communication functions such as JMPI_Isend() are used

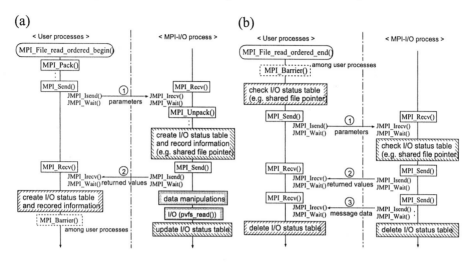

Figure 2.   Mechanisms of (a) `MPI_File_read_ordered_begin()` and (b) `MPI_File_read_ordered_end()` using PVFS I/O functions in remote MPI-I/O operations. MPI functions in solid line rectangles are MPI interfaces of Stampi. Internally, Stampi-supplied functions such as `JMPI_Isend()` are called by them. A vendor-supplied MPI function, `MPI_Barrier()`, in a dotted line rectangle is called among user processes.

for non-blocking TCP socket communications. After the message transfer, the I/O request and other parameters are unpacked by `MPI_Unpack()`. Then an I/O status table, which is used to manage non-blocking I/O operations, is created on the MPI-I/O process and the I/O request and related parameters including a shared file pointer are stored in it. In addition, a ticket number, which is issued to identify each I/O request on the MPI-I/O process, is also stored. After this operation, those parameters are sent to the user processes. Then, the user processes create own I/O status table and store the ticket number and the I/O related information in it. Besides, synchronization among the user processes is done by `MPI_Barrier()` in parallel with the I/O operation by the MPI-I/O process using PVFS I/O functions. On the MPI-I/O process, the stored information values such as the shared file pointer are updated in order of a rank-ID after the I/O operation.

To detect completion of the I/O operation, the split collective read function with an end statement is used. Once it is called, firstly synchronization by `MPI_Barrier()` is carried out among the user processes. Secondly, stored information values in the I/O status table of the user processes are retrieved, and the I/O request, the ticket number, and the related parameters are sent to the MPI-I/O process. The MPI-I/O process finds an I/O status table which has the same ticket number and retrieves the corresponding parameters. Finally, several parameters and read data are sent to the user processes, and both I/O status tables are deleted and the I/O operation finishes.

Table 1.   Specifications of PC clusters.

	PC cluster (I)	PC cluster (II)
	DELL PowerEdge 600SC ×4	DELL PowerEdge 1600SC ×5
CPU	Intel Pentium-4 2.4 GHz	Intel Xeon 2.4 GHz (dual)
Chipset	ServerWorks GC-SL	ServerWorks GC-SL
Memory	1 GByte DDR SDRAM	2 GByte DDR SDRAM
Local disk	40 GB (ATA-100 IDE)	73 GB (Ultra320 SCSI)
Ethernet interface	Intel PRO/1000 (on-board)	Intel PRO/1000-XT (PCI-X board)
Linux kernel	2.4.19-1SCORE	2.4.20-20.7smp (server node)
	(all nodes)	2.4.19-1SCOREsmp (computation nodes)
Network driver	Intel e1000 version 5.2.16	
MPI library	MPICH-SCore [8] based on MPICH [9] version 1.2.4	
Ethernet switch	NETGEAR GS108	3Com SuperStack4900

3.   Performance measurement

Performance of the MPI-I/O functions using a shared file pointer was measured on interconnected PC clusters using an SCore cluster system [7]. Specifications of the clusters are summarized in Table 1. A PC cluster I consisted
one server node and three computation nodes. As the server node also acted
as a computation node, total number of computation nodes was four. While
a PC cluster II had one server node and four computation nodes. Network
connections among PC nodes of the clusters I and II were established on 1
Gbps bandwidth network with full duplex mode via Gigabit Ethernet switches,
NETGEAR GS108 and 3Com SuperStack 4900, respectively. Interconnection between those switches was made with 1 Gbps bandwidth network with
full duplex mode. In the cluster II, PVFS (version 1.5.8) was available on the
server node. All the four computation nodes were used as I/O nodes for the
PVFS file system. Size of dedicated disk of each I/O node was 45 GByte,
and thus the PVFS file system with 180 GByte (4 × 45 GByte) was available.
During this test, default stripe size (64 KByte) of the PVFS was selected.

In performance measurement of round-trip communication, transfer rate
was calculated as (message data size)/(RTT/2), where RTT was a round trip
time for ping-pong communication between both clusters. In the remote MPI-
I/O operations, message data was split evenly among the user processes, and
they were transfered among user processes and an MPI-I/O process on a remote computer. Message data size was denoted as the whole message data size
to be transfered among them. A router process was not used in this test because
each computation node was able to communicate outside directly.

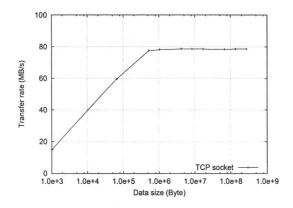

Figure 3.   Transfer rate values of inter-machine data transfer using raw TCP sockets between a computation node of a PC cluster I and a server node of a PC cluster II.

Inter-machine data transfer

Performance of inter-machine data transfer using raw TCP sockets between a computation node of the cluster I and a server node of the cluster II was measured because inter-machine data transfer in the remote MPI-I/O operations was carried out via the same communication path. In this test, TCP_NODELAY option was activated with the help of setsockopt(). Performance results are shown in Figure 3. Raw TCP socket connections achieved up to 78.7 MB/s for 8 MByte message data, thus up to 63 % ($\sim 78.7/125 \times 100$) of the theoretical bandwidth has been achieved. While raw TCP socket connections among PC nodes inside a PC cluster I and II via direct connection using a twisted-pair cross cable achieved up to about 80 MB/s and 112 MB/s, respectively. Thus this low performance was due to poor performance of an on-board Ethernet interface of a PC node in the cluster I.

Local I/O operations

To evaluate PVFS I/O functions, performance of local I/O operations on the PVFS file system was measured using native PVFS and UNIX I/O functions. In the PVFS I/O case, pvfs_write() and pvfs_read() were used for write and read operations, respectively. While write() and read() were used in the UNIX I/O case for write and read operations, respectively. Transfer rates in the both cases are shown in Figure 4. In the write operations, up to 111.6 MB/s for 16 MByte message data and 72.8 MB/s for 1 Mbyte message data were achieved in the PVFS and UNIX I/O cases, respectively. Thus up to 89 % ($\sim 111.6/125 \times 100$) and 58 % ($\sim 72.8/125 \times 100$) of the theoretical throughput were achieved in the PVFS and UNIX I/O cases, respectively. While 111.3 MB/s for 64 MByte and 77.9 MB/s for 16 MByte were achieved

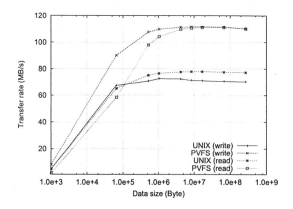

Figure 4.   Transfer rate values of local I/O operations on a PVFS file system of a PC cluster II, where *UNIX* and *PVFS* denote I/O operations using native UNIX and PVFS I/O functions, respectively. Besides, *write* and *read* in parentheses mean write and read operations, respectively.

in the read operations with the PVFS and UNIX I/O functions, respectively. Therefore up to 89 % ($\sim 111.3/125 \times 100$) and 62 % ($\sim 77.9/125 \times 100$) of the theoretical throughput were achieved in the PVFS and UNIX I/O cases, respectively. In the both I/O operations, the PVFS I/O case has performance advantage compared with the UNIX I/O case. In the UNIX I/O case, an I/O request is passed through to the block I/O layer of the Linux kernel on the server node, and then through to PVFS routines. While an I/O request bypasses the first path in the PVFS I/O case. The bottleneck in the former case is considered to be inefficiencies in the implementation of the block I/O layer.

Remote MPI-I/O operations

In performance measurement of remote MPI-I/O operations using PVFS I/O functions from the cluster I to the cluster II, performance of blocking and split collective MPI-I/O functions with a shared file pointer was measured. In this test, TCP_NODELAY option was activated by the Stampi start-up command to optimize inter-machine data transfer.

Execution times of write and read operations using the blocking and split collective MPI-I/O functions are shown in Figures 5 (a) and (b), respectively. Performance values of the blocking functions are almost the same with respect to the number of user processes in both I/O operations because the transfer of I/O requests which followed the former I/O request was blocked until the MPI-I/O process finished an I/O operation by the I/O request. In the read and write I/O operations, transfer rate values with more than 8 MByte data are about 48 MB/s and 38 MB/s, respectively. While estimated transfer rate is roughly calculated as 46 MB/s from the measured values in the inter-machine

(a)   (b)

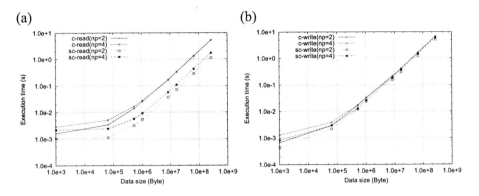

Figure 5.   Execution times of remote (a) read and (b) write MPI-I/O operations using blocking and split collective MPI-I/O functions from a PC cluster I to a PVFS file system of a
PC cluster II. *c-read* and *sc-read* in (a) denote I/O operations by MPI_File_read_ordered()
and MPI_File_read_ordered_begin(), respectively, while *c-write* and *sc-write* in (b) denote
I/O operations by MPI_File_write_ordered() and MPI_File_write_ordered_begin(), respectively. *np* in the parentheses denotes the number of user processes.

data transfer and the local I/O operations. Both values indicate that the inter-
machine data transfer is bottleneck due to the architectural constraints of the
blocking I/O function.

In the read operations, the execution times for the split collective function
are about 22 % and 33 % of those for the blocking function with more than
512 KByte message data in two and four user processes cases, respectively.
While the execution times for the split collective one in the write operations
are about 74 % and 84 % of those for the blocking one with more than 512
KByte message data in two and four user processes cases, respectively.

In the split collective case, the first I/O request was carried out by the MPI-
I/O process without blocking the user processes, but the following I/O requests
were blocked until the former I/O operation finished. Besides, bulk data was
also transfered in the write function, and a required time for the transfer was
dominant in the execution time for the function. As a result, minimizing effect
in the execution times is quite small compared with those in the read operations.

In both blocking and split collective cases, it was confirmed that message
data was written or read according to a rank-ID of each user process correctly.

4.   Summary

By introducing the PVFS system in the MPI-I/O mechanism of Stampi,
huge size of a parallel file system on a PC cluster is accessible from MPI processes on other computers using collective MPI-I/O functions with a shared
file pointer. In the remote MPI-I/O operations, user processes on a PC cluster

invoked an MPI-I/O process dynamically on the another PC cluster where the PVFS file system was available, and it played I/O operations using PVFS I/O functions on the file system. With the help of the PVFS system, distributed data management has been realized in the MPI-I/O mechanism. Execution times of split collective MPI-I/O functions using a shared file pointer were shorter than those of blocking collective ones, typically in read operations.

Acknowledgments

The author would like to thank Genki Yagawa, director of Center for Promotion of Computational Science and Engineering (CCSE), Japan Atomic Energy Research Institute (JAERI), for his continuous encouragement. The author would like to thank the staff at CCSE, JAERI, especially Toshio Hirayama, Norihiro Nakajima, Kenji Higuchi, and Nobuhiro Yamagishi for providing a Stampi library and giving useful information.

This research was partially supported by the Ministry of Education, Culture, Sports, Science and Technology (MEXT), Grant-in-Aid for Young Scientists (B), 15700079.

References

[1] Message Passing Interface Forum (1995). MPI: A message-passing interface standard.

[2] Message Passing Interface Forum (1997). MPI-2: Extensions to the message-passing interface standard.

[3] Imamura, T., Tsujita, Y., Koide, H., and Takemiya, H. (2000). An architecture of Stampi: MPI library on a cluster of parallel computers. In *Recent Advances in Parallel Virtual Machine and Message Passing Interface*, volume 1908 of *Lecture Notes in Computer Science*, pages 200–207. Springer.

[4] Tsujita, Y., Imamura, T., Takemiya, H., and Yamagishi, N. (2002). Stampi-I/O: A flexible parallel-I/O library for heterogeneous computing environment. In *Recent Advances in Parallel Virtual Machine and Message Passing Interface*, volume 2474 of *Lecture Notes in Computer Science*, pages 288–295. Springer.

[5] Carns, P., III, W. L., Ross, R., and Thakur, R. (2000). PVFS: A parallel file system for Linux clusters. In *Proceedings of the 4th Annual Linux Showcase and Conference*, pages 317–327. USENIX Association.

[6] Thakur, R., Gropp, W., and Lusk, E. (1999). On implementing MPI-IO portably and with high performance. In *Proceedings of the Sixth Workshop on Input/Output in Parallel and Distributed Systems*, pages 23–32.

[7] PC Cluster Consortium. http://www.pccluster.org/.

[8] Matsuda, M., Kudoh, T., and Ishikawa, Y. (2003). Evaluation of MPI implementations on grid-connected clusters using an emulated WAN environment. In *Proceedings of the 3rd IEEE/ACM International Symposium on Cluster Computing and the Grid (CCGrid 2003), May 2003*, pages 10–17. IEEE Computer Society.

[9] Gropp, W., Lusk, E., Doss, N., and Skjellum, A. (1996). A high-performance, portable implementation of the MPI Message-Passing Interface standard. *Parallel Computing*, 22(6):789–828.

AN APPROACH TOWARD MPI APPLICATIONS IN WIRELESS NETWORKS *

Elsa M. Macías,[1] Alvaro Suárez,[1] and Vaidy Sunderam[2]

[1]*Grupo de Arquitectura y Concurrencia (GAC)*
Dept. de Ingeniería Telemática, Las Palmas de G. C. University
emacias@dit.ulpgc.es, asuarez@dit.ulpgc.es

[2]*Dept. of Math and Computer Science*
Emory University, Atlanta, USA
vss@mathcs.emory.edu

Abstract   Many emerging situations and applications demand the reconciliation of the MPI model, which implicitly assumes well-connected-ness and unform network capabilities, with wireless and mobile networks that are subject to variations and intermittent connectivity. We describe middleware extensions that assist applications operating in such environments by providing pre-emptive Quality of Service information. By exploiting this data, undesirable deadlock or indefinite blocking scenarios can be effectively avoided. Based on experimentation with an MPI based optimization application, we also show that good performance is retained while providing the added value of state information about communication channels.

Keywords: IEEE 802.11, network-based computing, WLAN, network failures, MPI.

1.   Introduction

With the increasing widespread adoption of the MPI standard, it is becoming common for non-scientific distributed applications. Furthermore it is also common for such applications to execute on varied heterogeneous resources, including widely deployed IEEE 802.11 wireless networks. There are also many long running scientific applications that communicate relatively infrequently, in which it is not unreasonable to use MPI over wireless networks on mobile (or even stationary) devices. In previous work, we have shown that

*Research partially supported by Spanish CICYT under Contract TIC2001-0956-C04-03, The Canaries Regional Government under Contract Pi 2003/021-C and Las Palmas de G.C. University UNI2002/17, and by National Science Foundation grant ACI-0220183 and U.S. DoE grant DE-FG02-02ER25537

IEEE 802.11 WLANs can be efficiently combined with wired LANs to execute parallel-distributed applications [[Macías and Suárez, 2002]]. However, in these environments, sporadic wireless channel failures, abrupt disconnections of mobile computers (computers with wireless interfaces), congestion spikes and other variations in the quality of communications can adversely affect applications. Indeed, MPI applications written assuming certain levels of network quality (e.g. by setting small timeout values) may even behave erroneously, or may discontinue or fail. To permit graceful degradation in such situations, additional middleware functionality is required. To the best of our knowledge, LAM/MPI [[Burns et al., 1994]] and MPICH2 [[Gropp et al., 1996]] do not include this functionality because MPI was not devised for wireless networks although its use is feasible in wireless communications.

Other solutions have been proposed to solve the above issues. It is well known that Transmission Control Protocol (TCP) does not behave well for WLAN [[Huston, 2001]]. A TCP based mechanism that warns all applications could flood the wireless channel with a lot of irrelevant signalling information to a particular asynchronous MPI application. In [[18]] is presented the reliable socket connection a programmer could specify to recover the socket connection in case of sporadic failures during an interval of seconds (specified by the programmer). However, this interval of time is very difficult to adjust in order to detect, for example, that mobile computers are temporarily out of range. Moreover, to the best of our knowledge, reliable sockets have not yet been incorporated into any MPI implementation.

In previous work [[Macías et al., 2004]] we presented a low overhead mechanism (of the order of miliseconds) at the application level, that combined with our wireless network monitoring software detects wireless channel failures and warns MPI applications to help the programmer take appropriate action. In this paper we show how the user can restructure computations after detecting a channel failure. The performance of this technique is better than other alternatives, such as the traditional process migration scheme for WLAN [[Morita and Higaki, 2001]].

The rest of the paper is organized as follows. In section 2 we review the fault detection mechanism. In section 3 a practical implementation of the mechanism is applied to the parallel solution of unconstrained global optimization for n-dimensional functions. Then, some experimental results are presented. Finally we summarize with our conclusions and present directions for further research.

2.   Reviewing the Fault Detection Mechanism

Our LAMGAC middleware [[Macías et al., 2001]] maintains a registry of wireless computers that collaborate with the MPI program in question and uses a lightweight and efficient mechanism [[Macías et al., 2004]] to manage abrupt disconnections of computers with wireless interfaces.

LAMGAC_Fault_detection function implements our software mechanism at the MPI application level. The mechanism is based on injecting ICMP (Internet Control Message Protocol) echo request packets from a specialized node to the wireless computers and monitoring echo replies. The injection is only made if LAMGAC_Fault_detection is invoked and enabled, and replies determine the existence of an operational communication channel. This polling mechanism should not penalize the overall program execution. In order to reduce the overhead due to a long wait for a reply packet that would never arrive because of a channel failure, an adaptive timeout mechanism is used. This timeout is calculated with the collected information by our WLAN monitoring tool [[Tonev et al., 2002]].

3. Unconstrained Global Optimization for n-Dimensional Functions

One of the most interesting research areas in parallel nonlinear programming is that of finding the global minimum of a given function defined in a multidimensional space. The search uses a strategy based on a branch and bound methodology that recursively splits the initial search domain into smaller and smaller parts named *boxes*. The local search algorithm (*DFP* [[Dahlquist and Björck, 1974]]) starts from a defined number of random points. The box containing the smallest minimum so far and the boxes which contain a value next to the smallest minimum will be selected as the next domains to be explored. All the other boxes are deleted. These steps are repeated until the stopping criterion is satisfied.

Parallel Program Without Wireless Channel State Detection

A general scheme for the application is presented in Fig. 1. The master process (Fig. 1.b) is in charge of: sending the boundaries of the domains to be explored in parallel in the current iteration (in the first iteration, the domain is the initial search); splitting a portion of this domain into boxes and searching for the local minima; gathering local minima from slave processes (values and positions); doing intermediate computations to set the next domains to be explored in parallel.

The slave processes (Fig. 1.a and Fig. 1.c) receive the boundaries of the domains that are split in boxes locally knowing the process rank, the number of processes in the current iteration, and the boundaries of the domain. The boxes are explored to find local minima that are sent to the master process. The slave processes spawned dynamically (within LAMGAC_Awareness_update) by the

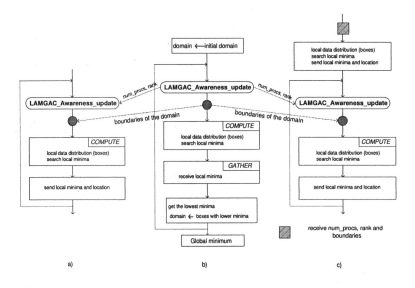

Figure 1. General scheme: a) slaves running on FC from the beginning of the application b) master process c) slaves spawned dynamically and running on PC

master process make the same steps as the slaves running from the beginning of the parallel application but the first iteration is made out of the main loop.

LAMGAC_Awareness_update sends the slaves the number of processes that collaborate per iteration (*num_procs*) and the process' rank (*rank*). With this information plus the boundaries of the domains, the processes compute the local data distribution (boxes) for the current iteration.

The volume of communication per iteration (Eq. 1) varies proportionally with the number of processes and search domains (the number of domains to explore per iteration is denoted as *dom(i)*).

$$comm(i) = A_1 * dom(i) * [1 + PC(i)] + A_2 * \sum_{k=1}^{PC(i)+FC} min(i)^{P_k} + A_3 \quad (1)$$

where FC is the number of computers with wired connections. A_1 represents the cost to send the boundaries (float values) of each domain (broadcasting to processes in FC and point to point sends to processes in PC), $PC(i)$ is the number of processes in the WLAN in the iteration i, $min(i)^{P_k}$ is the number of minima (integer value) calculated by k process in the iteration i, A_2 is the data bulk to send the computed minimum to master process (value, co-ordinates and box, all of them floats), and A_3 is the communication cost for LAMGAC_Awareness_update.

Eq. 2 shows the computation per iteration: $boxes(i)^{P_k}$ is the number of boxes that explores the k process in the iteration i, *random_points* are the total points per box, *DFP* is the DFP algorithm cost and *B* is the computation made by master to set the next intervals to be explored.

$$computation(i) = dom(i) * boxes(i)^{P_k} * random\_points * DFP + B \quad (2)$$

Parallel Program With Wireless Channel State Detection

A slave invalid process (*invalid process* in short) is the one that cannot communicate with the master due to sporadic wireless channel failures or abrupt disconnections of portable computers.

In Fig. 2.a the master process receives local minima from slaves running on fixed computers and, before receiving the local minima for the other slaves (perhaps running on portable computers), it checks the state of the communication to these processes, waiting only for valid processes (the ones that can communicate with the master).

Within a particular iteration, if there are invalid processes, the master will restructure their computations applying the *Cut and Pile* technique [[Brawer, 1989]] for distributing the data (search domains) among the master and the slaves running on FC. In Fig. 2.c we assume four invalid processes (ranks equal to 3, 5, 9 and 11) and two slaves running on FC. The master will do the tasks corresponding to the invalid processes with ranks equal to 3 and 11, and the slaves will do the tasks of processes with rank 5 and 9 respectively. The slaves split the domain in boxes and search the local minima that are sent to master process (Fig. 2.b). The additional volume of communication per iteration (only

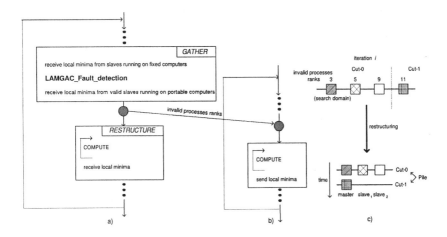

Figure 2. Modified application to consider wireless channel failures: a) master process b) slave processes running on FC c) an example of restructuring

in presence of invalid processes) is shown in Eq. 3.

$$comm(i) = C + A_2 * \sum_{k=1}^{N} min(i)^{P_k} \qquad (3)$$

$$N = \begin{cases} (\text{invalid(i)-1}) & \text{if } invalid(i) <= FC \\ FC & \text{if } invalid(i) > FC \end{cases}$$

C represents the cost to send the ranks (integer values) of invalid processes (broadcast message to processes in the LAN), and $invalid(i)$ is the number of invalid processes in the WLAN in the iteration i.

Eq. 4 shows the additional computation in the iteration i in presence of invalid processes: $boxes(i)^{P_k}_{P_j}$ is the number of boxes that explores the k process corresponding to the invalid processes (P_j).

$$computation(i) = dom(i) * boxes(i)^{P_k}_{P_j} * random\_points * DFP \qquad (4)$$

Experimental Results

The characteristics of computers used in the experiments are presented in Fig. 3.a. All the machines run under LINUX operating system. The input data for the optimization problem are: *Shekel* function for 10 variables, initial domain equal to [-50,50] for all the variables and 100 random points per box. For all the experiments shown in Fig. 3.b we assume a null user load and the network load is due solely to the application. The experiments were repeated 10 times obtaining a low standard deviation.

For the configurations of computers presented in Fig. 3.c, we measured the execution times for the MPI parallel (values labelled as A in Fig. 3.b) and for the equivalent LAMGAC parallel program without the integration with the wireless channel detection mechanism (values labelled as B in Fig. 3.b). To make comparisons we do not consider either input nor output of wireless computers. As is evident, A and B results are similar because LAMGAC middleware introduces little overhead.

The experimental results for the parallel program with the integration of the mechanism are labelled as C, D and E in Fig. 3.b. LAMGAC_Fault_detection is called 7 times, once per iteration. In experimental results we named C we did not consider the abrupt outputs of computers because we just only want to test the overhead of LAMGAC_Fault_detection function and the conditional statements added to the parallel program to consider abrupt outputs. The execution time is slightly higher for the C experiment compared to A and B results because of the overhead of LAMGAC_Fault_detection function and the conditional statements.

We experimented with friendly output of PC1 during the 4-th iteration. The master process receives results computed by the slave process running on PC1 before it is disconnected so the master does not restructure the computations (values labelled as D). We experimented with the abrupt output of PC1 during the step 4 so the master process must restructure the computations before starting the step 5. The execution times (E values) with 4 and 6 processors are higher than D values because the master must restructure the computations.

We measure the sequential time obtaining 124'18" on the slowest computer and 55'54" on the fastest computer. The sequential program generates 15 random points per box (instead of 100 as the parallel program) and the stopping criterion is less strict than for the parallel program, obtaining less accurate results. The reason for choosing these input data different from the parallel one is because otherwise the convergence is too slow in the sequential program.

4.   Conclusions and Future Work

A great concern in wireless communications is the efficient management of temporary or total disconnections. This is particularly true for applications that are adversely affected by disconnections. In this paper we put in practice our

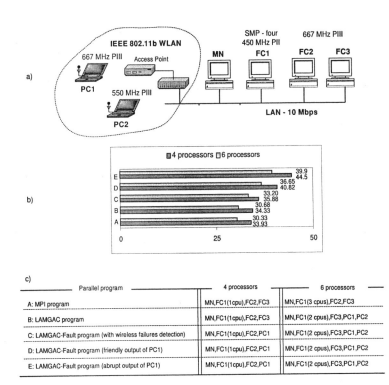

Parallel program	4 processors	6 processors
A: MPI program	MN,FC1(1cpu),FC2,FC3	MN,FC1(3 cpus),FC2,FC3
B: LAMGAC program	MN,FC1(1cpu),FC2,FC3	MN,FC1(2 cpus),FC3,PC1,PC2
C: LAMGAC-Fault program (with wireless failures detection)	MN,FC1(1cpu),FC2,PC1	MN,FC1(2 cpus),FC3,PC1,PC2
D: LAMGAC-Fault program (friendly output of PC1)	MN,FC1(1cpu),FC2,PC1	MN,FC1(2 cpus),FC3,PC1,PC2
E: LAMGAC-Fault program (abrupt output of PC1)	MN,FC1(1cpu),FC2,PC1	MN,FC1(2 cpus),FC3,PC1,PC2

Figure 3.   Experimental results: a) characteristics of the computers b) execution times (in minutes) for different configurations and parallel solutions c) details about the implemented parallel programs and the computers used

wireless connectivity detection mechanism applying it to an iterative loop carried dependencies application. Integrating the mechanism with MPI programs avoids the abrupt termination of the application in presence of wireless disconnections, and with a little additional programming effort, the application can run to completion.

Although the behavior of the mechanism is acceptable and its overhead is low, we keep in mind to improve our approach adding dynamic load balancing and overlapping the computations and communications with the channel failures management.

References

[Brawer, 1989] Brawer, S. (1989). *Introduction to Parallel Programming*. Academic Press, Inc.

[Burns et al., 1994] Burns, G., Daoud, R., and Vaigl, J. (1994). LAM: An open cluster environment for MPI. In *Proceedings of Supercomputing Symposium*, pages 379–386.

[Dahlquist and Björck, 1974] Dahlquist, G. and Björck, A. (1974). *Numerical Methods*. Prentice-Hall Series in Automatic Computation.

[Gropp et al., 1996] Gropp, W., Lusk, E., Doss, N., and Skjellum, A. (1996). A high-performance, portable implementation of the MPI message passing interface standard. *Parallel Computing*, 22(6):789–828.

[Huston, 2001] Huston, G. (2001). TCP in a wireless world. *IEEE Internet Computing*, 5(2):82–84.

[Macías and Suárez, 2002] Macías, E. M. and Suárez, A. (2002). Solving engineering applications with LAMGAC over MPI-2. In *9th European PVM/MPI Users' Group Meeting*, volume 2474, pages 130–137, Linz, Austria. LNCS, Springer Verlag.

[Macías et al., 2001] Macías, E. M., Suárez, A., Ojeda-Guerra, C. N., and Robayna, E. (2001). Programming parallel applications with LAMGAC in a LAN-WLAN environment. In *8th European PVM/MPI Users' Group Meeting*, volume 2131, pages 158–165, Santorini. LNCS, Springer Verlag.

[Macías et al., 2004] Macías, E. M., Suárez, A., and Sunderam, V. (2004). Efficient monitoring to detect wireless channel failures for MPI programs. In *12th Euromicro Conference on Parallel, Distributed and Network-Based Processing*, pages 374–381, A Coruña, Spain.

[Morita and Higaki, 2001] Morita, Y. and Higaki, H. (2001). Checkpoint-recovery for mobile computing systems. In *International Conference on Distributed Computing Systems*, pages 479–484, Phoenix, USA.

[Tonev et al., 2002] Tonev, G., Sunderam, V., Loader, R., and Pascoe, J. (2002). Location and network issues in local area wireless networks. In *International Conference on Architecture of Computing Systems: Trends in Network and Pervasive Computing*, Karlsruhe, Germany.

[Zandy and Miller, 2002] Zandy, V. and Miller, B. (2002). Reliable network connections. In *8th Annual International Conference on Mobile Computing and Networking*, pages 95–106, Atlanta, USA.

DEPLOYING APPLICATIONS IN MULTI-SAN SMP CLUSTERS

Albano Alves[1], António Pina[2], José Exposto[1] and José Rufino[1]

[1]*ESTiG, Instituto Politécnico de Bragança.*
{albano, exp, rufino}@ipb.pt

[2]*Departamento de Informática, Universidade do Minho.*
pina@di.uminho.pt

Abstract   The effective exploitation of multi-SAN SMP clusters and the use of generic clusters to support complex information systems require new approaches. On the one hand, multi-SAN SMP clusters introduce another level of parallelism which is not addressed by conventional programming models that assume a homogeneous cluster. On the other hand, traditional parallel programming environments are mainly used to run scientific computations, using all available resources, and therefore applications made of multiple components, sharing cluster resources or being restricted to a particular cluster partition, are not supported.

We present an approach to integrate the representation of physical resources, the modelling of applications and the mapping of application into physical resources. The abstractions we propose allow to combine shared memory, message passing and global memory paradigms.

Keywords: Resource management, application modelling, logical-physical mapping

1.   Introduction

Clusters of SMP (Symmetric Multi-Processor) workstations interconnected by a high-performance SAN (System Area Network) technology are becoming an effective alternative for running high-demand applications. The assumed homogeneity of these systems has allowed to develop efficient platforms. However, to expand computing power, new nodes may be added to an initial cluster and novel SAN technologies may be considered to interconnect these nodes, thus creating a heterogeneous system that we name multi-SAN SMP cluster.

Clusters have been used mainly to run scientific parallel programs. Nowadays, as long as novel programming models and runtime systems are developed, we may consider using clusters to support complex information systems, integrating multiple cooperative applications.

Recently, the hierarchical nature of SMP clusters has motivated the investigation of appropriate programming models (see [8] and [2]). But to effectively exploit multi-SAN SMP clusters and support multiple cooperative applications new approaches are still needed.

2.   Our Approach

Figure 1(a) presents a practical example of a multi-SAN SMP cluster mixing Myrinet and Gigabit. Multi-interface nodes are used to integrate sub-clusters (technological partitions).

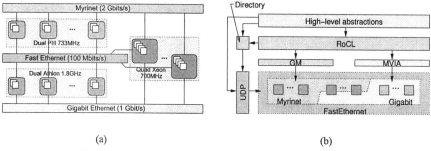

(a)   (b)

Figure 1.   Exploitation of a multi-networked SMP cluster.

To exploit such a cluster we developed RoCL [1], a communication library that combines GM – the low-level communication library provided by Myricom – and MVIA – a Modular implementation of the Virtual Interface Architecture. Along with a basic cluster oriented directory service, relying on UDP broadcast, RoCL may be considered a communication-level SSI (Single System Image), since it provides full connectivity among application entities instantiated all over the cluster and also allows to register and discover entities (see fig. 1(b)).

Now we propose a new layer, built on top of RoCL, intended to assist programmers in setting-up cooperative applications and exploiting cluster resources. Our contribution may be summarized as a new methodology comprising three stages: *(i)* the representation of physical resources, *(ii)* the modelling of application components and *(iii)* the mapping of application components into physical resources. Basically, the programmer is able to choose (or assist the runtime in) the placement of application entities in order to exploit locality.

3.   Representation of Resources

The manipulation of physical resources requires their adequate representation and organization. Following the intrinsic hierarchical nature of multi-SAN

SMP clusters, a tree is used to lay out physical resources. Figure 2 shows a resource hierarchy to represent the cluster of figure 1(a).

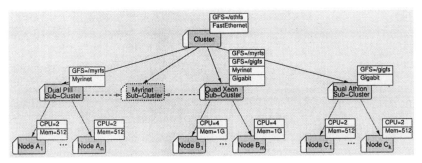

Figure 2. Cluster resources hierarchy.

Basic Organization

Each node of a resource tree confines a particular assortment of hardware, characterized by a list of properties, which we name as a domain. Higher-level domains introduce general resources, such as a common interconnection facility, while leaf domains embody the most specific hardware the runtime system can handle.

Properties are useful to evidence the presence of qualities – classifying properties – or to establish values that clarify or quantify facilities – specifying properties. For instance, in figure 2, the properties Myrinet and Gigabit divide cluster resources into two classes while the properties GFS=... and CPU=... establish different ways of accessing a global file system and quantify the resource *processor*, respectively.

Every node inherits properties from its ascendant, in addition to the properties directly attached to it. That way, it is possible to assign a particular property to all nodes of a subtree by attaching that property to the subtree root node. *Node A_1* will thus collect the properties GFS=/ethfs, FastEthernet, GFS=myrfs, Myrinet, CPU=2 and Mem=512.

By expressing the resources required by an application through a list of properties, the programmer instructs the runtime system to traverse the resource tree and discover a domain whose accumulated properties conform to the requirements. Respecting figure 2, the domain *Node A_1* fulfils the requirements (Myrinet) $\wedge$ (CPU=2), since it inherits the property Myrinet from its ascendant.

If the resources required by an application are spread among the domains of a subtree, the discovery strategy returns the root of that subtree. To combine the properties of all nodes of a subtree at its root, we use a synthesization mechanism. Hence, *Quad Xeon Sub-Cluster* fulfils the requirements (Myrinet) $\wedge$ (Gigabit) $\wedge$ (CPU=4*m).

Virtual Views

The inheritance and the synthesization mechanisms are not adequate when all the required resources cannot be collected by a single domain. Still respecting figure 2, no domain fulfils the requirements (Myrinet) $\wedge$ (CPU=2*n+4*m)[1]. A new domain, symbolizing a different view, should therefore be created without compromising current views. Our approach introduces the original/alias relation and the sharing mechanism.

An alias is created by designating an ascendant and one or more originals. In figure 2, the domain *Myrinet Sub-cluster* (dashed shape) is an alias whose originals (connected by dashed arrows) are the domains *Dual PIII* and *Quad Xeon*. This alias will therefore inherit the properties of the domain *Cluster* and will also share the properties of its originals, that is, will collect the properties attached to its originals as well as the properties previously inherited or synthesized by those originals.

By combining original/alias and ascendant/descendant relations we are able to represent complex hardware platforms and to provide programmers the mechanisms to dynamically create virtual views according to application requirements. Other well known resource specification approaches, such as the RSD (Resource and Service Description) environment [4], do not provide such flexibility.

4.   Application Modelling

The development of applications to run in a multi-SAN SMP cluster requires appropriate abstractions to model application components and to efficiently exploit the target hardware.

Entities for Application Design

The model we propose combines shared memory, global memory and message passing paradigms through the following six abstraction entities:

- domain - used to group or confine related entities, as for the representation of physical resources;

- operon - used to support the running context where tasks and memory blocks are instantiated;

- task - a thread that supports fine-grain message passing;

- mailbox - a repository to/from where messages may be sent/retrieved by tasks;

- memory block - a chunk of contiguous memory that supports remote accesses;

- memory block gather - used to chain multiple memory blocks.

Following the same approach that we used to represent and organize physical resources, application modelling comprises the definition of a hierarchy of nodes. Each node is one of the above entities to which we may attach properties that describe its specific characteristics. Aliases may also be created by the programmer or the runtime system to produce distinct views of the application entities. However, in contrast to the representation of physical resources, hierarchies that represent application components comprise multiple distinct entities that may not be organized arbitrarily; for example, tasks must have no descendants.

Programmers may also instruct the runtime system to discover a particular entity in the hierarchy of an application component. In fact, application entities may be seen as logical resources that are available to any application component.

A Modelling Example

Figure 3 shows a modelling example concerning a simplified version of SIRe[2], a scalable information retrieval environment. This example is just intended for explaining our approach; specific work on web information retrieval may be found eg in [3, 5].

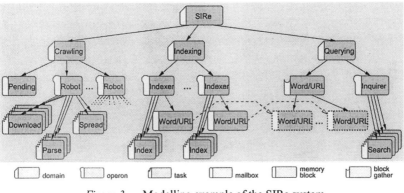

Figure 3. Modelling example of the SIRe system.

Each *Robot* operon represents a robot replica, executing on a single machine, which uses multiple concurrent tasks to perform each of the crawling stages. At each stage, the various tasks compete for work among them. Stages are synchronized through global data structures in the context of an operon. In short, each robot replica exploits an SMP workstation through the shared memory paradigm.

Within the domain *Crawling*, the various robots cooperate by partitioning URLs. After the parse stage, the spread stage will thus deliver to each *Robot* operon its URLs. Therefore *Download* tasks will concurrently fetch messages within each operon. Because no partitioning guarantees, by itself, a perfect balancing of the operons, *Download* tasks may send excedentary URLs to the mailbox *Pending*. This mailbox may be accessed by any idle *Download* task. That way, the cooperation among robots is achieved by message passing.

The indexing system represented by the domain *Indexing* is purposed to maintain a matrix connecting relevant words and URLs. The large amount of memory required to store such a matrix dictate the use of several distributed memory fragments. Therefore, multiple *Indexer* operons are created, each to hold a memory block. Each indexer manages a collection of URLs stored in consecutive matrix rows, in the local memory block, thus avoiding references to remote blocks.

Finally, the querying system uses the disperse memory blocks as a single large global address space to discover the URLs of a given word. Memory blocks are chained through the creation of aliases under a memory block gather which is responsible to redirect memory references and to provide a basic mutual exclusion access mechanism. Accessing the matrix through the gather *Word/URL* will then result in transparent remote reads throughout a matrix column. The querying system thus exploits multiple nodes through the global memory paradigm.

5.   Mapping Logical into Physical Resources

The last step of our methodology consists on merging the two separate hierarchies produced on the previous stages to yield a single hierarchy.

Laying Out Logical Resources

Figure 4 presents a possibility of integrating the application depicted in figure 3 into the physical resources depicted in figure 2.

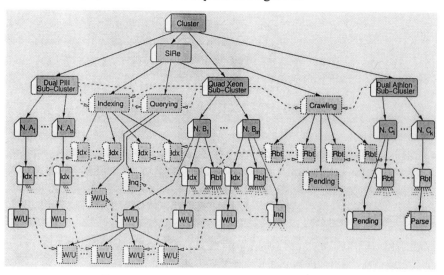

Figure 4.   Mapping logical hierarchy into physical.

Operons, mailboxes and memory block gathers must be instantiated under original domains of the physical resources hierarchy. Tasks and memory blocks are created inside operons and so have no relevant role on hardware appropriation. In figure 4, the application domain *Crawling* is fundamental to establish the physical resources used by the crawling sub-system, since the operons *Robot* are automatically spread among cluster nodes placed under the originals of that alias domain.

To preserve the application hierarchy conceived by the programmer, the runtime system may create aliases for those entities instantiated under original physical resource domains. Therefore, two distinct views are always present: the programmer's view and the system view.

The task *Parse* in figure 4, for instance, can be reached by two distinct paths: *Cluster* $\rightarrow$ *Dual Athlon* $\rightarrow$ *Node* C_k $\rightarrow$ *Robot* $\rightarrow$ *Parse* – the system view – and *Cluster* $\rightarrow$ *SIRe* $\rightarrow$ *Crawling* $\rightarrow$ *Robot*$^{(Alias)}$ $\rightarrow$ *Parse* – the programmer's view. No alias is created for the task *Parse* because the two views had already been integrated by the alias domain *Robot*; aliases allow to jump between views.

Programmer's skills are obviously fundamental to obtain an optimal fine-grain mapping. However, if the programmer instantiates application entities below the physical hierarchy root, the runtime system will guarantee that the application executes but efficiency may decay.

Dynamic Creation of Resources

Logical resources are created at application start-up, since the runtime system automatically creates an initial operon and a task, and when tasks execute primitives with that specific purpose. To create a logical resource it is necessary to specify the identifier of the desired ascendant and the identifiers of all originals in addition to the resource name and properties. To obtain the identifiers required to specify the ascendant and the originals, applications have to discover the target resources based on their known properties.

When applications request the creation of operons, mailboxes or memory block gathers, the runtime system is responsible for discovering a domain that represents a cluster node. In fact, programmers may specify a higher-level domain confining multiple domains that represent cluster nodes. The runtime system will thus traverse the corresponding sub-tree in order to select an adequate domain.

After discovering the location for a specific logical resource, the runtime system instantiates that resource and registers it in the local directory server. The creation and registration of logical resources is completely distributed and asynchronous.

6.   Discussion

Traditionally, the execution of high performance applications is supported by powerful SSIs that transparently manage cluster resources to guarantee high availability and to hide the low-level architecture eg [7]. Our approach is to rely on a basic communication-level SSI used to implement simple high-level abstractions that allow programmers to directly manage physical resources.

When compared to a multi-SAN SMP cluster, a metacomputing system is necessarily a much more complex system. Investigation of resource management architectures has already been done in the context of metacomputing eg [6]. However, by extending the resource concept to include both physical and logical resources and by integrating on a single abstraction layer *(i)* the representation of physical resources, *(ii)* the modelling of applications and *(iii)* the mapping of application components into physical resources, our approach is innovative.

Notes

1. *n* and *m* stand for the number of nodes of sub-clusters *Dual PIII* and *Quad Xeon*.

2. A research supported by FCT/MCT, Portugal, contract POSI/CHS/41739/2001.

References

[1] A. Alves, A. Pina, J. Exposto, and J. Rufino. RoCL: A Resource oriented Communication Library. In *Euro-Par 2003*, pages 969–979, 2003.

[2] S. B. Baden and S. J. Fink. A Programming Methodology for Dual-tier Multicomputers. *IEEE Transactions on Software Engineering*, 26(3):212–226, 2000.

[3] S. Brin and L. Page. The Anatomy of a Large-Scale Hypertextual Web Search Engine. *Computer Networks and ISDN Systems*, 30(1-7):107–117, 1998.

[4] M. Brune, A. Reinefeld, and J. Varnholt. A Resource Description Environment for Distributed Computing Systems. In *International Symposium on High Performance Distributed Computing*, pages 279–286, 1999.

[5] J. Cho and H. Garcia-Molina. Parallel Crawlers. In *11th International World-Wide Web Conference*, 2002.

[6] K. Czajkowski, I. Foster, N. Karonis, C. Kesselman, S. Martin, W. Smith, and S. Tuecke. A Resource Management Architecture for Metacomputing Systems. In *IPPS/SPDP'98*, pages 62–82, 1998.

[7] P. Gallard, C. Morin, and R. Lottiaux. Dynamic Resource Management in a Cluster for High-Availability. In *Euro-Par 2002*, pages 589–592. Springer, 2002.

[8] A. Gursoy and I. Cengiz. Mechanism for Programming SMP Clusters. In *PDPTA'99*, volume IV, pages 1723–1729, 1999.

III

PROGRAMMING TOOLS

EXAMPLES OF MONITORING AND PROGRAM ANALYSIS ACTIVITIES WITH DEWIZ

Rene Kobler, Christian Schaubschläger,
Bernhard Aichinger, Dieter Kranzlmüller, and Jens Volkert
GUP, Joh. Kepler University Linz
Altenbergerstr. 69, A-4040 Linz, Austria
kobler@gup.uni-linz.ac.at

Abstract   As parallel program debugging and analysis remain a challenging task and distributed computing infrastructures become more and more important and available nowadays, we have to look for suitable debugging environments to address these requirements. The Debugging Wizard DeWiz is introduced as modular and event-graph based approach for monitoring and program analysis activities. Example scenarios are presented to highlight advantages and ease of the use of DeWiz for parallel program visualization and analysis. Users are able to specify their own program analysis activities by formulating new event graph analysis strategies within the DeWiz framework.

Keywords: Event Graph, Monitoring, Program Analysis, User-defined Visualization

1.   Introduction

DeWiz (Debugging Wizard) was designed to offer a modular and flexible approach for processing huge amounts of program state data during program analysis activities. Our original fundament for the work on DeWiz was the Monitoring and Debugging environment MAD [4], essentially consisting of the monitoring tool NOPE and the tracefile visualization tool ATEMPT. A major difficulty of MAD was the amount of generated debugging data, some systems could even suffer from problems to store all produced trace data. Another reason for considering the development of an alternate debugging environment was MAD's limitation to message passing programs. DeWiz, the more universal solution, should enable program analysis tasks based on the event graph as representation of a program's behavior. Additionally, a modular, hence flexible and extensible approach as well as graphical representation of a program's behavior is desired [5].

Related work in this area includes P-GRADE [1] or Vampir [11]. P-GRADE supports the whole life cycle of parallel program development. Monitoring as well as program visualization possibilities are both offered by the P-GRADE environment. GRM which is part of P-GRADE is responsible for program monitoring tasks, users are able to specify filtering rules in order to reduce recorded trace data. PROVE, also part of P-GRADE, takes on the part of visualization of message-passing programs in form of space-time diagrams. Vampir, result of a cooperation of Pallas and Technical University of Dresden, provides a large set of facilities for displaying the execution of MPI-programs. An interesting feature of Vampir is the ability to visualize programs in different levels of detail. Additionally many kinds of statistical evaluation can be peformed. On the other hand, EARL [13] which stands for Event Analysis and Recognition Language allows to construct user- and domain- specific event trace analysis tools. Paradyn [8] is rather laid out for performance analysis and optimizations of parallel programs. Its main field of application is the location of performance bottlenecks. Many other tools exist which adress the area of parallel program observation and performance analysis, a couple of them (all of them considering MPI programs) are reviewed in [10].

Unlike DEWIZ, most of the previously mentioned developments suffer from their limitation to certain programming paradigms. The paper is organized as follows: Section 2 introduces the basics of DEWIZ. Afterwards, Section 3 presents concrete examples, concerning monitoring and program analysis using DEWIZ. VISWIZ expatiated in Section 4 introduces a novel way for user-defined program visualizations. The paper is summarized by concluding and giving an outlook on future work.

2.   Overview of DEWIZ

The event graph acts as a basic principle in the DEWIZ infrastructure; it consists of a set of events and a set of happend-before relations connecting them [3]. By linking such DEWIZ modules together, a kind of event-graph processing pipeline is built. Basically we distinguish between three kinds of modules, that are *event graph generation modules*, *automatic analysis modules* and *data access modules*.

Event graph generation modules are responsible for generating event graph streams while automatic analysis modules process these streams by means of different criteria. Data access modules present results produced by predecessing modules to the user. According to this module-oriented structure, a protocol has been specified to define the communication between different modules. The event graph stream consists of two kinds of data structures. For events we use the structure $(p, i, type, data)$, where i indicates the timestamp of occurence on process/thread p. The field $type$ usually determines the content of $data$ where additional event data can be stored. (p, i, q, j) characterizes a happend-before relation, connecting corresponding events.

In addition, modules in a DEWIZ system have to be organized in some way. A special module called *Sentinel* assumes this function. Modules have to register to the sentinel to be part of a DEWIZ system by sending special control messages to this module. On his part the sentinel has to confirm a registration request by returning a special control message to the inquiring module.

The required functionality is offered to DEWIZ-modules by the DEWIZ framework, currently available in C/C++ and Java, respectively. An important feature of this framework is the supply of a controller module which is a visual representation of the information collected and processed by the Sentinel. By dint of the controller control messages can be issued to the sentinel to affect the behavior of a DEWIZ system. A sample DEWIZ system including a dialog for submitting control messages is displayed in Figure 1. Further needed functionalities will be exemplified in the course of the upcoming sections.

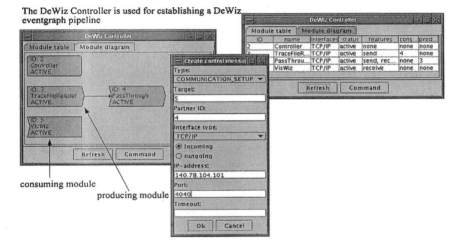

Figure 1. Controller module, once as diagram, once as table + control message dialog

After explaining the basics of DEWIZ, we now present a few extensions and applications to show the underline of this approach. The following list gives a preview of contents of the following sections:

- Visualization of OpenMP Programs

- Online Monitoring with OCM

- User-Defined Visualizations

3. Analysis of OpenMP and PVM Pograms with DEWIZ

As clusters of SMP's gained more and more importance in the past few years, it's essential to provide program analysis environments which support debugging of shared-memory programs. Since OpenMP has emerged to a quasi - standard for programming shared-memory architectures, this section demonstrates how OpenMP programs can be visualized in a DEWIZ-based system. Our DEWIZ module observes the execution of omp_set_lock as well as omp_unset_lock operations using the POMP performance tool interface [9]. DEWIZ-events and happend-before relations will be generated during program execution and forwarded to a consuming visualization module. Figure 2 illustrates the execution of an OpenMP program consisting of 5 threads in a sample scenario. The small circles indicate set- and unset-events (for establishing a critical region) whereas the arrows denote that the ownership of a semaphore changes from one thread to another.for a more detailed description of this implementation please refer to [2].

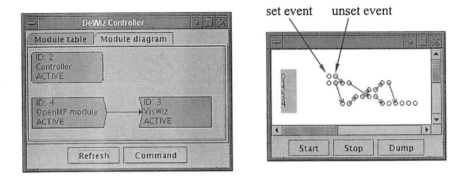

Figure 2.   OpenMP Program Visualization

The next example outlines a DEWIZ system for on-line visualizing PVM-programs as well as for finding communication patterns in such programs. Figure 3 shows an overview of the system where the doted rectangle contains the DEWIZ modules.

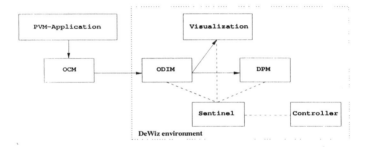

Figure 3.   Program visualization and pattern matching in a PVM-based environment using DEWIZ

PVM-programs are monitored using a concrete implementation of OMIS (Online Monitoring Interface Specification) [7], which defines a universally usable on-line monitoring interface. Due to its event-action-model it is well suited for being integrated in a DEWIZ-based environment. Another good reason for applying OMIS-based program observation is its on-line characteristic. Occured events in our investigated PVM-program can immediately be generated using the OCM (Omis Compliant Monitoring) monitoring system [12] which is a reference implementation of the OMIS specification. The ODIM module (OMIS DEWIZ Interface Module) bridges the gap between a OMIS-based monitoring system and DEWIZ, moreover it is responsible for generating a DEWIZ-specific event-graph stream. In our sample system this stream is sent to a visualization module as well as to a pattern matching module (DPM). Program visualization in terms of a space-time-diagram is carried out on-the-fly during its execution (see Figure 4). The horizontal lines represent the execution of the particular processes (in Figure 4 we have 4 processes), the spots indicate send and receive events, respectively. At present the DPM-module provides only text-based output. Communication patterns, i.e the two hinted in the space-time-diagram are currently being detected.

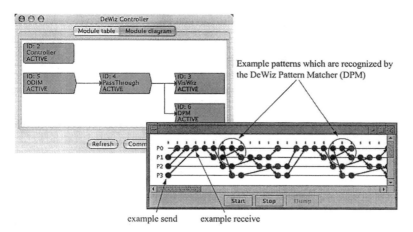

Figure 4. DEWIZ-Controller and Visualization of the PVM-Program

4. User-defined Visualization of Event-Graphs using the VISWIZ-Client

As visualization is indispensable for parallel program activities, this section introduces VISWIZ, the Visualization Wizard for creating user-defined visualizations of events graphs. Some of the available tools offer a variety of diagrams or animations to support program analysis activities. Some of them requires special program instrumentation to achieve the desired kind of visualization. Most tools are also concentrated on certain programming paradigms. The abstract description of runtime information and program states using the event graph decouples from programming paradigms. We try to map events on graphical objects to facilitate different visualizations of event graphs. VISWIZ is the implementation of a DEWIZ consumer module which takes on the task of user-defined visualization. As visualization tools should not be restricted on a small amount of applications, the modular- and event-graph-based concept of DEWIZ enables certain pre-processing activities and paradigm- and platform-independent visualization.

DEWIZ pursues on-line analysis which means that there is no point of time where the event graph is fully available within the VISWIZ system. To achieve a correct visualization, VISWIZ has to accomplish following steps:

1 Description of event-datatypes

2 Rearrangement of the event graph

3 Processing of the particular events

As alluded in Section 2, DEWIZ events may contain additional data depending on the event-type. Therefore it's crucial to know which events are generated by a corresponding producer module during analysis activities. Some default event-types exist, that are substantial for event processing in VISWIZ. The type names *send* and *receive* characterize such event types and should not be redefined by the user. DEWIZ has no knowledge of the whole configuration of the event graph. As it is possible that more than one producing module forwards event data to one consuming module and interconnection network latencies may cause out-of-order receipts, the order of the graph has to be effectuated by a seperate module (see step 2). The so-called *HBR-Resolver* (currently integrated in VISWIZ) is conceived as a pass-through module and takes on the reordering of events. It works with the aid of additional process buffers, every send and receive event is inserted in its corresponding buffer. When receiving a happend-before relation two possibilities arise:

- if both participated events are inside the process buffers, the corresponding send event will be further processed.

- if only one or none of the participated events are inside the process buffers, the happend-before relation is saved and processed after receiving both participated events.

Logical clocks are adapted after removing events from the process buffers for further processing. According to Lamport [6] receive event's logical clocks will be revised by adding the corresponding send's logical clock. After the work of HBR-Resolver, all happend-before events are removed from the event stream. Thus, after the work of this pass-through module we do not have an eventgraph anymore, according to its definition.

After step 2 VISWIZ proceeds with step 3 by mapping each event to its dedicated graphical object. Therefore the user has to specify mapping rules inside a XML-File. The following listing shows an example which denotes how the mapping of events to graphical objects takes place:

```
<eventconfig>
    <event type="send" processid="1">
        <parameter name="blocking" value="blocking">
        <parameter name="commname" value="mpi_send">
        <parameter name="messagesize" value="10" min="0" max="128">
    </event>
    <eventrep>...</eventrep>
</eventconfig>
```

The `<eventrep>`-tag contains different `<class>`-elements; each of these elements include an object class as parameter which is responsible for the description of graphical objects. The SVG standard [14] serves as basis for specifying these objects. The following example should indicate how the representation of an event is accomplished. The `<circle>`-tag creates a circle for each event at the given coordinate:

```
<class name="visualization.objects.NativeSVG" reuse="false">
    <svg xmlns="http://www.w3.org/2000/svg">
        <circle cx="#[40+${logclock}*20]" cy="#[30+${processid}*20]"
            r="6" fill="blue" stroke="red"/>
    </svg>
</class>
```

Event-type declarations as well as mapping rules are stored in configuration files which are loaded when starting VISWIZ. VISWIZ additionally supports the creation of so-called adaptors. Adaptors are applied when statistical data over the program execution is required. They are specified using the XML language as well. Figure 5 illustrates the implementation of an adaptor, which denotes the communication times of the particular processes.

Basically VISWIZ is used like any other consumer module in the DEWIZ environment. Additionally to the registration process, VISWIZ users also have to select files for configuring the event mapping and the visualization, respectively. After loading the configuration data a dialog is opened where the user has to start the visualization process. Alternatively to this, users have the possibility to pause and resume the visualization as well as dumping the currently displayed information in form of a SVG-document for debugging purposes. Figure 6 pictures an event-graph as space-time-diagram, the window in the foreground shows a halted visualization.

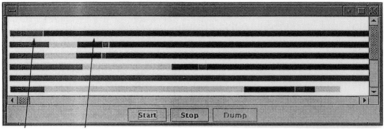

– dark grey and black bars denote comm. times of send and receive events, respectively
– the grey horicontal lines indicate the time–lines for the particular processes

Figure 5.   VisWiz module showing execution times of send and receive events

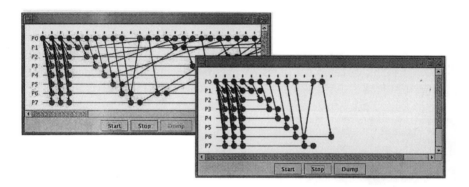

Figure 6.   Event graph visualization, once in running mode, once in stopped mode

5.   Conclusions and Future Work

Apart from DEWIZ's programming paradigm independency, its modular attempt makes it predestinated to cope with demands brought with newer computing environments like the Grid. Modules can be arranged arbitrarily, i.e. in the sample DEWIZ system outlined in Section 3 the OpenMP module could be placed at an OpenMP-friendly computing architecture, while the program visualization could be done on a simple low-end PC. Basic improvements compared to earlier DEWIZ versions have been made in the area of program visualization. The corresponding module VISWIZ (introduced in Section 4) offers completely user-defined visualizations in a very easy way. At the moment our efforts are concentrated in adapting the DEWIZ framework to run on a grid-based environment, additionally the pattern matching module is extended to present detected patterns in a more intuitive way.

Acknowledgements.   Thanks to Roland Wismüller for his input to the OCM related DeWiz modules. Furthermore, our colleagues at GUP Linz provided some valuable input to this work, and we are most grateful to Michael Scarpa and Reinhard Brandstätter.

References

[1] Kacsuk P. *Visual Parallel Programming on SGI Machines.* Proc. of the SGI Users' Conference, Krakow, Poland (2000).

[2] Kobler R., Kranzlmüller D., and Volkert J. *Online Visualization of OpenMP Programs in the DeWiz Environment.* Proc. of the 5th International Conference on Parallel Processing and Applied Mathematics (PPAM 2003), Czestochowa, Poland (September 2003).

[3] Kranzlmüller, D. *Event Graph Analysis for Debugging Massively Parallel Programs.* PhD Thesis, GUP Linz, Joh. Kepler University Linz (September 2000). http://www.gup.uni-linz.ac.at/~dk/thesis

[4] Kranzlmüller D., Schaubschläger Ch., and Volkert J. *A Brief Overview of the MAD Debugging Activities.* Proc. of the Fourth International Workshop of Automated Debugging (AADEBUG 2000), Munich, Germany (August 2000).

[5] Kranzlmüller D., Schaubschläger Ch., Scarpa M., and Volkert J. *A Modular Debugging Infrastructure for Parallel Programs.* Proc. ParCo 2003, Dresden, Germany (September 2003).

[6] Lamport L. *Time, clocks, and the ordering of events in a distributed system.* Communications of the ACM, Vol. 21, No. 7 (July 1978).

[7] Ludwig T., and Wismüller R. *OMIS 2.0 – A Universal Interface for Monitoring Systems.* Proc. of the 4th European PVM/MPI Users' Group Meeting, Cracow, Poland (November 1997).

[8] Miller B.P., Callaghan M.D., Cargille J.M., Hollingsworth J.K., Irvin R.B., Karavanic K.L., Kunchithapadam K., and Newhall T. *The Paradyn Parallel Performance Measurement Tools.* IEEE Computer 28(11), (November 1995).

[9] Mohr, B., Mallony, A., Hoppe, H.-C., Schlimbach, F., Haab, G., Hoefinger, J. and Shah. S. *A Performance Monitoring Interface for OpenMP.* Proc. of the 4th European Workshop on OpenMP (EWOMP'02), Rome, Italy (September 2002).

[10] Moore, S., Cronk, D., London, K., and Dongarra, J. *Review of Performance Analysis Tools for MPI Parallel Programs.* Proc. of the 8th European PVM/MPI Users' Group Meeting, Santorini, Greece (September 2001).

[11] Nagel W.E., Arnold A., Weber M., and Hoppe H.-C. *Vampir: Visualization and Analysis of MPI Resources.* Supercomputer 63, Vol. 12, No. 1 (1996).

[12] Wismüller R. *Interoperability Support in the Distributed Monitoring System OCM.* Proc. of the 3rd International Conference on Parallel Processing and Applied Mathematics (PPAM'99), Kazimierz Dolny, Poland (September 1999)

[13] Wolf F., and Mohr B. *EARL - A Programmable and Extensible Toolkit for Analyzing Event Traces of Message Passing Programs.* Technical Report FZJ-ZAM-IB-9803, Forschungszentrum Jülich, Zentralinstitut für Angewandte Mathematik (April 1998).

[14] World Wide Web Consortium (W3C). *Scalable Vector Graphics (SVG) 1.1 spezification.* Technical Report, http://www.w3.org/TR/SVG11.

INTEGRATION OF FORMAL VERIFICATION AND DEBUGGING METHODS IN P-GRADE ENVIRONMENT*

Róbert Lovas, Bertalan Vécsei
Computer and Automation Research Institute, Hungarian Academy of Sciences (MTA SZTAKI)
[rlovas|vecsei]@sztaki.hu

Abstract   In this paper we present a combined method, which enables the collaboration of parallel debugging techniques with simulation and verification of parallel program's coloured Petri-net model in the frame of an integrated development environment. For parallel applications, written in the hybrid graphical language of P-GRADE, the coloured Petri-net model can be automatically generated. The Occurrence Graph (a kind of state-space) is constructed straight away from the model by the GRSIM simulation engine, which allows examining and querying the Occurrence Graph for critical information, such as dead-locks, wrong termination, or the meeting the temporal logic specification. Based on the obtained information the macrostep-based execution can be steered towards the erroneous situations assisting to users to improve the quality of their software.

Keywords: parallel programming, debugging, formal methods, Petri-net, temporal logic

1.   Introduction to P-GRADE and DIWIDE

P-GRADE is an integrated programming environment for development and execution of parallel programs on various platforms [3][16]. It consists of several software tools, which assist the different steps of software development; it can be used to create, execute, test and tune parallel applications. In P-GRADE, parallel programs can be constructed with GRED graphical editor according to the syntax and semantics of GRAPNEL [3] language. GRAPNEL is a hybrid programming language in the sense that it uses both graphical and textual representations to describe the whole parallel application.

In this paper we introduce the further development of macrostep based DIWIDE debugger in the frame of P-GRADE environment. A particular chal-

---

*The research described in this paper has been supported by the following projects and grants: Hungarian OTKA T042459, and Hungarian IHM 4671/1/2003 project.

lenge is the handling of non-determinism, which may arise in message passing programs from wildcard receive operations, i.e., receive operations that non-deterministically accept messages from different communication partners. The DIWIDE debugger in P-GRADE environment applies the technique of macrostep [9] and it allows the user to test the application in various timing conditions.

The idea of *macrostep* is based upon the concept of collective breakpoints, which are placed on the inter-process communication primitives in each GRAPNEL process. The set of executed code regions between two consecutive collective breakpoints is called a macrostep. Assuming that sequential program parts between communication instructions are already tested, we can handle each sequential code region as an atomic operation. In this way, the systematic debugging of a parallel program requires to debug the parallel program by pure macrosteps. The macrostep-by-macrostep execution mode of parallel programs can be defined as follows. In each macrostep the program runs until a collective breakpoint is hit thus, the boundaries of the macrosteps are defined by series of global breakpoint sets, and the consecutive consistent global states of parallel program are generated automatically.

At replay, the progress of tasks are controlled by the stored collective breakpoints and the program is automatically executed again macrostep-by-macrostep as in the execution phase. The execution path is a graph whose nodes represent the end of macrosteps (i.e. consistent global states) and the directed arcs indicate the possible macrosteps (i.e. the possible state transitions

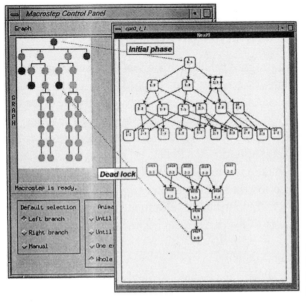

Figure 1 The execution tree (left window) and a part of the corresponding Occurrence Graph (right window)

between consecutive global states). The *execution tree* (see Figure 1, debugging a wrong implementation of producer-consumer problem) is the generalisation of the execution path; it can contain all the possible execution paths of a parallel program assuming that the non-determinism of the current program is inherited from wildcard message passing communications.

The behaviour of sequential programs can be described with run-time assertions expressed in the language of temporal logic (TL) [5], which is an effective way of increasing the code's reliability and thus, the developer's confidence in a program's correct behaviour.

During the extension of the debugging capabilities of P-GRADE, our major goal was to support the following mechanism (see Figure 2) besides using temporal logic assertions.

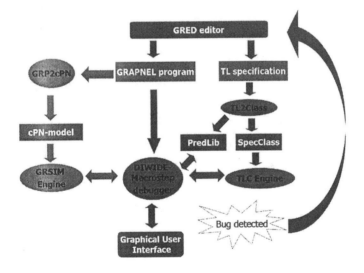

Figure 2.   The structure of debugging cycle in P-GRADE

When the user already specified with temporal logic specification the correctness properties (i.e. the expected program behavior) of GRAPNEL application, and this application was compiled successfully, the GRP2cPN tool [4] generates the coloured Petri-net model of the program. Then, the DIWIDE distributed debugger in co-operation with TLC engine [5] compares the specification to the observed program behaviour macrostep by macrostep, meanwhile the GRSIM simulator steers the traversing of state-space towards suspicious situations. If an erroneous situation is detected, the user is able to inspect (with GUI) either the global state of the application or the state of the individual processes as well. Depending on the situation, the user may fix the programming bug by means of GRED editor, or replay the entire application to get closer to the origin of the detected erroneous situation.

In this way, two isolated subsystems support in detecting bugs in macrostep mode. On one hand, the TLC engine and its related modules [5] are able to deal with the past and present program states during the actual execution of the program. On the other hand, the coloured Petri-net based modeling and simulation can look forward to the future steering automatically the actual execution towards the detected errorenous situations without any user's interaction.

2.   Coloured Petri-net and Occurrence Graph

Coloured Petri-nets [3] (CPN) allow system designers and analysts to move the often difficult task of working directly with real systems into the more tractable and inexpensive computerised modeling, simulation, and analysis. CP nets provide an effective dynamic modeling paradigm and a graphical structure with associated computer language statements. The primary components of a CP net are data entities, places, markings, transitions, arcs and guards but the effective CPN modeling requires the ability to distribute a net across multiple hierarchical pages.

The core of our experimental GRSIM system is Design/CPN toolset [2] that is equipped by several facilities, such as simulation and analysis capabilities, or a C-like standardised meta-language (CPN/ML) for defining guards for transitions, compound tokens, etc. It offers two mechanisms for interconnecting net structure on different pages: substitution transitions and fusion places. In order to add details to a model without losing overview, a (substitution) transition can be associated with it a separate page of CP net structure, called as a subpage. The page that holds the transition is called the superpage. A place that is connected to a substitution transition on a subpage is called a port, and it will appear on a superpage as a socket. These two places compose one functional entity.

The *Occurrence Graph* (OCC graph) (see Figure 1) of a given CPN model is a directed graph where each node represents a possible token distribution (i.e. marking), and each arc represents a possible state transition between two consecutive token distributions.

3.   Transformation steps from GRAPNEL to CPN

The programming model employed in P-GRADE is based on the message passing paradigm. The programmer can define processes which perform the computation independently in parallel, and interact only by sending and receiving messages among themselves. Communication operations always take place via communication ports which belong to processes and are connected by channels.

In GRAPNEL programs, there are three distinguished hierarchical design levels [3], the application level (for definition of processes, ports and channels ensuring the inter-process communication, see Figure 4), the process level (applying a control flow graph like technique for the definition of the inner structure of a process including communication actions such as input, output and alternative input), and the textual level (define C code for sequential elements and conditional or loop expressions, or port protocols inside a process).

One of the main challenges during the automatic generation [4][6][7] of a Petri-net model equivalent to the GRAPNEL application was placing the net in a hierarchical mode on pages and connecting these components together.

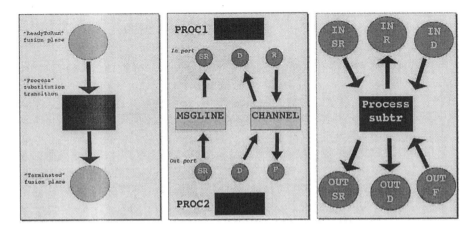

Figure 3. Representation of GRAPNEL process, channel, and port in Petri-net model

Looking into the generation, GRP2cPN kept the logical hierarchy of GRAPNEL and the application level is described on the highest level superpage (MainPage, see Figure 3) where a substitution transition connected with 'ReadyToRun' (by placing a token here it allows the process to execute) and 'Terminated' (if a token appears here, execution of the process finished) fusion places stands for every process. Accordingly, a process is represented on a subpage including the previously mentioned two fusion places.

On the application level a GRAPNEL input type synchronous port [3] is transformed into three fusion places: 'SenderReady' (SR); a token on this place indicates that the partner process is ready for communication, 'ReceiverReady' (RR) the execution is pending on the communication input action waiting for the partner, and 'Data' (D) the place for data to be arrived fusion places. A GRAPNEL output type port is converted into CPN with other three fusion places: 'SenderReady' (SR), 'Data' (D); data to be sent should be placed here in the form of a token (its type determined by the port protocol), 'Finished'

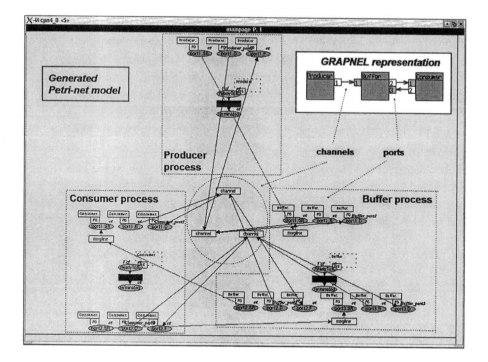

Figure 4.   Petri-net representation of the producer-consumer program at application level

(F) whether the execution of sender process may go further fusion places (see Figure 3).

The communication channel between two processes is converted to CPN 'Channel' (responsible for the whole communication action to occur), and 'MsgLine' (may fire if there is a token in 'SenderReady') simple transitions. When a process wants to send some data to its partner, first it must send a sign through the 'MsgLine' transition to inform the other process about the current situation. If the partner is in 'ReceiverReady' state the data described in the protocol may be transferred through the 'Channel' transition. The detailed description of all transformation steps can be found in [4][7].

4.   Steering the macrostep debugger based on simulation

The pure Petri-net simulation and analysis of entire program is usually not feasible due to the combinatorial explosion of program states, and the simulation is based on the model of the program that neglects numerous physical constraints and real programming bugs. However, the simulation can traverse the different program states much faster than the real execution by orders of magnitude, and we can take the advantage of this fast simulation during the idle periods of macrostep-by-macrostep (or in background mode).

The idea and the goal of this research is that during the execution of each macrostep the simulation engine has to build up an undiscovered part of the OCC graph based on the Petri-net model of GRAPNEL program. On the other hand, using OCC graph analysis the simulation engine can steer the traversing of Execution Tree and can direct the user's focus to deadlocks, wrong terminations, and other erroneous situations that may occur in the future. The starting point of the Petri-net simulation (the first marking from where the simulation starts) is always related to the current consistent global state, i.e. the current node of the Execution Tree that is discovered by the macrostep engine using a depth-first searching strategy [9]. Then the simulation is running concurrently with the real program execution until the next macrostep starts. During the simulation an undiscovered sub-graph of OCC is generated automatically applying a breadth-first searching strategy since it cannot be predicted easily, which are the most possible timing conditions (occurring in the future). The simulator is able to detect some simple classes of erroneous situations that require low-cost analysis, such as deadlocks or wrong process terminations. Meanwhile, the analyser is trying to find other erroneous situations (which require deeper analysis) in the OCC subgraph generated during the previous macrosteps. When either the simulator tool or the analyser tool detects an erroneous situation, the macrostep engine gets a message on the type of error and the list of timing constraints that lead to the erroneous situation. Thus, the macrostep engine can steer the program execution towards the erroneous node of Execution Tree, and the user can uncover the reasons of the error deploying the distributed debugging facilities of DIWIDE debugger.

In the *experimental implementation* two scenarios are proposed to get use of OCC graph; with an automatic verification offered by Design/CPN or with predefined own custom queries using some built-in general query functions derived from the users' TL specification [5].

In the *first case* independently on the actual debug session, when the OCC graph for a CP-net is constructed by the simulator, the reporting facilities of Design/CPN can be utilized to generate a standard report providing information about: Statistics (e.g. size of Occurrence Graph), Boundedness Properties (integer and multi-set bounds for place instances), Home Properties (home markings), Liveness Properties (dead markings, dead/live transition instances), Fairness Properties (impartial/fair/just transition instances).

The contents of the report file can be interpreted and translated automatically to GRAPNEL program behaviour properties, especially keeping a close watch on suspicious situations.

One of the main goals is to detect dead-locks which are equivalent of dead markings in the OCC graph. For all dead markings (ListDeadMarkings) the

GRSIM calls the 'Reachable' function that determines whether there exists an occurrence sequence from the marking of the first node (the actual or initial marking) to the marking of the second node. It means the search in OCC graph to find a directed path between these nodes. When this search is finished, GRSIM gains information about the paths leading to dead-lock situations. The syntax of the output of our queries (the paths) is defined by Design/CPN [2]. The GRSIM gets use of these paths by converting them to a standard form (specified by the input/output interface of macrostep debugger) that allows the user to replay the execution-path from an input file. During this conversion GRSIM traverses the nodes of the OCC path and also converts the proper states into the standard file form of execution tree. For this purpose, the path is segmented into series of nodes, which are corresponding to a macrostep, taking into consideration the transitions, which represent a message passing (particularly where an alternative input receives a message). Relying on the cross-reference file, which is generated during the Petri-net model generation, the segments of OCC path (the reachable coloured Petri-net markings) are translated back and stored as the nodes of execution tree (reachable states of executed program). While the user replays the execution macrostep-by-macrostep through the path ending in dead-lock searching for the cause of dead-lock, it is possible to inspect the actual values of variables, the composition of stack, the instruction pointer in every process with DIWIDE debugger.

The *second option* is to create custom queries in the meta-language and built-in functions [2] of Design/CPN derived from the TL specification [5]. The base function to take into consideration is 'SearchNodes' [2], which traverses the nodes of the OCC graph:

```
SearchNodes(Area, Pred, Limit, Eval, Start, Comb)
begin
  Result := Start; Found := 0;
  for all n in Area do
    if Pred(n) then begin
                    Result := Comb(Eval(n),Result)
                    Found  := Found + 1
                    if Found = Limit then stop for-loop
                 end
  end
end.
```

At each node the specified calculation is performed and the results of these calculations are combined, in the specified way, to form the final result. GRSIM takes the converted form of the negation of our temporal logic expression that must be evaluated to true as the 'Pred' parameter of 'SearchNodes'. The conversion is needed because the introduced TL specification [5] is another description level of program expected behaviour than the approach applied in Design/CPN. The 'SearchNodes' function can be invocated by GRSIM with the following parameters: *SearchNodes(EntireGraph, Pred, NoLimit, fun Eval(n) = n, [], fun Comb(new,old) = new::old)*. As the result of this method GRSIM gets all the places where TL specification fails. From this stage the task remaining is the same as it was described at the end of the first case.

5. Related works

We followed the active control approach, similarly to other state-of-the-art debugging frameworks [8][10][11][12]. There are existing approaches [13] [14][15] to detect erroneous program behaviour based on Petri-net analysis, especially dead-locks, but these techniques developed mainly theoretically with less practical results, and not integrated into a high-level unified framework.

Our attempt is an extension of a parallel programming environment providing automatic support as much as possible preventing the user from the unnecessary interactions; such as automatic generation of Petri-net model. However, the presented experimental debugging framework is strongly tightened to the GRAPNEL graphical language thus; it cannot be applied directly for real-size legacy parallel application contrary to MAD environment [8]. Other solutions, such as FIDDLE [12], address the flexibility of the debugging environment making an open framework for debugging.

6. Summary, future goals

With the introduced technique the debugging of the parallel application becomes more efficient in P-GRADE. The users get easy-to-understand information about the program's possible abnormal behaviour enabling easier bug detection in the same environment, where the program is under development.

The automated analysis of OCC graphs will give efficient support for debugging P-GRADE programs; one possible scenario is to have the GRSIM engine run continuously in the background when a new test version of the application released. In another scenario, the simulation is running simultaneously during the macrostep-based debugging utilising the idle time, when the user inspects the current state of the application.

In both cases, whenever a dead-lock, wrong-termination, live-lock or some other critical events based on the temporal logic specification become predictable by queries on the OCC graph, GRSIM can warn the tester and give the exact path(s) of execution tree leading the erroneous state for further inspection.

The introduced toolset has been implemented partially (some components require manual interactions by the user) and tested with some basic problems, such as the presented producer-consumer or the dinning philosophers problem.

References

[1] Kacsuk, P., Dozsa, G. and Fadgyas, T.: Designing Parallel Programs by the Graphical Language GRAPNEL. Microprocessing and Microprogramming, No. 41 (1996), pp. 625-643

[2] Meta Software Corporation: Desgin/CPN. A Tool Package Supporting the Use of Colored Petri Nets. Technical Report, Cambridge, MA, USA, 1991

[3] Jensen, K.: Coloured Petri Nets. Basic Concepts, Analysis Methods and Practical Use. Volume 2, Analysis Methods. Monographs in Theoretical Computer Science, Springer-Verlag, 1994. ISBN: 3-540-58276-2

[4] Vecsei, B., Lovas, R.: Debugging Method for Parallel Programs Based on Petri-net Representation. Proc. of microCAD International Scientific Conference, 18-19 March 2004, pp. 413-420

[5] Kovacs, J., Kusper, G., Lovas, R., Shreiner, W.: Integrating Temporal Assertions into a Parallel Debugger. Proc. of the 8th International, Euro-Par Conference, Paderborn, Germany, pp. 113-120, 2002

[6] Tsiatsoulis, Z., Dozsa, G., Cotronis, Y., Kacsuk, P.: Associating Composition of Petri Net Specifications with Application Designs in Grade. Proc. of the Seventh Euromicro Workshop on Parallel and Distributed Processing, Funchal, Portugal, pp. 204-211, 1999.

[7] Lovas, R., Kacsuk, P., Horvath, A., Horanyi, A.: Application of P-GRADE Development Environment in Meteorology. Journal of Parallel and Distributed Computing Practices, Special issue on DAPSYS 2002, Nova, Science Publishers (accepted for publication)

[8] Kranzlmuller, D., Rimnac, A.: Parallel Program Debugging with MAD - A Practical Approach. Proc. of International Conference on Computational Science 2003, pp. 201-212

[9] Kacsuk, P.: Systematic Macrostep Debugging of Message Passing Parallel Programs. Journal of Future Generation Computer Systems, Vol. 16, No. 6, pp. 609-624, 2000.

[10] Tarafdar, A., Garg, V.K.: Predicate control for active debugging of distributed programs. Proc. of IPPS/SPDP-98, pages 763-769, Los Alamitos, March 30-April 3 1998.

[11] Frey, M., Oberhuber, M.: Testing and Debugging Parallel and Distributed Programs with Temporal Logic Specifications. Proc. of Second Workshop on Parallel and Distributed Software Engineering 1997, pages 62-72, Boston, May 1997.

[12] Lourenco, J., Cunha, J.C.: Fiddle: A Flexible Distributed Debugging Architecture. Proc. of ICCS 2001, San Francisco, CA, USA, 2001, pp. 821-830

[13] Bruneton, E., Pradat-Peyre, J.-F.: Automatic verification of concurrent Ada programs. Ada-Europe'99 International Conference on Reliable Software Technologies (Santander, Spain), pp. 146–157.

[14] Rondogiannis, P., Cheng, M.H.M: Petri-net-based deadlock analysis of Process Algebra programs. Science of Computer Programming, 1994. Vol. 23 (1), pp. 55-89.

[15] Dwyer, M.B., Clarke, L.A., Nies, K.A.: A compact petri net representation for concurrent programs. Technical Report TR 94-46, University of Massachusetts, Amherst, 1994.

[16] Kacsuk, P. et al.: P-GRADE: a Grid Programming Environment. Journal of Grid Computing Volume 1, Issue 2, 2003, pp. 171-197

TOOLS FOR SCALABLE PARALLEL PROGRAM ANALYSIS - VAMPIR NG AND DEWIZ

Holger Brunst[1], Dieter Kranzlmüller[1,2], Wolfgang E. Nagel[1]

[1] *Center for High Performance Computing*
Dresden University of Technology, Germany
{brunst, nagel}@zhr.tu-dresden.de

[2] *GUP - Institute of Graphics and Parallel Processing*
Joh. Kepler University Linz, Austria/Europe
kranzlmueller@gup.jku.at

Abstract   Large scale high-performance computing systems pose a tough obstacle for to-days program analysis tools. Their demands in computational performance and memory capacity for processing program analysis data exceed the capabilities of standard workstations and traditional analysis tools. The sophisticated approaches of Vampir NG (VNG) and the Debugging Wizard DeWiz intend to provide novel ideas for scalable parallel program analysis. While VNG exploits the power of cluster architectures for near real-time performance analysis, DeWiz utilizes distributed computing infrastructures for distinct analysis activities. A comparison of these two complimentary approaches delivers some promising ideas for future solutions in the area of parallel and distributed program analysis.

Keywords: scalability, program analysis, performance tuning, debugging, tracing

1.   Introduction

The constantly increasing need for computing power and memory resources is a major driving factor of modern computer science. Yet, while standard computer architectures are getting ever more powerful by following Moore's law, the most powerful machines achieve their performance through utilization of massively parallel processing and cluster technology. This fact is clearly demonstrated by the Top500 supercomputer list [17], which contains an increasing number of high performance computer systems with hundred or more processors. At the same time, the continuing interests and application of grid computing infrastructures [5] push the numbers of interconnected computing resources even further.

Consequently, the characteristics of the underlying computer architecture must also be addressed by software development tools. A key factor of software tools is scalability which means that arbitrary numbers of processes, from a few up to 10.000 and more, must be supported. This is unfortunately not the case in todays development environments. Most existing tools support only small numbers of processes, ranging at best up to 32 or 64.

This paper describes two distinct approaches for parallel and distributed program analysis, which try to overcome the above mentioned barrier[1]. The Vampir Next Generation tool VNG [3] is a completely re-designed version of the well-known program analysis tool Vampir [13], while the Debugging Wizard DeWiz is a research prototype based on the technology of the Monitoring And Debugging environment MAD [12]. Both tools address the issue of scalability by exploiting parallelism for program analysis tasks, although different ideas are incorporated in each representative.

The goal of this paper is to provide an overview of these two program analysis tools, and to highlight the provided functionality for scalable program analysis. The paper is organized as follows: Section 2 describes the current situation in the domain of parallel program analysis tools, emphasizing the limitations of related work and the functionality of VNG's and DeWiz's predecessors. Section 3 describes the high performance program analysis tool VNG in more detail, followed by an overview of DeWiz in Section 4. A comparison of both approaches as well as a summary of insights is presented in Section 5, before an outlook on future work in both projects concludes the paper.

2.   Tools for Parallel Program Analysis

Many problems of software engineering emerge during the program analysis phase, which distinguishes between error debugging and performance tuning. Corresponding tools are used to improve the reliability and efficiency of the code, and thus the overall quality of the software. To support this in the best possible way, tool developers have to follow the developments of the hardware on the one hand and the requests of the users on the other hand, while at the same time managing the ever increasing complexity of software applications.

As a consequence, there exists a large number of software tools, which offer more or less sophisticated analysis functionality for different tasks of the program analysis phase. Example surveys of program analysis tools are provided in [15],[6],[9], and [1]. Some of the best known tools for parallel program analysis are AIMS [18], MAD [12], Paje [4], Paradyn [14], ParaGraph [7], P-GRADE [10], TAU [16], and Vampir [13]. While each of these tools has a set of distinguished features and characteristics, their goals are quite comparable: To support users during program analysis activities. Unfortunately, the support offered by these tools is usually limited in the number of supported processes[2]. For example, the ParaGraph tool, often mentioned as one of the first successful tools in this domain, supports a large number of different displays. Yet, the number of processes supported in these displays is limited by 16 in most cases, and 64 in some cases.

Interesting enough is one statement of the ParaGraph manual [8], which says that "ParaGraph's speed of execution is determined primarily by the drawing speed of the workstation". With the advance of computer graphics capabilities on todays workstations, this is clearly no longer a factor in todays software tools. The limiting factor today is mainly given by the number of operations performed on the amount of trace data, including file I/O operations to access the trace data on the disks.

In order to manage the trace data, each of these tools offers a different approach. The idea of the on-line program analysis tool Paradyn is to limit the data gathering during monitoring to the most important regions, and to increase the monitoring only dynamically when more information is required. Consequently, the amount of data being processed by the analysis tool can be defined by the user during the execution of the running program. The drawbacks of this method are, that user interaction is required to obtain the data – which can be difficult for long-running parallel programs – and that some analysis techniques are not applicable during on-line monitoring.

A different idea is chosen by MAD and Vampir, the latter being one of the few commercially available tools for high performance computers. Both tools offer sophisticated mechanisms, which allow to investigate the trace data on different levels of abstraction. In MAD, this is achieved with process grouping and hiding [11], while Vampir provides summary overviews of the program's execution [2]. Nevertheless, each of these tools gets close to its limits, when facing really large amounts of trace data. A typical yardstick is the amount of available main memory. As long as the trace data fits into the main memory of the applied workstation, displaying the contents of the trace data and performing analysis activities is possible. As soon as the trace data exceeds the available memory, or the trace data has to be moved over long distance networks, the analysis tasks become increasingly tedious for the human user.

A solution of this problem is parallelization. Only through parallelism, the amount of memory and the computational performance available and usable for computation can be increased. We believe that this standard approach of high-performance computing to cope with large-scale problems must also be adopted for program analysis tools in order to facilitate tools for todays software development projects. The following two sections introduce two distinct tools, which apply this parallelization approach.

3.   High-Performance Program Analysis with VNG

The distributed architecture of the parallel program analysis tool VNG outlined in this section has been newly designed based on the experience gained from the development of the program analysis tool Vampir. The new architecture uses a distributed approach consisting of a parallel analysis server running on a segment of a parallel production environment and a visualization client running on a remote graphics workstation. Both components interact with each other over the Internet through a socket based network connection. The major goals of the distributed parallel approach are:

1 Keep event trace data close to the location where they were created.

2 Analyze event data in parallel to achieve increased scalability
   (# of events $\sim 1.000.000.000$ and # of streams (processes) ~ 10.000).

3 Provide fast and easy to use remote performance analysis on end-user platforms.

VNG consists of two major components: an analysis server (vngd) and a visualization client (vng). Each is supposed to run on a different machine. Figure 1 shows a high-level view of the VNG architecture. Boxes represent modules of the components whereas arrows indicate the interfaces between the different modules. The thickness of the arrows gives a rough measure of the data volume to be transferred over an interface, whereas the length of an arrow represents the expected latency for that particular link.

In the top right corner of Figure 1 we can see the analysis server, which runs on a small interactive segment of a parallel machine. The reason for this is two-fold. Firstly, it allows the analysis server to have closer access to the trace data generated by an application being traced. Secondly, it allows the server to execute in parallel. Indeed, the server is a heterogeneous parallel program, implemented using MPI and pthreads, which uses a master/worker approach. The workers are responsible for storage and analysis of trace data. Each of them holds a part of the overall data to be analyzed. The master is responsible for the communication to the remote clients. He decides how to distribute analysis requests among the workers. Once the analysis requests are completed, the master merges the results into a single response package that is subsequently sent to the client.

The bottom half of Figure 1 depicts a snapshot of the VNG visualization client which illustrates the timeline of an application run with 768 independent tasks. The idea is that the client is not supposed to do any time consuming calculations. It is a straightforward sequential GUI implementation with a look-and-feel very similar to performance analysis tools listed in Section 2. For visualization purposes, it communicates with the analysis server according to

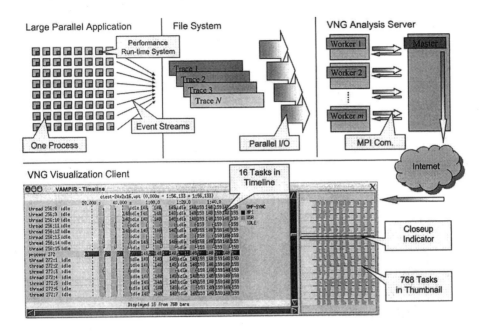

Figure 1.   VNG Architecture Overview

the user's preferences and inputs. Multiple clients can connect to the analysis server at the same time, allowing simultaneous viewing of trace results.

4.   Distributed Program Analysis with DeWiz

The Debugging Wizard DeWiz is a program analysis tool comparable to VNG. However, in contrast to VNG, DeWiz is more a research prototype and a proof-of-concept than a tool for the high performance computing market.

This major distinction allows DeWiz to apply a more radical approach to scalable parallel program analysis, and some features of DeWiz can therefore be seen as the logical extension to VNG. In fact, one of the ideas in the design of DeWiz was to evaluate the feasibility of using distributed computing infrastructures, such as clusters and computational grids, for parallel and distributed program analysis activities. Therefore, the most important characteristic of DeWiz is modularity. Each analysis activity is performed by a distinct analysis module, and the overall analysis strategy is defined by assembling and interconnecting selected DeWiz modules.

A basic necessity in this approach is the definition of a protocol between the modules, such that analysis data can be exchanged. Simplified, this module transports only two different kinds of elements, a variable-sized event structure and a fixed-sized happened-before relation structure. The event structure contains information about the event type, the ordering of this event with respect to other events, the executing object (e.g. the process, on which the event occurred), and the event attributes. The data stored in the event attributes is defined by the event type and the amount of tracing performed. For instance, a send event would contain the message length, the message type, and the destination address as event attributes. The happened-before relation structure contains information about the interconnection of arbitrary events on distinct executing objects. For example, a pair of corresponding send and receive events would generate an additional happened-before relation to express the temporal and causal relation between these two operations.

The analysis activities of DeWiz are based on these two data structures. The foundation of this approach is provided by the event graph model, which describes the execution of a program over the course of time. Consequently, the DeWiz modules are implementations of event graph operations, which process the event graph stream provided with the two data structures described above.

An example of DeWiz during operation is shown in Figure 2. The structure of the applied DeWiz system is given in the top left picture. Each box in the diagram represents a distinct DeWiz module, and the arcs between the boxes indicate their interconnection. The same information is provided in the table of the Controller module on the right bottom side.

On the left hand side of the diagram, monitoring modules are used to produce the data or read corresponding trace files. This data is forwarded to analysis modules, which transform the observed data or try to extract useful information for the analysis activities.

The modules on the right of the diagram display in Figure 2 are used to present the results of the analysis activities to the user. An example of a display module is given in the bottom left corner. The space-time view provides a glimpse of the program analysis activities, with another window given detailed information about a selected event. In addition to this standard display of program execution, DeWiz can also be used to forward events to a series of other display systems. An example is given with the picture of a mobile phone in the top right of Figure 2, which highlights the occurrence of a failure (in this case, a MPI error code).

5.   Comparison and Insights

As described above, both tools, VNG and DeWiz, utilize the capabilities of parallel execution environments to address the possibly huge amounts of trace data. Based on these descriptions, we can identify the following characteristics within either or both of these approaches:

- *Parallelization of analysis activities*: Each tool applies concurrent threads of execution distributed over distinct processing units to perform

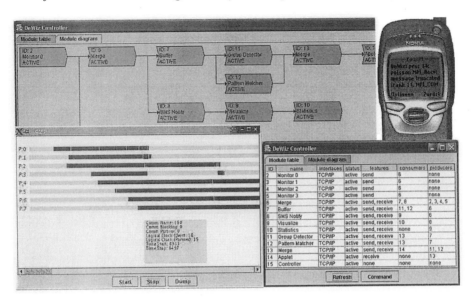

Figure 2. DeWiz Architecture and Analysis Example

partial operations on the trace data. The advantage of this approach is (a) the increased amount of memory available to store the trace data and (b) the additional computing power to perform the analysis operations. The drawback is (comparable to parallel computing applications) the need for distribution and reduction operations in order to produce total results from the generated partial results. Yet, as long as enough trace data is being processed, this additional overhead is acceptable [3].

- *Modularity and programming paradigm*: As a consequence of parallelization, each tool performs the analysis activities in some kind of subunits, in DeWiz called modules. The approaches of VNG and DeWiz are comparable to the two parallelization approaches, SPMD and MPMD. In VNG, the SPMD (Single Program Multiple Data) paradigm is utilized. Each VNG worker process performs the same operation on different sets of data. In DeWiz, the MPMD (Multiple Program Multiple Data) is utilized to provide different modules for distinct analysis activities.

The obvious advantage of VNG is the ease of use of cluster architectures, where the same code is loaded and executed on all processes. On contrary, the initialization process of DeWiz is much more complicated, requiring explicit instructions to load specific modules on specific hardware. However, once the modules are loaded, DeWiz offers more flexibility in terms of utilized hardware resources.

- *Data transportation*: Another major distinction between VNG and DeWiz is the transportation of data between the distribution processing units. On the one hand, the approach used in VNG facilitates parallel I/O capabilities, which are typically available in todays cluster environments. On the other hand, DeWiz requires a dedicated protocol to exchange data over communication links, and may thus be more likely subject to communication failures.

- *Abstraction levels*: Besides processing the data, an important factor of program analysis is the presentation of the analysis results to the user. Especially with large amounts of trace data, users are often overwhelmed and confused, if corresponding functionality is missing. Both, VNG and DeWiz, provide dedicated features for managing the trace data on different, hierarchical levels of abstraction, such that users are able to navigate through the trace data using overview and summary information whenever needed.

- *Analysis goals*: A historic distinction between VNG and DeWiz is their area of application. While both tools can be used for arbitrary analysis activities, VNG is more focused on the performance tuning aspects, while DeWiz originally started as an error debugging tool. However, as clearly shown by the functionality of both tools, these areas are more and more merging, leading to integrated tools for the users.

- *Target of program analysis*: In terms of the targets for program analysis, both tools should be capable of addressing arbitrary codes, which is demonstrated by the fact, that message-passing (e.g. MPI) as well as shared-memory programs (e.g. OpenMP) are supported. The key to universality in this area is the program model utilized by the two analysis tools.

- *Connection to monitoring*: While this paper does not address the problems of scalable program monitoring, there are some aspects of monitoring that obviously influence the analysis activities. For example, the abstraction levels described above would be best supported by a hierarchical trace format, which is unfortunately not available today. At the same time it is interesting to see, how each of the tools accesses the observation data. Usually, on-line and post-mortem analysis activities are distinguished, and both VNG and DeWiz are capable of supporting both types of connections to the monitoring system.

6.   Summary and Future Work

The problem of large-scale parallel and distributed program analysis is ever more immanent with todays availability of large-scale and possibly distributed computing resources. Consequently, performing program analysis activities requires dedicated functionality from software tools, and parallelism is the only choice, if applications on large-scale computing infrastructures are being investigated. In fact parallelization is the key to scalable program analysis, as shown by the two example tools VNG and DeWiz.

The implementations of VNG and DeWiz have offered interesting insights into the problem area of large-scale analysis activities. Many open questions remain for the future, e.g. the issue of scalable monitoring and – associated with it – the development of a suitable trace file format. Additionally, some more advanced analysis features are currently being integrated in VNG and DeWiz, including sophisticated pattern matching of program execution traces. Finally, the increasing availability of grid infrastructures represents an interesting area to deploy program analysis activities, and first ideas to utilize the grid for VNG and DeWiz are currently being investigated.

Acknowledgments

The VNG tool developed at Dresden University of Technology and the DeWiz tool developed at Joh. Kepler University Linz are the results of several years of research and software engineering, supported by many of our colleagues to whom we are most grateful.

Notes

1. Please note, that we only address the program analysis tasks, assuming that a monitoring tool is capable of gathering and storing the monitoring data. The latter is a difficult enough challenge by itself.

2. With processes, we mean the more general term representing executing entities such as threads, tasks, and actual processes, e.g. within the context of MPI.

References

[1] Browne, S., Dongarra, J.J., London, K., "Review of Performance Analysis Tools for MPI Parallel Programs", Technical Report, NHSE, Computer Science Department, University of Tennessee, Knoxville, TN, USA, http://www.cs.utk.edu/Λbrowne/perftools-review/review.html (1999).

[2] Brunst, H., Hoppe, H.Ch., Nagel, W.E., Winkler, M., "Performance Optimization for Large Scale Computing: The Scalable VAMPIR approach", Proc. ICCS 2001, Intl. Conference on Computational Science, Springer-Verlag, LNCS, Vol. 2074, San Francisco, CA, USA (May 2001).

[3] Brunst, H., Nagel, W.E., Malony, A.D., "A Distributed Performance Analysis Architecture for Clusters", IEEE International Conference on Cluster Computing, Cluster 2003, IEEE Computer Society, Hong Kong, China, pp. 73-81 (December 2003).

[4] Chassin de Kergommeaux, J., Stein. B., "Paje: An Extensible Environment for Visualizing Multi-Threaded Program Executions", Proc. Euro-Par 2000, Springer-Verlag, LNCS, Vol. 1900, Munich, Germany, pp. 133-144 (2000).

[5] Foster, I., Kesselman, C., "The Grid: Blueprint for a New Computing Infrastructure", Morgan-Kaufman (1999).

[6] Gu, W., Vetter, J., Schwan, K., "An Annotated Bibliography of Interactive Program Steering", ACM SIGPLAN Notices, Vol. 29, No. 9, pp. 140-148 (September 1994).

[7] Heath, M.T., Etheridge, J.A., "Visualizing the Performance of Parallel Programs", IEEE Software, Vol. 8, No. 5, pp. 29-39 (September 1991).

[8] Heath, M.T., Etheridge, J.A., "ParaGraph: A Tool for Visualizing the Performance of Parallel Programs", Technical Report, Oak Ridge National Laboratory, http://www.netlib.org/paragraph/ (1994).

[9] Hondroudakis, A., "Performance Analysis Tools for Parallel Programs", Version 1.0.1, Edinburgh Parallel Computing Centre, The University of Edinburgh, available at: http://www.epcc.ed.ac.uk/epcc-tec/documents.html (July 1995).

[10] Kacsuk, P., Cunha, J.C., Dozsa, G., Lourenco, J., Fadgyas, T., Antao, T., "A Graphical Development and Debugging Environment for Parallel Programs", Journal of Parallel Computing, Haring, G., Kacsuk, P., Kotsis, G., (Eds.), "Distributed and Parallel Systems: Environments and Tools", Elsevier Publisher, Vol. 22, No. 13, pp. 1699-1701 (1997).

[11] Kranzlmller, D., Grabner, S., Volkert, J., "Event Graph Visualization for Debugging Large Applications", Proc. SPDT'96, ACM SIGMETRICS Symposium on Parallel and Distributed Tools, Philadelphia, PA, USA, pp. 108-117 (May 1996).

[12] Kranzlmller, D., Grabner, S., Volkert, J., "Debugging with the MAD Environment", Journal of Parallel Computing, Dongarra, J.J., Tourancheau, B., (Eds.), "Environments and Tools for Parallel Scientific Computing III", Elsevier Publisher, Vol. 23, No. 1-2, pp. 199-217 (Apr. 1997).

[13] Nagel, W.E., Arnold, A., Weber, M., Hoppe, H.-C., Solchenbach, K., "VAMPIR: Visualization and Analysis of MPI Resources", Supercomputer 63, Volume XII, Number 1, pp. 69-80 (Jan. 1996).

[14] Miller, B.P., Callaghan, M.D., Cargille, J.M., Hollingsworth, J.K., Irvin, R.B., Karavanic, K.L., Kunchithapadam, K., Newhall, T., "The Paradyn Parallel Performance Measurement Tool", IEEE Computer, Vol. 28, No. 11, pp. 37-46 (November 1995).

[15] Pancake, C.M., Netzer, R.H.B., "A Bibliography of Parallel Debuggers, 1993 Edition", Proc. of the 3rd ACM/ONR Workshop on Parallel and Distributed Debugging, San Diego, CA, USA (May 1993), reprinted in: ACM SIGPLAN Notices, Vol. 28, No. 12, pp. 169-186 (Dec. 1993).

[16] Shende, S., Cuny, J., Hansen, L., Kundu, J., McLaugry, S., Wolf, O., "Event and State-Based Debugging in TAU: A Prototype", Proc. SPDT'96, ACM SIGMETRICS Symposium on Parallel and Distributed Tools, Philadelphia, PA, USA, pp. 21-30 (May 1996).

[17] TOP 500 Supercomputer Sites, http://www.top500.org/ (2004).

[18] Yan, J.C., H.H. Jin, H.H., Schmidt, M.A., "Performance Data Gathering and Representation from Fixed-Size Statistical Data", Technical Report NAS-98-003, http://www.nas.nasa.gov/Research/Reports/Techreports/1998/nas-98-003.pdf, NAS System Division, NASA Ames Research Center, February 1999.

PROCESS MIGRATION IN CLUSTERS AND CLUSTER GRIDS *

József Kovács
MTA SZTAKI
Parallel and Distributed Systems Laboratory
H1518 Budapest, P.O.Box 63 Hungary
smith@sztaki.hu

Abstract   The paper describes two working modes of the parallel program checkpointing mechanism of P-GRADE and its potential application in the nationwide Hungarian ClusterGrid (CG) project. The first generation architecture of ClusterGrid enables the migration of parallel processes among friendly Condor pools. In the second generation CG Condor flocking is disabled, so a new technique is introduced to somehow interrupt the whole parallel application and take it out of the Condor scheduler with checkpoint files. The latter mechanism enables a parallel application to be completely removed from the Condor pool after checkpointing and to be resumed under another non-friendly Condor pool after resubmission. The checkpointing mechanism can automatically (without user interaction) support generic PVM programs created by the P-GRADE Grid programming environment.

Keywords: message-passing parallel programs, graphical programming environment, checkpointing, migration, cluster, grid, pvm, condor

1.   Introduction

Process migration in distributed systems is a special event when a process running on a resource is redeployed on another one in a way that the migration does not cause any change in the process execution. In order to provide this capability special techniques are necessary to save the whole memory image of the target process and to reconstruct it. This technique is called checkpointing. During checkpointing a tool suspends the execution of the process, collects all those internal status information necessary for resumption and terminates the

*The work presented in this paper has been supported by the Hungarian Chemistrygrid OMFB-00580/2003 project, the Hungarian Supergrid OMFB-00728/2002 project, the Hungarian IHM 4671/1/2003 project and the Hungarian Research Fund No. T042459.

process. Later a new process is created and all the collected information is restored for the process to continue its execution without any modification.

Such migration mechanism can be advantageously used in several scenarios like load balancing, utilisation of free resources (high throughput computing), fault tolerant execution or resource requirement driven migration. When using a job scheduler most of the above cases can only be supported by some external checkpointing mechanism, since automatic checkpointing of parallel jobs is rarely solved within a job scheduler. For example, the Condor [11] system can only guarantee the automatic checkpointing of sequential jobs but only provides user level support for fault-tolerant execution of Master/Worker PVM jobs.

When building a huge ClusterGrid we should aim at making the Grid [4] capable of scheduling parallel applications effectively, otherwise these applications will fail due to the dynamic behaviour of the execution environment.

Beyond the execution of a parallel program another important aspect of a Grid end-user - among others - is the creation of a Grid application. Unfortunately, there are no widely accepted graphical tools for high-level development of parallel applications. This is exactly the aim of the P-GRADE [9] (Parallel Grid Run-time and Application Development Environment) Grid programming environment that has been developed by MTA SZTAKI. P-GRADE currently generates [3] either PVM or MPI code from the same graphical notation according to the users' needs.

In this paper we show how an external checkpointing mechanism can be plugged into a scheduler by our tool without requiring any changes to the scheduler, and making a huge nationwide ClusterGrid be capable of executing parallel application with full support of automatic checkpointing. The paper details two working modes: migration among friendly (flocked) Condor pools and migration among non-friendly (independent) condor pools. Both are related to the different layouts of the evolving Hungarian ClusterGrid project.

2.   The Hungarian ClusterGrid Project

The ClusterGrid project was started in the spring of 2002, when the Hungarian Ministry of Education initiated a procurement project which aimed at equipping most of the Hungarian universities, high-schools and public libraries with high capacity computational resources.

The ClusterGrid project aims to integrate the Intel processor based PCs into a single, large, countrywide interconnected set of clusters. The PCs are provided by the participating Hungarian institutes, the central infrastructure and the coordination is provided by NIIF/HUNGARNET, the operator of the Hungarian Academic Network. Every contributor uses their PCs for their own purposes during the official work hours, such as educational or office-like purposes, and offers the infrastructure for high-throughput computation whenever they do not use them for other purposes, i.e. during the night hours and the unoccupied week-ends. The combined use of "day-shift" (i.e. individual mode) and "night-shift" (i.e. grid mode) enables us to utilise CPU cycles (which would have been lost anyway) to provide firm computational infrastructure to the national research community.

By the end of summer 2002, 99 PC-labs had been installed throughout the country; each lab consisting of 20 PCs, a single server and a firewall machine. The resources of PCs in each lab were accumulated by the Condor software and the pools were flocked to each other creating a huge Condor pool containing 2000 machines. A Virtual Private Network was built connecting all the nodes and a single entry point was defined to submit applications. This period is referred as 1st generation architecture of ClusterGrid.

From September 2003, a new grid layout has been established referred to as 2nd generation architecture. It was changed to support decentralised submission of applications and to add an intelligent brokering layer above the condor pools that are not flocked to each other any more.

Currently both sequential jobs and parallel jobs parallelized by Parallel Virtual Machines (PVM) library are supported. Automatic checkpointing works for statically linked sequential jobs only, thus no parallel jobs can run longer than 10 hours (the duration of a night-shift operation) or 60 hours (the duration of a week- end operation). User-level check-pointing can be applied to both sequential and parallel jobs without any execution time restriction. For more detailed information, please refer to [12]

3. The P-GRADE software development tool

P-GRADE [5] provides a complete, integrated, graphical solution (including design, debugging, testing, monitoring, load balancing, checkpointig, performance analysis and visualization) for development and execution of parallel applications on clusters, Grid systems and supercomputers. The high-level graphical environment of P-GRADE reduces the need for programming competence thus, non-professional programmers can use the same environment on traditional supercomputers, clusters, or Grid solutions. To overcome the execution time limitation for parallel jobs we introduced a new checkpointing technique in P- GRADE where different execution modes can be distinguished.

In interactive mode the application is started by P-GRADE directly, which means it logs into a cluster, prepares the execution environment, starts a PVM or MPI application and takes care of the program. In this case it is possible to use the checkpoint system with a load balancer attached to it.

In job mode the execution of the application is supervised by a job scheduler like Condor or SGE after submission. When using the Condor job scheduler P-

GRADE is able to integrate automatic checkpointing capability into the application. In this case the parallel application can be migrated by Condor among the nodes of its pool or it is even possible to remove the job from the queue after checkpointing and transfer the checkpoint files representing the interrupted state to another pool and continue the execution after it is resubmitted to the new pool.

To enable one of the execution modes mentioned above the user only needs to make some changes in the "Application Settings" dialog of P-GRADE and submit the application. No changes required in the application code.

4.   Migration in the 1st generation ClusterGrid

P-GRADE compiler generates [3] executables which contain the code of the client processes defined by the user and an extra process, called the grapnel server which is coordinating the run-time set-up of the application. The client processes contain the user code, the message passing primitives and the so called grapnel (GRAPhical NEt Language) library that manages logical connections among them. To set-up the application first the Grapnel Server (GS) (see Figure 1 comes to life and then it creates the client processes containing the user computation.

Before starting the execution of the application, an instance of the Checkpoint Server (CS) is started in order to transfer checkpoint files to/from the dynamic checkpoint libraries dynamically linked to the application. Each process of the application automatically loads the checkpoint library at start-up that checks the existence of a previous checkpoint file of the process by connecting to the Checkpoint Server. If it finds a checkpoint file for the process, resumption of the process is automatically initiated by restoring the process image from the checkpoint file otherwise the process is started from the beginning. To provide an application-wide consistent checkpointing, the communication primitives are modified to perform the necessary protocol among the user processes and among the user processes and the server.

In a Condor based Grid, like the 1st generation ClusterGrid, the P-GRADE checkpoint system is prepared to the dynamic behaviour of the PVM virtual machine organised by Condor. Under Condor the PVM runtime environment is slightly modified by Condor developers in order to give fault-tolerant execution support for Master-Worker (MW) type parallel applications.

The basic principle of the fault-tolerant MW type execution in Condor is that the Master process spawns workers to perform the calculation and it continuously monitors whether the workers successfully finish their calculation. In case of a failure the Master process simply spawns new workers passing the unfinished work to them. The situation when a worker fails to finish its calculation usually comes from the fact that Condor removes the worker because

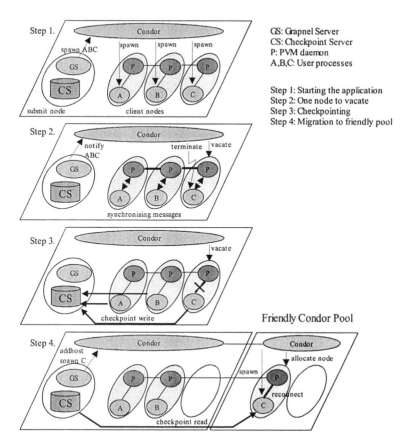

Figure 1. Migration phases under Condor.

the executor node is no longer available. This action is called vacation of the machine containing the PVM process. In this case the master node receives a notification message indicating that a particular node has been removed from the PVM machine. As an answer the Master process tries to add new PVM host(s) to the virtual machine with the help of Condor and gets notified when it is done successfully. Afterwards it spawns new worker(s).

For running a P-GRADE application, the application continuously requires the minimum amount of nodes to execute the processes. Whenever the number of the nodes decreases below the minimum, the Grapnel Server (GS) tries to extend the number of PVM machines above the critical level. It means that the GS process works exactly the same way as the Master process in the Condor MW system.

Whenever a process is to be killed (e.g. because its node is being vacated), an application-wide checkpoint is performed and the exited process is resumed on another node. The application-wide checkpointing is driven by the GS, but can be initiated by any user process (A, B, C) which detects that Condor tries to kill it. After the notification the GS sends a checkpoint signal and message to every user process, which results in the user processes to make a coordinated checkpoint. It is started with a message synchronisation among the processes and finishes with saving the memory image of the individual processes. Now, that the application is saved, terminating processes exit to be resumed on another node.

At this point the GS waits for the decision of Condor that tries to find underloaded nodes either in the home Condor pool of the submit machine or in a friendly Condor pool. The resume phase is performed only when the PVM master process (GS) receives a notification from Condor about new host(s) connected to the PVM virtual machine. For every new node a process is spawned and resumed from the stored checkpoint file. When every terminated process is resumed on a new node allocated by Condor, the application can continue its execution.

This working mode enables the PVM application to continuously adapt itself to the changing PVM virtual machine by migrating processes from the machines being vacated to some new ones that have just been added. Figure 1 shows the main steps of the migration between friendly Condor pools. This working mode is fully compatible with the first generation architecture of the nationwide Hungarian ClusterGrid project.

5.   Migration in the 2nd generation ClusterGrid

Notice that in the previous solution the Application Server (GS) and Checkpoint Server (CS) processes must remain in the submit machine during the whole execution even if every user process (A,B,C in Figure 1) of the application migrates to another pool through flocking. Since flocking is not used in the 2nd generation ClusterGrid, the application must be checkpointed and removed from the pool. Then a broker allocates a new pool, transfers checkpoint files and resubmits the job. Then, the application should be able to resume its execution.

In order to checkpoint the whole application, the checkpoint phase is initiated by the broker (part of the ClusterGrid architecture) by simply removing the application from the pool. In this case the application server detects to be killed, it performs a checkpoint of each process of the application, shuts down all user processes, checkpoints itself and exits. This phase is similar to the case when all the processes are prepared for migration but completes with an additional server self-checkpointing and termination. As a preparation the server creates a file status table in its memory to memorise the open files used by the application and also stores the status of each user process.

When the broker successfully allocates a new pool it transfers the executable, checkpoint and data or parameter files and resubmits the application. When resubmitted, the server process first comes to life and the checkpoint library linked to it automatically checks for proper checkpoint file by querying the checkpoint server. The address of the checkpoint server is passed by parameters (or optionally can be taken from environment variable). When it is found, the server (GS) resumes, data files are reopened based on the information stored in the file status table and finally every user process is re-spawned, the application is rebuilt.

This solution enables the parallel application to be migrated among different sites and not limited to be executed under the same condor pool during its whole lifetime. Details of the checkponting mechanism can be found in [6].

6. Performance and Related Work

Regarding the performance of checkpointing overall time spent for migration are checkpoint writing, reading, allocation of new resources and some coordination overhead. The overall time a complete migration of a process takes also includes the response time of the resource scheduling system e.g. while Condor vacates a machine, the matchmaking mechanism finds a new resource, allocates it, initialises pvmd and notifies the application. Finally, the cost of message synchronisation and costs used for coordination processing are negligible, less than one percent of the overall migration time.

Condor [8], MPVM [1], DPVM [2], Fail-Safe PVM [7], CoCheck [10] are other software systems supporting adaptive parallel application execution including checkpointing and migration facility. The main drawbacks of these systems are that they are modifying PVM, build complex execution system, require special support, need root privileges, require predefined topology, need operating system support, etc. Contrary to these systems our solution makes parallel applications be capable of being checkpointed, migrated or executed in a fault tolerant way on specific level and we do not require any support from execution environment or PVM.

7. Conclusion

In this paper a checkpointing mechanism has been introduced which enables parallel applications to be migrated partially among friendly Condor pools in the 1st generation Hungarian ClusterGrid and to be migrated among independent (non- friendly) Condor pools in the 2nd generation ClusterGrid.

As a consequence, the P-GRADE checkpoint system can guarantee the execution of any PVM job in a Condor-based Grid system like ClusterGrid. Notice that the Condor system can only guarantee the execution of sequential jobs and special Master/Worker PVM jobs. In case of generic PVM jobs Condor cannot provide checkpointing. Therefore, the developed checkpointing mechanism significantly extends the robustness of any Condor-based Grid system.

An essential highlight of this checkpointing system is that the checkpoint information can be transferred among condor pools, while native condor checkpointer is not able provide this capability, so non-flocked condor pools cannot exchange checkpointed applications not even with help of an external module.

The migration facility presented in this paper does not even need any modification either in the message-passing layer or in the scheduling and execution system. In the current solution the checkpointing mechanism is an integrated part of P-GRADE, so the current system only supports parallel applications created by the P-GRADE environment. In the future, roll-back mechanism is going to be integrated to the current solution to support high-level fault-tolerance and MPI extension as well.

References

[1] J. Casas, D. Clark, R. Konuru, S. Otto, R. Prouty, and J. Walpole, "MPVM: A Migration Transparent Version of PVM", Technical Report CSE-95-002, 1, 1995

[2] L. Dikken, F. van der Linden, J.J.J. Vesseur, and P.M.A. Sloot, "DynamicPVM: Dynamic Load Balancing on Parallel Systems", In W.Gentzsch and U. Harms, editors, Lecture notes in computer sciences 797, High Performance Computing and Networking, volume Proceedings Volume II, Networking and Tools, pages 273-277, Munich, Germany, April 1994. Springer Verlag

[3] D. Drótos, G. Dózsa, and P. Kacsuk, "GRAPNEL to C Translation in the GRADE Environment",Parallel Program Development for Cluster Comp.Methodology,Tools and Integrated Environments, Nova Science Publishers, Inc. pp. 249-263, 2001

[4] I. Foster, C. Kesselman, S. Tuecke, "The Anatomy of the Grid." Enabling Scalable Virtual Organizations, Intern. Journal of Supercomputer Applications, 15(3), 2001

[5] P. Kacsuk, "Visual Parallel Programming on SGI Machines", Invited paper, Proc. of the SGI Users Conference, Krakow, Poland, pp. 37-56, 2000

[6] J. Kovács and P. Kacsuk, "Server Based Migration of Parallel Applications", Proc. of DAP-SYS'2002, Linz, pp. 30-37, 2002

[7] J. Leon, A. L. Fisher, and P. Steenkiste, "Fail-safe PVM: a portable package for distributed programming with transparent recovery". CMU-CS-93-124. February, 1993

[8] M. Litzkow, T. Tannenbaum, J. Basney, and M. Livny, "Checkpoint and Migration of UNIX Processes in the Condor Distributed Processing System", Technical Report #1346, Computer Sciences Department, University of Wisconsin, April 1997

[9] P-GRADE Parallel Grid Run-time and Application Development Environment: http://www.lpds.sztaki.hu/pgrade

[10] G. Stellner, "Consistent Checkpoints of PVM Applications", In Proc. 1st Euro. PVM Users Group Meeting, 1994

[11] D. Thain, T. Tannenbaum, and M. Livny, "Condor and the Grid", in Fran Berman, Anthony J.G. Hey, Geoffrey Fox, editors, Grid Computing: Making The Global Infrastructure a Reality, John Wiley, 2003

[12] http://www.clustergrid.iif.hu

IV

P-GRADE

GRAPHICAL DESIGN OF PARALLEL PROGRAMS WITH CONTROL BASED ON GLOBAL APPLICATION STATES USING AN EXTENDED P-GRADE SYSTEM

M. Tudruj*,**   J. Borkowski*   D. Kopanski*
*Polish-Japanese Institute of Information Technology, ul. Koszykowa 86, 02-008 Warsaw, Poland
**Institute of Computer Science of the Polish Academy of Sciences, ul. Ordona 21, 01-237 Warsaw, Poland
{tudruj, janb, damian}@pjwstk.edu.pl

Abstract: An extension of the graphical parallel program design system P-GRADE towards specification of program execution control based on global application state monitoring is presented. De-coupled structured specifications of computational and control elements of parallel programs are assumed. Special synchronizer processes collect process state messages supplied with time interval timestamps and construct strongly consistent application states. Control predicates are evaluated on these states by synchronizers. As a result, control signals can be sent to application processes to stimulate desired reactions to the predicates. The signals can cause asynchronous computation activation or cancellation. Implementation of a parallel program of Traveling Salesman Problem (TSP) solved by branch-and-bound (B&B) method is described to illustrate properties of the new system.

Key words: parallel program design, graphical support tools, synchronization-based control, global program states.

1.   INTRODUCTION

Parallel program execution control defined with the use of high level predicates based on global application states is an emerging method that opens new design possibilities in programs for distributed memory systems. The essential concept is here that the control predicates enable influencing the behavior of programs by means of generalized synchronization of global states of processes located in separate parallel processors [TK98, JB00]. It is different to what exists in the standard practice, where the control is always derived from a local state inside a processor. P-GRADE [KDF97] allows users to specify graphically parallel processes, their interconnections and the internal structure of each process. A programmer specifies a program by the use of a graphical user interface and does not need to know any technical details of communication libraries. Inter-process synchronization in standard P-GRADE is based on message passing facilities including a barrier. We have extended the existing P-GRADE environment with global level synchronization and control mechanisms. The control is de-coupled from computational code of a program. Such a methodology improves standard methods where the code responsible for the synchronization and control is usually scattered in the program code in an unstructured way.

The paper is composed of 2 main parts. The first part describes the extension of the P-GRADE system. The second part describes a TSP parallel program implementation for the new GRADE system.

2. PS-GRADE - SYNCHRONIZATION -ORIENTED P-GRADE SYSTEM

The extended P-GRADE environment incorporates new mechanisms based on high-level synchronization and communication methods. A parallel program control environment includes the global control level and the process level. The global control level is based on special globally accessible processes called synchronizers. They are responsible for monitoring execution states of parallel processes in application programs, computing predicates on these states and issuing control signals depending on the predicate values, to application processes. A global application state is a vector of local states of all constituent processes A global state is strongly consistent if it contains pair wise concurrent local states, according to the chosen precedence relation. The process level describes how application processes report their states to synchronizers and how the processes react to control signals coming from synchronizers. We suggest to reduce the use of passive waiting in program control and to keep programs doing some useful computations potentially all the time. The computations can be suspended temporally if there are more important actions to be performed. When a synchronization condition is met, selected processes are signaled. The signals can trigger execution of dedicated new computations, which are integral parts of the whole application. Alternatively, computations can be cancelled on signals, if for some reason there is no point in continuing them. In distributed systems, inter-process communication is generally subject to various delays, so, state messages can arrive to synchronizers in unpredictable order. Therefore, the state messages are supplied with timestamps based on partially synchronized processor clocks. Based on the timestamps, the synchronizers construct precedence relation on process states and determine global or regional (partial) strongly consistent states (SCS) [JB04, MN91, S00], before control predicates are evaluated. Evaluation of a predicate starts when the synchronizer finds a new pertinent SCS. The clock synchronization is based on the Network Time Protocol [RFC]. Soon, hardware counters controlled from a global clock and the RBS protocol [EGE02] will be used with clock tolerance of few microseconds.

Two components of the synchronization-based program control - global control level and process level are directly mapped onto GRADE application window and process windows, respectively. There are 3 new features introduced to GRADE in the application window: synchronizer processes, synchronizer input ports with potentially many processes connected to each port and synchronizer output ports with potentially many processes connected to each port. By clicking on a synchronizer icon, a synchronizer condition window is opened. It enables specification of all synchronizer's conditions (generalized predicates) as control flow diagrams supported by code in C.

To design a parallel program with execution control based on predicates computed on global application states, we should prepare an overall image of the application program. We have to decompose the program into a set of parallel application processes and a set of synchronizers. In the application processes, we should identify the states, which will be monitored by synchronizers and used for global program control. We have to determine how state representation will be sent to synchronizers. Then, we define the regions in the program code, which are sensitive to synchronization signals sent back from synchronizers. Next, we prepare the reactions to synchronization signals, which are received. Having all this, we start editing the code (the block and flow diagrams) using the graphical design tool.

3. EXAMPLE: A TSP SOLVED BY B&B METHOD

A parallel program design for a Travelling Salesman Problem solved by a branch and bound method [WA99] will illustrate the PS-GRADE system. Execution of the algorithm is based on a set of worker parallel processes, which receive search tasks from a central coordinator process. In this algorithm some state tables are used to monitor current load of each worker process (how much work is left), the upper bound of the sub-problem being solved by each search (worker) process and the best solution found so far. Two synchronization conditions are checked: is there a worker process out of work and are there worker processes solving sub-problems, which are not prospective any more (i.e. their upper bounds are below the best solution found). The first condition is responsible for parallel search task farming with dynamic load balancing. The second condition is responsible for canceling solving non-productive sub-problems.

The new GRADE windows for the TSP program are shown below. Fig 1 presents the application layer window. The program consists of a set of worker processes workerXj, workerYj, workerZj and four synchronizers Synchi. The synchronizers are mutually connected in a hierarchical structure with the Synch0 at the top. Synch0 is connected with each lower level synchronizer by one state channel and one signal channel. Workers are connected to synchronizers using three channels: two state channels from

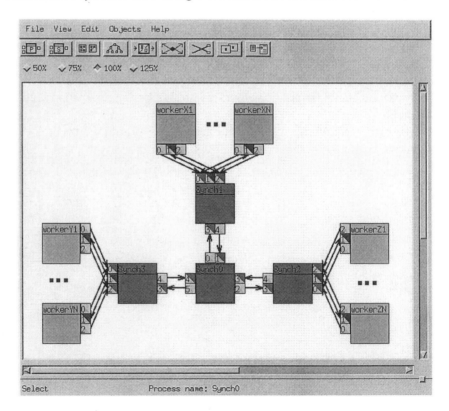

Figure 1. Application window of TSP program

workers to the synchronizers and one reverse channel with two types of signals (new search data signal and new MinDist signal). The synchronizers Synch1, ..., Synch3 react to state messages received from workers and signals from Synch0. They have some pools of search data previously sent to them by the Synch0. If they can satisfy the data requests, they send some new search data to workers. Otherwise, they send new search data pool requests states to Synch0. In response, Synch0 can send new search data to lower level synchronizer to be dispatched among requesting workers. In response to received LocMinDist states, Synch1, ..., Synch3 compare the received values with the best results they know, dispatch the better-than-known results among their local workers and inform Synch0 if a better result than known to it has been found. Synch0 evaluates the best-known result and dispatches it to lower level synchronizers for further parallel dispatching to workers.

The Synch0 condition window is shown in Fig. 2. It shows condition (predicate) blocks MinDist, DataRequesti, which are used to control program behavior. A condition flow graph can be edited after clicking on the condition block. Each condition has input state ports and output ports for sending signals to processes. Conditions DataRequesti are defined on regional states Dreqi, respectively and MinDist is based on Nmini states . DReqi correspond to new search data pool requests from lower level synchronizers and NMini, correspond to current minimal search results from Synch1, Synch2, Synch3. The conditions input/output ports are connected to external synchronizer ports using special assignment windows. Each lower level synchronizer has 2 conditions: DataRequest triggered by any of regional states: Dreq or Dsend, and MinDist, triggered by any of two regional states: NMin and Emin. NMin corresponds to a MinDist result for local workers. Emin corresponds to MinDist for all workers.

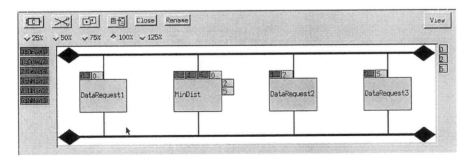

Figure 2 Condition window of Synch0

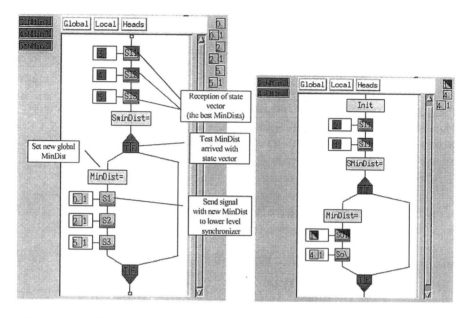

Figure 3. Control flow diagram of Synch0 condition MinDist (left) and control flow diagram of Synch1 conditions MinDist (right)

Fig. 3 shows the flow diagrams of MinDist conditions of Synch0 and Synch1. In condition handling, state vectors are first read, the data associated with state messages are tested, predicates are evaluated and control signal decisions are taken and executed. Based on received Nmin states a local best result SminDist for all workers of Synch1 is computed. If the new SminDist is better the current condition's best MinDist, new MinDist is associated with a signal sent to all the workers of Synch1 and also it is sent to Synch0 in a state message Nmin1. In response to Emin signal received from Synch0, the new SminDist is computed and distributed to all local workers of Synch1 if it is better than the best locally known.

Fig 4 shows the control flow diagram of a worker process. This diagram consists of two parts: computation code and signal handling code. Workers send search data requests to lower level synchronizers and receive new search data or the new MinDist values for further search activity. Depending on what control signal has been received by a worker from its synchronizer, the execution of the worker program is interrupted and the new global MinDist value is substituted (NewMinDist block) or the new search task is installed in the processors (NewData block). If an inconsistent MinDist has been received, an error is displayed to the user. After each of these actions, program returns to the point where it was interrupted.

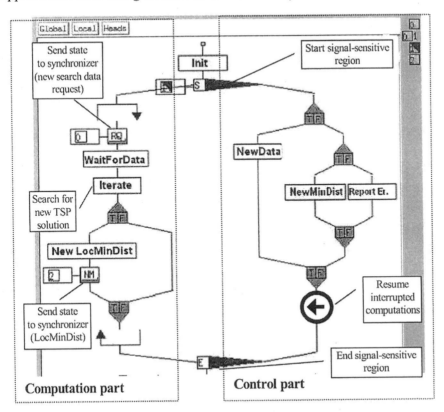

Figure 4. Control flow diagram of a worker process

4.   CONCLUSIONS

We have presented a new P-GRADE-based graphical parallel programming environment with extended parallel program synchronization and control features. The assumed de-coupled specification of synchronization and control in programs is consistent with current tendencies of systematic design of parallel systems. The control in a parallel application program is based on asynchronous evaluation of higher level control predicates. Global predicates used to control program execution are combined with asynchronous activation and cancellation mechanism. Global predicates can implement application control and synchronization, which is correct by construction. The use of the evolved synchronization can improve efficiency of many parallel application programs. Computational data transmissions can be de-coupled from synchronization and control transmissions. In the final implementation of the system, computational data exchange is assumed to be done by the Gigabit Ethernet, while state and control messages will be exchanged by a FireWire network.

Parallel implementation of the travelling salesman problem TSP in the new program design environment has been presented in the paper. Comparative experiments have shown that implementation of parallel TSP programs, which applies new control features of PS-GRADE is more efficient than that using standard P-GRADE features.

Acknowledgements. The authors wish to thank cordially the Laboratory of Parallel and Distributed Systems of SZTAKI Institute (Institute of Computers and Automation of the Hungarian Academy of Sciences) in Budapest for so fruitful co-operation while designing the PS-GRADE system and having made the source code of the P-GRADE system available.

This work has been partially sponsored by the KBN Grant N. 4T11C 007 22 and internal PJIIT research grants.

5. BIBLIOGRAPHY

[BKT03] J. Borkowski, D. Kopanski, M. Tudruj, Implementing Control in Parallel Programs by Synchronization-Driven Activation and Cancellation, 11-th Euromicro Conference on Parallel Distributed and Network based Processing, Genoa - Italy February, 5-7, 2003, IEEE Computer Society Press, pp. 316-323.

[JB00] J. Borkowski, Towards More Powerful and Flexible Synchronization Primitives, in Proc. of Inter. Conf. on Parallel Computing in Electrical Engineering PARELEC 2000, August 2000, Trois-Rivieres, Canada. IEEE Computer Society, pp.18-22.

[JB04] J. Borkowski, Strongly Consistent Global State Detection for On-line Control of Distributed Applications, 12-th Euromicro Conference on Parallel Distributed and Network-Based Processing, PDP 2004, La Coruna, Spain, Feb., 2004, IEEE Computer Society, pp. 126-133.

[KDF97] Kacsuk, P., Dózsa, G. and Fadgyas, T., GRADE: A Graphical Programming Environment for PVM Applications Proc. of the 5th Euromicro Workshop on Parallel and Distributed Processing, London, 1997, pp. 358-365.

[KDFL99] The GRED Graphical Editor for the GRADE Parallel Program Development Environment, P .Kacsuk, G. Dózsa, T. Fadgyas and R. Lovas, Future Generation Computer Systems, No. 15 (1999), pp. 443-452.

[MN91] K. Marzullo and G. Neiger Detection of Global StatePredicates, in: Distributed Algorithms, 5th Int. Workshop, WDAG '91, Delphi, Greece, 1991, Proceedings, LNCS 579, Springer 1992.

[RFC] Request for Comment RFC1305 Network Time Protocol (Version 3) Specification, Implementation and Analysis.

[S00] Scott D. Stoller: "Detecting Global Predicates in Distributed Systems with Clocks". Distributed Computing, Vol. 13, Issue 2 (2000), pp 85-98.

[TK98] M. Tudruj, P. Kacsuk, Extending Grade Towards Explicit Process Synchronization in Parallel Programs, Computers and Artificial Intelligence, Vol 17, 1998, No. 5, pp 507-516.

[WA99] B. Wilkinson, M. Allen, Parallel Programming, Techniques and Applications Using Networked Workstations and Parallel Computers, Prentice Hall, 1999.

PARALLELIZATION OF A QUANTUM SCATTERING CODE USING P-GRADE: A CASE STUDY

Ákos Bencsura and György Lendvay
Institute of Chemistry, Chemical Research Center, Hungarian Academy of Sciences,
P. O. Box 17, H- 1525 Budapest, Hungary
bencsura, lendvay@chemres.hu

Abstract   We used P-GRADE, a graphical tool and programming environment to parallelize atomic level reaction dynamics codes. In the present case study ABC, a quantum reactive scattering code written in FORTRAN has been parallelized. We used the possibly coarsest grain parallelization, i.e. a complete calculation at each total energy is performed on a node. From the automatic schemes offered by P-GRADE, the task farm was selected. The FORTRAN code was separated into an input/output and a working section. The former, enhanced by a data transfer section operates on the master, the latter on the slaves. Small sections for data transfer were written in C language. The P-GRADE environment offers a user-friendly way of monitoring the efficiency of the parallelization. On a 20-processor NPACI Rocks cluster the speed-up is 99 percent proportional to the number of processors. P-GRADE proved to be user-friendly and made the programmer's work very efficient.

Keywords: P-GRADE, quantum scattering, parallelization

1. Introduction

Computer simulation of dynamical processes at the atomic level has been actively pursued for decades. Although the foundations of the methods were laid down long ago, really efficient application of the techniques started only in the last few years when the speed and amount of computers achieved a critical level, because calculations in reaction dynamics are computationally very intensive. The current tendency for speeding up the calculations is that one uses multiple processors on a supercomputer or a cluster, or a Grid, [1, 2, 3]. The purpose of this report is a brief overview of the issues arising when a user experienced in modeling molecular processes decides to switch to parallel programming. Our overview is strictly user-oriented, and we hope to help others familiar with scientific FORTRAN programming in finding efficient ways of parallelizing existing dynamics codes, without going through extensive education in computer science.

Computer codes written for application in the field of molecular modeling are generally prepared for sequential execution. When a code is mdified for parallel execution, the algorithm of the calculation has to be re-organized so that the possibility that several processors perform calculations at the same time could be allowed and exploited. The steps of the algorithm have to be set so that the computational tasks could be assigned to processors running simultaneously. Of course, the programmer still needs to take care of proper organization of data flow between processors, of assigning tasks to processors, and of collecting the final data. The bottleneck is generally that one needs to know the commends that perform the communication. Parallelization, however, can be made easy by the use of software that takes care of implementing the communication between processors. We have been using for this purpose P-GRADE (Parallel Grid Run-time and Application Development Environment) developed at SZTAKI [4, 5, 6, 7]. P-GRADE is a graphical program development tool and running environment. It provides users with prepared clichés for different data flow models from which one can build the graph of the code using graphical tools. P-GRADE then generates a code using PVM or MPI that enables parallel execution. The execution can be monitored and optimized using the "Prove" tool of P-GRADE, which graphically displays in real time how the processors are utilized, what time is spent on communication etc. The software can also prepare codes that can be run on the Grid. In out earlier test of P-GRADE we parallelized a classical trajectory code that has since been routinely used to calculate reactive cross sections of chemical reactions [9]. We found P-GRADE to be easy to learn. There are manuals and instructions available on the web [8]. Some case studies have also been presented in the literature [10, 11].

In the present case study we describe how we parallelized a quantum scattering code that is used to calculate the main dynamical characteristics of an elementary chemical reaction of atom A with a diatomic molecule BC. In the following we first describe how the algorithm was adapted for multiprocessor use in Section 2, then in Section 3 we detail how the code was modified using P-GRADE, and finally we present some data on the performance.

2.   Re-structuring of the FORTRAN code

Numerical solution of quantum scattering equations requires a complicated computer code and is computationally fairly intensive [12]. We do not detail the theory here (see e.g. [13, 14, 15]). Briefly, the time-independent solution of the coupled channel (CC) equations has to be performed at each total energy selected. Generally one is interested in reactive and inelastic cross sections at several total energies. The calculations at separate total energies can be made indepent from each other. From the computational point of view the solution of the CC equations involves the calculation of some large matrices (e.g. the **R** matrix or the logarithmic derivative matrix of the wavefunction of the size of about 2000x2000) that are then used to calculate state-to state **S** matrix elements, whose absolute value is necessary for the calculation of reactive cross sections. The calculation of the individual elements of the large matrices is time-consuming; a major contributor to their computation is the calculation of the potential energy. The individual elements are not needed once the bf S-matrix elements are calculated, and can be disposed of. The actual code we parallelized is the reactive quantum scattering code for triatomic systems, ABC [16], made available for us by Dr. D. E. Manolopoulos. The time-independent Schrödinger equation is solved using a log-derivative method [17]. In this method, the logarithmic derivate of the wavefunction is propagated along the scattering coordinate (the hyperradius) which is divided into sectors. From the computational point of view, the propagation is the most time-consuming step. It has to be done at each set of parameters J, the total angular momentum, p, parity, E, the total energy. The wavefunction is expanded in term of a basis set the size of which, in principle, can be varied with the total energy: one can optimize the basis set size for various ranges of energy in test calculations by selecting the smallest basis that guarantees a required convergence of the **S** matrix elements.

The basic steps of the code are:

- input of parameters that include J, p, E_{max} and the set of total energies to be considered;
- setting up the basis set, i.e. calculation of the rovibrational eigenfunctions of the possible diatomic molecules that can be constructed from atoms A, B, and C; these are used at the end of the propagation to determine the elements of the rearrangement-dependent **S** matric elements;
- in a loop over sectors (steps in the hyperradius) calculate the basis functions corresponding to the sector and write them to disk; calculate the transformation matrix from the sector to the next one and write it to disk
- in a loop over total energies perform the log-derivative propagation, write the data to a scratch file
- in a loop over total energies read the matrices from the scratch file and calculate the **S** matrix elements by matching the wavefunction at the end of the propagation with the diatomic basis of the molecule corresponding to each arrangement.

A disadvantage of this arrangement is that the scratch files can grow too large (e.g. 40GB) and exceed the available limit because their size is proportional to the number of energies to be run.

In order to test the capabilities of P-GRADE, we have reorganized this algorithm according to the following principle: we perform the propagation of the log-derivative wavefunction *and* the analysis of the result of the propagation separately for each energy. This way the calculation at each energy can be assigned to a different processor. After completing a job, the processor can get a new energy to be calculated. This algorithm can use the task-farm model. The FORTRAN code requires minimal modifications: after reading the parameters and setting up the total energies to be calculated, *subroutine solve* is called, but one energy is calculated in each call. This way calculation at each energy is separated. This set-up has an advantage, namely, that each processor generates its own scratch file, and there is no need for massive data transfer between processors. In addition, the scratch files remain small because each contains only data needed for one energy. A disadvantage of this arrangement is that the sector basis functions are re-calculated by every processor. The time lost this way is smaller than that needed for propagation at one energy, so in our case, when each processor calculates more than 10 energies, this time loss is acceptable, especially when considering that the transfer of the large basis set matrices would also require some time. We are working on reducing this time loss by a somewhat different strategy.

In order to use the P-GRADE environment the code needs the following alterations at the FORTRAN level:
- the main program has to be made a subroutine
- instructions for starting an energy have to be inserted
- the calculation at an energy needs to be separated into a distinct set of subroutines
- the output to disk file needs has to be moved to the main subroutine
- the FORTRAN segments have to be compiled on each operating system that will be involved in the computation.
All the other steps can be performed using P-GRADE.

3.   Setting up the parallel code using P-GRADE

P-GRADE is a high-level graphical environment providing a general tool to develop parallel applications. It offers a graphical programming environment and graphical tools for the whole program development. It has a graphical editor for program development and a debugger for interactive testing and monitoring of the performance.

The current version of the program can create MPI, PVM or MPICH-G2 jobs. It inserts the interface commands into the program so that when compiled, the whole code becomes an individual program. This way the user does not need to learn the language of the message passing software. The user can see a "coarse grain" graphical representation of the parallel code in the sense that a flow chart is visible and the fine details are automatically taken care of by P-GRADE.

P-GRADE has a visual programming language, GRAPNEL, and an easy to use graphical editor. The visual editor helps one to set up the graph of the code The units of the graph can be sets of instructions written either in C or pre-compiled FORTRAN subroutines. Currently, FORTRAN commands can not be be used in these boxes so that a certain familiarity with C is necessary.

In order to gain access to variables used in the FORTRAN COMMON blocks, one needs to declare those variables in the P-GRADE code by typing the declarations into the appropriate box. This can be fairly time consuming if many COMMON block are transferred.

The upper part of Fig. 1 shows the pre-built FARM architecture. Arrows between the boxes are graphical representations of parallel data transfer.

The lower left panel of Fig. 1 displays the P-GRADE representation of the master program. The program starts with an initialization and reading the input parameters. The next line is a data broadcasting instruction where all the necessary input parameters are transferred to the slaves. When a slave receives the last piece of data, it starts a calculation. The item in the graph is the main calculating loop. Here we collect results from the slave that sends a signal that it has finished an energy, do some bookkeeping and send back a flag to the slave instructing it whether to start a new calculation or not. Then the master waits for signal from the next slave that finishes its task. After collecting the required number of energies, each slave gets a "do not continue" signal, and the master analyzes and writes to disk the results.

The lower right panel of Fig. 1 represents the slave program. After receiving data from the master, the slave initializes the variables needed for the calculation and goes into the slave loop. Here it calculates the next energy, and sends the results back to master, receives the signal whether to continue or not; if so, it goes back to the beginning of the loop; if not, then quits.

4. Program performance analysis

Parallel execution of the program was tested on our 20 processor cluster running Rocks v3.0 [18]. The efficiency of the parallelization was examined with the P-GRADE Monitor that collects trace information about the different events during the program execution. The collected data can be visualized with the PROVE visualization tool of P-GRADE in real time or later from a saved trace file. A result of a test run with 8 processors can be seen in Fig. 2.

In Fig. 2 different horizontal bars represent different processors with the master in the center. Shades on each bar indicate different process activity, black means calculation, gray (green in color print) communication. The arrows represent the direction of communication between processors. The top

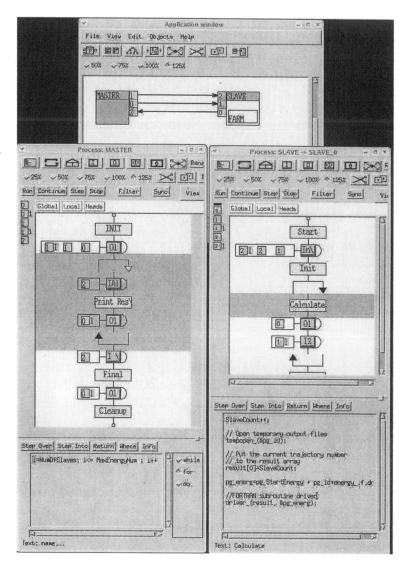

Figure 1.   P-GRADE representation of the quantum scattering program

of the figure shows the different parallel execution options available in P-GRADE. The bars corresponding to the slaves are all colored black indicating that there is no idling. We found that during the total execution the slave nodes spend more than 99 percent of the time by doing calculations.

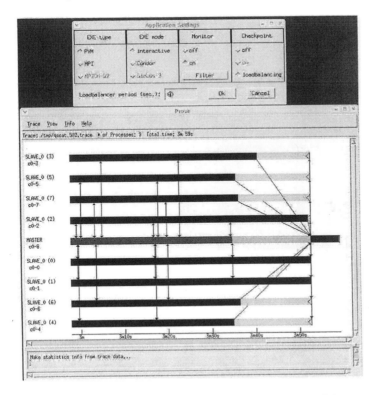

Figure 2. PROVE visualization of the last minute of parallel execution of the quantum reactive scattering program (from 3min till 3min50sec)

5. Summary

A quantum reactive scattering program written as a sequential code was parallelized using the P-GRADE graphical environment. P-GRADE made it possible to quickly parallelize the code for users not familiar with message passing based on the following algorithm: 1. re-design the parallel algorithm corresponding to the existing sequential code (this requires deep understanding how the existing code has been built) . 2. separate the FORTRAN or C code into units of the parallel algorithm and compile those subprograms 3. draw the graph of the algorithm using P-GRADE 4. fill in any missing boxes with the necessary program units (using C or C++ within the boxes in P-GRADE if no separate codes are available) 5. compile, check efficiency and run. This algorithm has proved to be efficient and useful in several applications.

Acknowledgments

Financial support by the Hungarian Ministry of Education (IKTA 00137) and by the Hungarian National Scientific Research Fund (OTKA T29726) is gratefully acknowledged. This work is part of the workgroup METACHEM [3] supported by COST of EU. We thank Prof. P. Kacsuk, Drs. R. Lovas and G. Hermann for their help with P-GRADE.

References

[1] A. Laganá, A. Riganelli. Computational reaction and molecular dynamics: from simple systems and rigorous methods to complex systems and approximate methods it Lecture Notes in Chemistry, **75**, 1-12,(2000)

[2] A. Laganá, Towards a Grid-based Molecular Simulator, in: Theory of Chemical Reaction Dynamics, A. Laganá, G. Lendvay, Eds., Kluwer, New York, in press

[3] COST Action No. D23, *METACHEM: Metalaboratories for complex computational applications in chemistry* http://costchemistry.epfl.ch

[4] P-GRADE Graphical Parallel Program Development Environment: http://www.lpds.sztaki.hu/index.php?menu=pgrade&load=pgrade.php

[5] P. Kacsuk, G. Dózsa: From Supercomputing Programming to Grid Programming by P-GRADE, WESIC 2003, Lillafured, 2003, pp. 483-494

[6] P. Kacsuk: Development and Execution of HPC Applications on Clusters and Grid by P-GRADE, European Simulation and Modelling Conference, Naples, Italy, 2003, pp. 6-13.

[7] P. Kacsuk, G. Dózsa, R. Lovas: The GRADE Graphical Parallel Programming Environment, Parallel Program Development for Cluster Computing: Methodology, Tools and Integrated Environments (Chapter 10), Nova Science Publishers, New York, 2001, pp. 231-247

[8] http://www.lpds.sztaki.hu/pgrade/p_grade/tutorial/tutorial.html

[9] A. Bencsura and G. Lendvay: Parallelization of reaction dynamics codes using P-GRADE: a case study, *Lecture Notes in Chemistry*, **3044**, 290-299, 2004.

[10] R. Lovas, et al., : Application of P-GRADE Development Environment in Meteorology., Proc. of DAPSYS'2002, Linz, pp. 30-37, 2002

[11] R. Lovas, P. Kacsuk, I. Lagzi, T. Turányi: Unified development solution for cluster and grid computing and its application in chemistry *Lecture Notes in Chemistry*, **3044**, 226-235, 2004.

[12] Supercomputer Algorithms for Reactivity, Dynamics and Kinetics of Small Molecules, edited by A. Laganá (Kluwer, Holland, 1989)

[13] Gunnar Nyman and Hua-Gen Yu : Quantum Theory of Bimolecular Chemical Reactions, Rep.Progr.Phys. **63** 1001, 2000.

[14] J.Z.H. Zhang: Theory and applications of quantum molecular dynamics World Scientific, Singapore, 1999

[15] G. C. Schatz: Quantum Mechanics of Interacting Systems: Scattering Theory, in Encyclopedia of Chemical Physics and Physical Chemistry, J. H. Moore and N. D. Spencer eds., Institute of Physics Publ, Bristol, pp. 827-863, 2001

[16] D. Skouteris, J.F. Castillo, D.E. Manolopoulos, ABC: a quantum reactive scattering program, *Comp. Phys. Comm.* **133** 128-135, 2000.

[17] Manolopoulos D. E. *J. Chem. Phys.* **85** 6425-6429, 1986.

[18] P.M. Papadopulos, M.J. Katz, G. Bruno: NPACI Rocks: Tools and Techniques for Easily Deploying Manageble Linux Clusters, Cluster 2001 http://rocks.npaci.edu

TRAFFIC SIMULATION IN P-GRADE AS A GRID SERVICE

T. Delaitre, A. Goyeneche, T. Kiss, G. Terstyanszky, N. Weingarten,
P. Maselino, A. Gourgoulis, and S.C. Winter.
Centre for Parallel Computing,
Cavendish School of Computer Science,
University of Westminster,
115 New Cavendish Street,
London, W1W 6UW,
Email: testbed-discuss@cpc.wmin.ac.uk

Abstract   Grid Execution Management for Legacy Code Architecture (GEMLCA) is a general architecture to deploy existing legacy applications as Grid services without re-engineering the original code. Using GEMLCA from the P-Grade portal, legacy code programs can be accessed as Grid services and even participate in complex Grid workflows. The parallel version of MadCity, a discrete time-based traffic simulator, was created using P-Grade. This paper describes how MadCity is offered as a Grid service using GEMLCA and how this solution is embedded into the P-Grade portal.

Keywords: Grid service, GEMLCA, traffic simulation, Grid portal, P-Grade.

1.   Introduction

Computational simulations are becoming increasingly important because in some cases it is the only way that physical processes can be studied and interpreted. These simulations may require very large computational power and the calculations have to be distributed on several computers using clusters or Grids.

MadCity [1], a discrete time-based traffic simulator, was developed by the research team of the Centre for Parallel Computing at the University of Westminster and a parallel version of the program was created with the P-Grade [2] (Parallel Grid Run-time and Application Development Environment) development environment.

MadCity, in common with many other legacy code programs, has been designed and implemented to run on a computer cluster and does not offer the necessary interfaces in order to be published as a Grid service. One approach to create a Grid service version of the simulator would be to re-engineer the original code; implying significant effort. However, using GEMLCA [3] (Grid Execution Management for Legacy Code Architecture), a general solution to deploy legacy code programs as Grid services, the traffic simulator can be run from a Grid service client without any modification to the original code.

This paper describes how MadCity is offered as a Grid service using the GEMLCA architecture and how GEMLCA and MadCity visualisation are connected to the P-Grade portal [4] and workflow solutions [5].

2.   Traffic simulation using P-Grade

MadCity simulates traffic on a road network and shows how individual vehicles behave on roads and at junctions. It consists of the GRaphical Visualiser (GRV) and the SIMulator (SIM) tools. The GRaphical Visualiser helps to design a road network file. The SIMulator of MadCity models the movement of vehicles using the network file. After completing the simulation, the SIM creates a trace file, which is loaded on the GRV to display the movement of vehicles.

The computational performance of the simulator depends on a number of parameters, such as number of vehicles, junctions, lane cut points and roads. These parameters increase the amount of computational resources required. The road network can contain thousands of vehicles, roads and junctions. Lane Cut Points (LCP) [6] are used to maintain the continuity of the simulation between cluster nodes. LCPs allow vehicles to move from one network partition to an adjacent partition residing on a different cluster node. Hence, the number of LCPs affect the amount of communications between cluster nodes.

The traffic simulator must be parallelised to meet the real-time requirements for large road networks. The SIM of MadCity is parallelised using P-Grade. Figure 1 shows the parallel simulation structure of MadCity using a parent node and four children nodes in the P-Grade graphical environment. The parent process sends the network file to each child process together with a partition identifier. Each node executes a particular road partition to provide simulation locality and allow efficient parallelisation of the simulator. As shown in Figure 1, neighbouring road partitions (or nodes) communicate by exchanging vehicles moving from one partition to another. The LCP buffer stores the vehicles leaving one partition and entering another. The vehicles are retrieved from the LCP buffer by the neighbouring node through synchronous communications.

The traffic simulator can be parallelised using either non-scalable or scalable designs as shown in Figure 1. Using the non-scalable design, users have to modify the application code each time when adding more nodes (or processes). Scalability can also be addressed by using P-Grade templates to set the number of nodes (or processes) without modifying the application code.

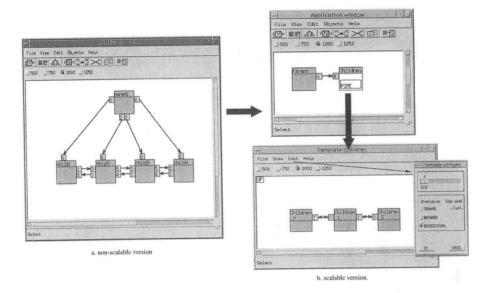

Figure 1.   MadCity in the P-Grade graphical environment.

In the traffic simulator, the P-Grade pipeline template is used where all nodes perform the same task but on different data. Figure 1(b) shows the pipeline template-based traffic simulation architecture. The template attributes window shows that four children nodes (SIZE=4) will participate in the traffic simulation. The number of nodes can be increased or decreased according to the simulation requirements by specifying the size in the template attributes window.

3. Grid Execution Management for Legacy Code Architecture

GEMLCA is a general architecture to deploy legacy code programs as Grid services without re-engineering the original code. To offer a legacy application as an OGSA Grid service, the GEMLCA architecture has to be installed and the applications have to be registered with it. Following this, the legacy code programs can be accessed from a Grid service client that can be created by using either the universal GEMLCA Stubs for Java or the GEMLCA WSDL [7] file. GEMLCA design is a three-layer architecture. The front-end layer, called "Grid Services Layer", is published as a set of Grid Services and it is the only access point for a Grid client to submit jobs and retrieve results. The internal or "Core Layer" is composed of several classes that manage the legacy code program environment and job behaviour. Finally, a back-end, currently

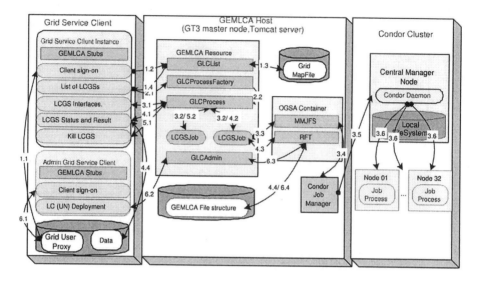

Figure 2.   GEMLCA architecture.

called "GT3 Layer", offers services to the Core Layer that is closely related to Globus Toolkit 3 [8] and will be updated following the Globus Alliance road-maps.

Figure 2 describes the GEMLCA implementation and its life-cycle. The scenario for using GEMLCA is described as follows: A Grid Client, after signing-on his credential, contacts a GEMLCA Grid Service (GLCList) that returns the available Legacy Code Grid Services (LCGS) to the client (1.1-1.4). From the returned list and using the Grid Legacy Code Factory (GLCProcessFactory) the client creates a new Legacy Code Process Instance (GLCProcess) (2.1-2.2) and gets the LCGS interfaces and parameters that can be changed in order to submit several Jobs (LCGSJob) to the defined job manager, in this case Condor. (3.1-3.6). As far as the client credentials are not expired and the GLCProcess is still alive, the client contacts GEMLCA for checking job status and retrieve partial or final results any time (4.1-4.4). The client can terminate a particular job or the GLCProcess (5.1-5.2). Legacy Code deployment is managed by the GEMLCA GLCAdmin Grid Service. In order to deploy a Legacy Code, a configuration file needs to be created and deployed together with the binary. This file exposes the Legacy Code environment: Process description, Executable, Job Manager, Maximum number of jobs accepted, maximum and minimum processors (for multi-processor job managers) standard output and input and also a list and description of parameters: name, input , output, mandatory, order, file, command-line, fixed.

4. Integrating GEMLCA with the P-Grade portal

Grid portals are an essential facility to make Grid applications available from a Web browser. By connecting GEMLCA to a Grid portal such as the P-Grade portal, legacy codes applications are available as Grid services through the Web.

The functionalities of the P-Grade development environment are available from the P-Grade portal [4]. All of the P-Grade portal services are provided by one or more portal servers that can be connected to various Grid systems. P-Grade portal is currently composed of three key Grid services needed by Grid end-users and application developers: (1) Grid certificate management, (2) creation, modification and execution of workflow applications on Grid resources and (3) visualisation of workflow progress as well as each component job. The portal is developed using the GridSphere [9, 10] development framework where a number of portlets have been created to implement the P-Grade portal end-user Grid services described previously.

University of Westminster and SZTAKI collaborate to enhance the P-Grade portal in order to execute GEMLCA legacy codes within a workflow. GEMLCA legacy code is either a sequential or a parallel binary program published as a Grid service. The portal contains a graphical editor to draw a workflow graph which defines a set of cooperating sequential or parallel jobs. Integrating GEMLCA with the P-Grade portal consists of three phases: (1) for the workflow editor to get a list of legacy code(s) and their Grid services interfaces available in GEMLCA resources, (2) for the P-Grade workflow manager to be able to submit and get results back of legacy codes available through a GEMLCA resource, and (3) for the P-Grade portal to be able to manage legacy codes such as adding, modifying or removing legacy codes within a GEMLCA resource. GEMLCA resource is considered as a GEMLCA instance running on a particular host.

The PGRADE portal is integrated with GEMLCA as shown in Figure 3. The workflow editor has been modified to interface with the GLCList Grid service to get a list of legacy codes available in a GEMLCA resource. The workflow manager has been enhanced to submit jobs and get results back from the workflow nodes to the GLCProcessFactory Grid services and to manage GEMLCA legacy codes by interfacing to the GLCAdmin Grid service.

The integration of the P-Grade portal with GEMLCA, enables the execution of the parallel version of MadCity from a web browser and to visualise the simulated traffic densities on a road network by using a macroscopic traffic visualisation applet. The applet is being deployed as a GridSphere portlet within the P-Grade portal. Westminster developed an applet to display the traffic densities on a road network such as the Greater Manchester area as shown in Figure 4. The applet requires a macroscopic trace file generated by Madcity

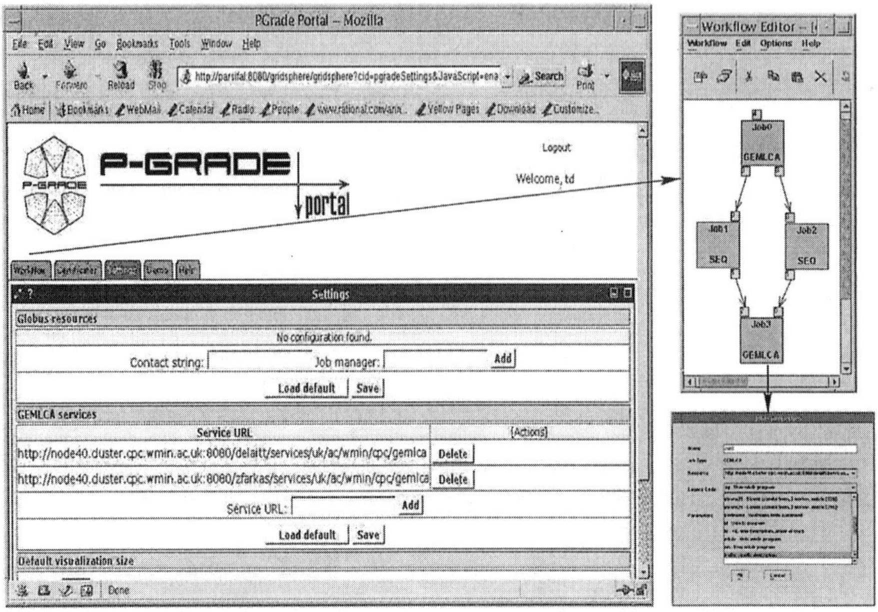

Figure 3.   GEMLCA integration with PGRADE portal.

and a description of the simulated road network as input. For each simulation
time step, the road network is displayed using different colours to represent
the density of traffic on each road. Figure 4(a) shows the Macroscopic visualisation output for the full Greater Manchester Road Network. Figure 4(b)
shows visualisation output for a zoomed in area of Greater Manchester Road
Network, with individual roads visible.

5.   Conclusion

This paper described a Grid environment in which legacy code applications
like Madcity can be deployed in a service-oriented Grid architecture and accessed through a user-friendly Web interface. The simulator can be parame-
terised and run from a web browser. The results can be visualised from the
same web browser. The solution utlised the P-Grade development environment, GEMLCA, P-Grade portal and a visualisation applet for traffic densities
in the following way:

- a parallel version of Madcity was designed and implemented using the
  P-Grade development environment,

- a MadCity legacy code is offered as an OGSA compliant Grid service
  using the GEMLCA architecture,

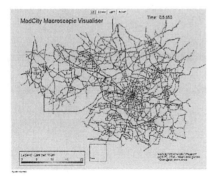
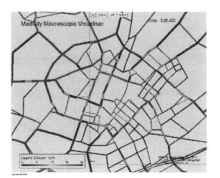
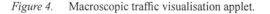

(a) Full Greater Manchester Road Network

(b) zoomed in area of Greater Manchester Road Network

Figure 4. Macroscopic traffic visualisation applet.

- in order to make the legacy code applications available from a Web browser, P-Grade portal has been enhanced for connecting to GEMLCA,

- legacy codes can be part of complex Grid workflows using P-Grade workflow solution and its connection to GEMLCA,

- an applet has been developed and is being deployed as a portlet for visualising traffic densities of a road network.

Acknowledgments

The work presented in this paper is supported by an EPSRC funded project (Grant No.: GR/S77509/01).

The authors wish to acknowledge the support and contributions of Damian Igbe, in the traffic simulation aspects, Kreeteeraj Sajadah in investigating GT3 security from University of Westminster, Zoltan Farkas and Tamas Boczko from SZTAKI.

References

[1] A. Gourgoulis, G. Terstyansky, P. Kacsuk, S.C. Winter, Creating Scalable Traffic Simulation on Clusters. PDP2004. Conference Proceedings of the 12th Euromicro Conference on Parallel, Distributed and Network based Processing, La Coruna, Spain, 11-13th February, 2004.

[2] P. Kacsuk, G. Dozsa, R. Lovas: The GRADE Graphical Parallel Programming Environment, In the book: Parallel Program Development for Cluster Computing: Methodology, Tools and Integrated Environments (Chapter 10), Editors: C. Cunha, P. Kacsuk and S.C. Winter, pp. 231-247, Nova Science Publishers New York, 2001.

[3] T. Delaitre, A. Goyeneche, T. Kiss and S.C. Winter, Publishing and Executing Parallel Legacy Code using an OGSI Grid Service, Conference proceedings of the 2004 International Conference on Computational Science and its Applications. Editors: A. Lagana et al. LNCS 3044, pp. 30-36, S. Maria degli Angeli, Assisi(PG), Italy, 2004.

[4] Z. Németh, G. Dózsa, R. Lovas and P. Kacsuk, The P-GRADE Grid Portal, Conference proceedings of the 2004 International Conference on Computational Science and its Applications. Editors: A. Lagana et al. LNCS 3044, pp. 10-19, 2004, S. Maria degli Angeli, Assisi(PG), Italy.

[5] R. Lovas, G. Dózsa, P. Kacsuk, N. Podhorszki, D. Drótos, Workflow Support for Complex Grid Applications: Integrated and Portal Solutions, Proceedings of 2nd European Across Grids Conference, Nicosia, Cyprus, 2004.

[6] D.Igbe, N Kalantery, S. Ijaha, S.Winter, An Open Interface for Parallelization of Traffic Simulation. Proc 7th IEEE International Symposium on Distributed Simulation and Real Time Applications (DS-RT 2003), http://www.cs.unibo.it/ds-rt2003/ Oct 23-25 2003 Delft, The Netherlands, in conjunction with 15th European Simulation Symposium (ESS 2003), http://www.scs-europe.org/conf/ess2003/ October 26-29, 2003 Delft, The Netherlands.

[7] Web Services Description Language (WSDL) Version 1.2, http://www.w3.org/TR/wsdl12

[8] The Globus Project, http://www.globus.org

[9] GridSphere consortium; (2003), GridSphere Tutorial, GridSphere, http://www.gridsphere.org/gridsphere/docs/index.html

[10] Jason Novotny, (2004), Developing grid portlets using the GridSphere portal framework, Max-Planck Institute for Gravitational Physics, http://www-106.ibm.com/developerworks/grid/library/gr-portlets/?ca=dgrgridw11GSPortFrame

DEVELOPMENT OF A GRID ENABLED CHEMISTRY APPLICATION*

István Lagzi[1], Róbert Lovas[2], Tamás Turányi[1]

[1]*Department of Physical Chemistry, Eotvos University (ELTE)*
lagzi@vuk.chem.elte.hu, turanyi@garfield.chem.elte.hu

[2]*Computer and Automation Research Institute, Hungarian Academy of Sciences (MTA SZTAKI)*
rlovas@sztaki.hu

Abstract   P-GRADE development and run-time environment provides high-level graphical support to develop scientific applications and to execute them efficiently on various platforms. This paper gives a short overview on the parallelization of a simulator algorithm for chemical reaction-diffusion systems. Applying the same user environment we present our experiences regarding the execution of this chemistry application on non-dedicated clusters, and in different grid environments.

Keywords: programming environment, grid, cluster, computational chemistry

1.   Introduction

Beside the widely applied PC clusters and supercomputers, different computational grid systems [1] are becoming more and more popular among scientists, who want to run their simulations (having high computational and storage demands) as fast as possible. In such grid systems, large number of heterogeneous resources can be interconnected in order to solve complex problems.

One of the main aims of a joint national project, *Chemistry Grid and its application for air pollution forecast* is to investigate some aspects of Grids, such as their application as high performance computational infrastructure in chemistry, and to find practical solutions. The Department of Physical Chemistry (ELTE) applied P-GRADE environment to parallelise an existing sequential

*The research described in this paper has been supported by the following projects and grants: Hungarian IHM 4671/1/2003 project, Hungarian OTKA T042459 and T043770 grants, OTKA Instrument Grant M042110, Hungarian IKTA OMFB-00580/2003, and EU-GridLab IST-2001-32133.

simulator for chemical reactions and diffusions in the frame of the Chemistry Grid project.

In this paper we introduce briefly the fundamental problems of reaction-diffusion systems (see Section 2) and its parallelisation with P-GRADE programming environment (see Section 3). We present our experiences in details regarding the execution and performance of this chemistry application on non-dedicated clusters (see Section 4) taking the advantages of the built-in dynamic load balancer of P-GRADE run-time environment. Finally, its successful execution in Condor and Globus based Grids are also presented (see Section 5).

2. Reaction-diffusion equations

Chemical pattern formation arises due to the coupling of diffusion with chemistry, such as chemical waves [3], autocatalytic fronts [4], Turing structures [5] and precipitation patterns (Liesegang phenomenon) [6]. Evolution of pattern formation can be described by second-order partial differential equations:

$$\frac{\partial c_i}{\partial t} = D_i \nabla^2 c_i + R_i(c_1, c_2, \ldots, c_n), \quad i = 1, 2, \ldots, n, \qquad (1)$$

where c_i is the concentration, D_i is the diffusion coefficient and R_i is the chemical reaction term, respectively, of the ith chemical species, and t is time. The chemical reaction term R_i may contain non-linear terms in c_i. For n chemical species, an n dimensional set of partial differential equations is formed describing the change of concentrations over time and space.

The operator splitting approach is applied to equations (1), decoupling transport (diffusion) from chemistry, i.e.

$$c_{i,\hat{t}+\Delta t} = T_D^{\Delta t} T_C^{\Delta t} c_{i,\hat{t}}$$

where T_D and T_C are the diffusion and the chemistry operators, respectively, and $c_{i,\hat{t}+\Delta t}$ and $c_{i,\hat{t}}$ are the concentration of the ith species at time $\hat{t}$ and $\hat{t}+\Delta t$, where Δt is the time step.

The basis of the numerical method for the solution of the diffusion operator is the spatial discretisation of the partial differential equations on a two-dimensional rectangular grid. In these calculations, the grid spacing (h) is uniform in both spatial directions. A second order Runge-Kutta method is used to solve the system of ODEs arising from the discretisation of partial differential equations with no-flux boundary conditions on a 360×100 grid. The Laplacian is calculated using nine-point approximation resulting in an error of $O(h^2)$ for the Laplacian.

The equations of the chemical term have the form

$$\frac{dc_i}{dt} = R_i(c_1, c_2, \ldots, c_n), \quad i = 1, 2, \ldots, n. \qquad (2)$$

The time integration of system (2) is performed with the BDF method using the CVODE package [7, 8], which can solve stiff chemical kinetics equations.

3. Parallel implementation in P-GRADE

In order to parallelise the sequential code of the presented reaction-diffusion simulation the domain decomposition concept was followed; the two-dimensional grid is partitioned along the x space direction, so the domain is decomposed into horizontal columns. Therefore, the two-dimensional subdomains can be mapped onto e.g. a pipe of processes (see Figure 1, *Template: sim* window). An equal partition of subdomains among the processes gives us a well balanced load during the solution of the reaction-diffusion equations assuming a dedicated and homogeneous cluster or a dedicated supercomputer as the execution platform.

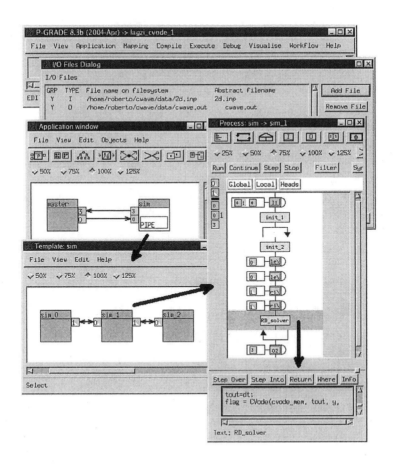

Figure 1. Parallel code of reaction-diffusion simulation in P-GRADE

During the calculation of the diffusion of the chemical species communications are required to exchange information on the boundary concentrations between the nearest neighbour subdomains, which are implemented via communication ports, channels (see Figure 1, *Template: sim* window, arcs between small rectangles), and communication actions (see Figure 1, *Process: sim* → *sim_1*, icons labelled as 'le' and 'ri' in the control flow like description).

For the calculation the process invokes external sequential functions (see Figure 1, bottom of *Process: sim* → *sim_1* windows), which are available as sequential third-party code [7, 8] written in C. The implementation is published in details in [13].

4.   Performance results on non-dedicated cluster

The parallel version of reaction-diffusion simulation has been tested and fine tuned [13] on SZTAKI cluster using it as a dedicated resource. This self-made Linux cluster contains 29 dual-processor nodes (Pentium III/500MHz) connected via Fast Ethernet.

Generally the exclusive access and use of a cluster (e.g. at universities) can not be guaranteed. Sometimes the application is implemented inefficiently, and it may cause unbalanced load (and less effective execution) on the cluster nodes. In both cases the dynamic load balancer [9] of P-GRADE environment can be applied.

In case of the reaction-diffusion simulator the parallel application showed balanced CPU loads [13] on a homogenous and dedicated cluster but we experienced significant slow-down if any of the nodes get an extra calculation intensive task or the node can not deliver the same performance as the other ones. The reason for this phenomenon is that the application must synchronise the boundary conditions at each simulation steps, and they have to wait for the slowest running process. Such situation can be inspected in Figure 2, *Prove* visualisation window when the application was executed on the *n2, n3, n4*, and *n5* nodes in the first 3 minutes (see the details in Figure 2, smaller *Prove* window in left). The space-time diagram presents a task bar for each process, and the arcs between the process bars are showing the message passing between the processes. In all the diagrams of PROVE tool, the black colour represents the sequential calculations, and two different colours; green for incoming and grey for outgoing communication used for marking the message exchanges.

Thus, we turned on the load balancing support in P-GRADE and re-compiled the application under PVM (see Figure 2, *Application settings* dialog window). In our case, the actual period was set to *180 seconds* when the load balancer has to evaluate the execution conditions based on the gathered information and to make decisions [9].

As the on-line visualisation tool depicts (see Figure 2, *Prove* window) at the beginning of the 4th minute the load balancer initiated the migration of processes to new nodes: *n19*, *n13*, *n21*, and *n0* (see Figure 2, *Prove* window in right). One message was sent before the migration from the node *n2* (process *sim_0*) and delivered just after the migration to the node *n19* (process *sim_1*); the co-ordinated checkpointer in P-GRADE can handle such situations (on-the-fly messages) without any problems.

We could focus on the interesting parts of the trace (see Figure 2, smaller *PROVE* windows) using its zooming facilities. According to statistics the application was executed almost optimally from the 5th minute. The migration took about 1 min and 57 sec due to mainly the large memory images of processes (more than 95 MB/process), that must be transferred from the actual nodes, stored at the checkpoint server, and must be retrieved during the recov-

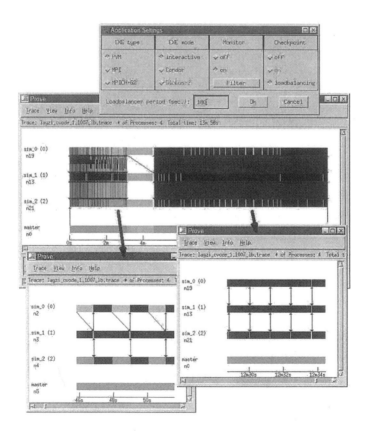

Figure 2.   Performance visualisation on non-dedicated cluster

ery phase of migration on the new nodes. Since the current P-GRADE version launches only one checkpoint server to store these checkpoint files, the network connection of the single checkpoint server may be a serious performance bottle neck. In our case the migration caused almost 800 MB network traffic on the Fast Ethernet network interface of the checkpoint server.

However, the cost of migration is still acceptable since the application continued its execution more than 2 times faster during the remaining calculation; one simulation step needed 1.5-1.7 seconds contrary to the earlier measured 3.5-5 seconds. Our application needed only 14 minutes (with 500 simulation steps) instead of 25 minutes without the intervention of load balancer tool. Obviously, with more simulation steps we could get more significant speedup.

5.   Performance results in the Grid

The simulation has been also tested with 10.000 iterations [13]; the parallel application was able to migrate automatically to another friendly Condor [10] pool when the actual pool had become overloaded, as well as to continue its execution from the stored checkpoint files [2].

The application has been also executed successfully on Globus [16] based Grid. In order to support the transparent execution of applications on local and remote (interactive or Grid) resources, P-GRADE provides a new I/O file abstraction layer (see Figure 1, *I/O Files Dialog* window), where the physical data files of the application can be assigned to logical names, which can be referenced in the application by file operations. We defined the input and output files and, in this way, all the necessary I/O files can be automatically transferred to and from the remote site, and the executable can be also staged by P-GRADE run-time system.

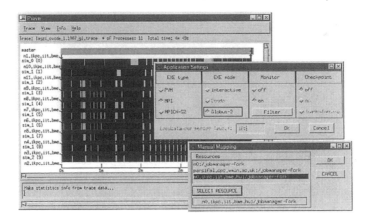

Figure 3.   Performance results in Globus mode

Having a valid certificate to deploy a Globus resource (instead of the local resources), the user can turn on the Globus mode with MPI support in P-GRADE (see Figure 3, *Application settings*). On-line monitoring and visualisation is also possible on Globus resources using the GRM/Mercury monitoring infrastructure [11]; only a re-compilation is needed for the utilization of the Globus/MPI/Monitoring facilities.

The user can select the specific Globus resource where the entire application will be executed in the *Manual Mapping* Window (see Figure 3) (in MPICH-G2 mode, processes can be mapped individually to different Globus resources but this mode showed poor performance in our application due to the frequent message exchanges between simulation steps). The monitoring infrastructure provides on-line view similarly to the local execution of job (see Figure 3, *PROVE* window). In the presented case, we executed the 10-process pipe version of the application as a Globus job. The initial time before the real execution and the transfer of output files back (i.e. the 'cost' of Grid based execution from the user's point of view) was within 1 minute because we selected the *fork* job-manager on the Grid site, the cluster was not overloaded, the size of transferred files was relatively small (less then 4MB), and the Hungarian academic network (HBONE) provided high bandwidth between the sites.

6. Related works

P-GRADE has been successfully applied for the parallelisation of different algorithms; e.g. Institute of Chemistry, Chemical Research Centre of the Hungarian Academy of Sciences has recently parallelised a classical trajectory calculation written in FORTRAN [12] in the frame of Chemistry Grid project. Some other development systems, such as ASSIST [14], or CACTUS [15], target the same research community (biologist, chemists, etc.), and they can offer several useful facilities similarly to P-GRADE. On the other hand, P-GRADE is able to provide more transparent run-time support for parallel applications without major user interactions, such as code generation to different platforms (Condor [10] or Globus-2 [16] based Grids, PVM or MPI based clusters and supercomputers), migration of parallel jobs across grid sites (or within a cluster) based on automatic checkpointing facilities [2], or application monitoring of parallel jobs [11] on various grid sites, clusters, or supercomputers [11].

7. Summary

P-GRADE is able to support the entire life-cycle of parallel program development and the execution of parallel applications both for parallel systems and the Grid [2]. One of the main advantages of P-GRADE is the transparency; P-GRADE users do not need to learn the different programming methodologies for various parallel systems and the Grid, the same environment is applicable either for supercomputers, clusters or the Grid. As the presented work illustrates, P-GRADE enables fast parallelisation of sequential programs providing an easy-to-use solution even for non-specialist parallel and grid application developers, like chemists.

References

[1] Foster, I., Kesselman, C.: Computational Grids, Chapter 2 of The Grid: Blueprint for a New Computing Infrastructure, Morgan-Kaufman, (1999)

[2] Kacsuk, P., Dozsa, G., Kovacs, J., Lovas, R., Podhorszki, N., Balaton, Z., Gombas, G.: P-GRADE: a Grid Programming Environment. Journal of Grid Computing Volume 1, Issue 2, 2003, pp. 171-197

[3] Zaikin, A. N., Zhabotinsky, A. M.: Concentration wave propagation in two-dimensional liquid-phase self-oscillating system. Nature 225 (1970) 535-537

[4] Luther, R.: Raumliche fortpflanzung chemischer reaktionen. Zeitschrift fur Elektrochemie 12 (1906) 596-600

[5] Turing, A. M.: The chemical basis of morphogenesis. Philosophical Transactions of the Royal Society of London series B 327 (1952) 37-72

[6] Liesegang, R. E.: Ueber einige eigenschaften von gallerten. Naturwissenschaflichee Wochenschrift 11 (1896) 353-362

[7] Brown, P. N., Byrne, G. D., Hindmarsh, A. C.: Vode: A variable coefficient ode solver. SIAM Journal of Scientific and Statistical Computing 10 (1989) 1038-1051

[8] Cohen, S. C., Hindmarsh, A. C.: CVODE User Guide. Lawrence Livermore National Laboratory technical report UCRL-MA-118618 SIAM Journal of Scientific and Statistical Computing (1994) pp. 97

[9] Toth, M., Podhorszki, N., Kacsuk, P.: Load Balancing for P-GRADE Parallel Applications. Proceedings of DAPSYS 2002, Linz, Austria, pp. 12-20

[10] Thain,D., Tannenbaum, T., Livny, M.: Condor and the Grid. In F. Berman, A. J. G. Hey, G. Fox (eds), Grid Computing: Making The Global Infrastructure a Reality, John Wiley, 2003

[11] Balaton, Z., Gombas, G.: Resource and Job Monitoring in the Grid. Proceedings of EuroPar'2003 Conference, Klagenfurt, Austria, pp. 404-411

[12] Bencsura, A., Lendvay, Gy.: Parallelization of reaction dynamics codes using P-GRADE: a case study. Computational Science and Its Applications, ICCSA 2004, LNCS, Vol. 3044, pp. 290-299

[13] Lovas, R., Kacsuk, P., Lagzi, I., Turanyi, T.: Unified development solution for cluster and grid computing and its application in chemistry. Computational Science and Its Applications, ICCSA 2004, LNCS, Vol. 3044, pp. 226-235

[14] Vanneschi, M.: The programming model of ASSIST, an environment for parallel and distributed portable applications. Parallel Computing 28 (2002) 1709-1732

[15] Goodale, T., et al.: The Cactus Framework and Toolkit: Design and Applications. 5th International Conference on Vector and Parallel Processing, 2002, pp. 197-227

[16] Foster, I., Kesselman, C.: The Globus Project: A Status Report. Proc. IPPS/SPDP '98 Heterogeneous Computing Workshop, pp. 4-18, 1998.

V

APPLICATIONS

SUPPORTING NATIVE APPLICATIONS IN WEBCOM-G

John P. Morrison, Sunil John and David A. Power
Centre for Unified Computing,
Dept. Computer Science,
National University of Ireland,
University College Cork,
Cork,
Ireland.
{j.morrison, s.john, d.power}@cs.ucc.ie

Abstract   The area Grid Computing has been the center of much research recently. Grids can provide access to vast computing resources from hardware to software. Despite all the attention Grid Computing has received, the development of applications for execution on grids still requires specialist knowledge of the underlying grid architecture. This paper describes a programming environment for the WebCom-G project. This programming environment is used to support the execution of legacy applications on the WebCom-G system.

WebCom-G is a multi layer platform for executing distributed applications. Applications are separate from the underlying computing infrastructure and are specified as Condensed Graphs. Condensed Graphs are used to specify tasks and the sequencing constraints associated with them. They provide a mechanism for specifying Control Driven, Coercion Driven and Demand Driven computations in one uniform formalism. WebCom-G supports fault tolerance, load balancing, scheduling and security at different levels within its architecture. WebCom-G seeks to provide Grid access to non specialist users and from the application developer and end user's perspectives hide the underlying Grid.

Keywords: WebCom, Grid Computing, Distributed Computing, Application Execution

1.   Introduction

The computing power offered by Grids has caught the imagination of many researchers. Grids offer the potential to access vast resources available in heterogeneous and high performance computing systems. However, access to Grid Computing is typically restricted to those in the scientific and academic community. This is mainly due to the specialist knowledge required to create Grid aware applications.

Globus[9, 10] is one of the more common Grid Computing infrastructures in use. It promotes the use of a Grid Information Service[5, 7] to provide access to distributed resources. Job managers such as Condor[6], Portable Batch System[18] or the Load Sharing Facility[17] are used to marshal job execution. Applications are developed using libraries and API's provided by PVM[11] and MPI[8], for example.

One of the reasons why the Grid is still unpopular among non-specialists users is the complexity of application development for this environment. The developer must provide all the support for communications, fault tolerance and load balancing in addition to the mechanisms for solving the original problem. This has to be repeated for each application.

For Grid computing to become more widely accepted, mechanisms to free the programmer from the underlying architectural details have to be provided. WebCom-G[14, 16, 19] is a fledgling Grid Operating System. The WebCom-G project is a grid enabled version of the WebCom[15] metacomputer. It separates the application from the execution platform. This is achieved by providing a multi-layer system implementation. Each layer has particular responsibilities in achieving task execution. These range from an application execution engine, to layers that carry out scheduling, load balancing, fault tolerance and security. By separating the application from the underlying infrastructure, the programmer is free to concentrate on providing a solution to the problem specified rather than the provision of a complete distributed computing platform to solve the problem.

Applications executing on the WebCom-G platform are expressed as Condensed Graphs[13]. A Condensed Graph represents a program as a directed, acyclic graph. The semantics of Condensed Graphs permit programs to express data-driven, demand-driven and control driven computations using a single, uniform, formalism.

Grid Computing involves the utilisation of resources whose availability is ever changing in a highly dynamic heterogeneous environment. To cater for this, a powerful programming model is needed in order to develop applications to utilise these resources. Examples of programming environments for the Grid computing area include Ibis [20], BioOpera [3] and Iktara [4].

In this paper, a programming environment for WebCom-G is described. This programming environment is used to support execution of native applications by WebCom-G. This is achieved by using specialised compilers to compile existing source code, and interpret script files. The output from these compilers is a Condensed Graphs representation of the application, capable of being executed by WebCom-G. Expressing these applications as Condensed Graphs exposes any parallelism present and allows them to avail the advantages of WebCom-G such as it's fault tolerance, load balancing, scheduling and security mechanisms.

2. Program Execution in WebCom-G

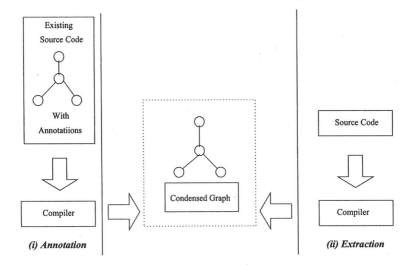

Figure 1. Annotation and Extraction.

Within WebCom-G task sequencing is expressed as a Condensed Graph[13]. Task execution is carried out using appropriate Execution Engine modules. Support for legacy applications is provided by compiling or translating existing code into an intermediate representation expressed as a Condensed Graph. This support is provided by two methodologies called *Extraction* and *Annotation*.

Extraction

Extraction is a process of translating higher level specifications into Condensed Graph representation. This process is suitable for specification languages such as the Globus Resource Specification Language (RSL)[12], for example. RSL specifies the list of tasks to be executed and their associated configurations. During extraction, tasks specified in the RSL will be expressed as nodes in a Condensed Graph. In addition, the task sequencing constraints specified in the RSL script are represented as arcs in the resulting Condensed Graph. For extraction, this Condensed Graph can be specified as an XML document. WebCom-G can dynamically load and execute Condensed Graphs specified in XML.

Condensed Graph applications executed by WebCom-G receive all the benefits of the WebCom-G system including transparent support for fault tolerance, load balancing, scheduling and security. Hence, tasks extracted from RSL scripts also benefit from these WebCom-G features. For example, if the

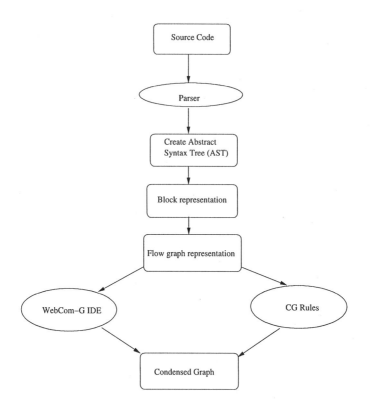

Figure 2.   The process of generating a Condensed Graph from sequential code.

job should fail to execute, WebCom-G will reschedule the job for execution at a later time.

A different approach has to be adopted for traditional high level languages like C, C++ and Java. These languages are typically not optimised for execution in distributed environments, as they normally consist of sequential code. Attempting to parallelise sequential code is not trivial. A Condensed Graphs compiler is used to parallelise sequential applications, Figure 2. This compiler converts existing code into an XML representation of the associated Condensed Graph. The compiler takes existing code and performs a data dependency analysis, using well known compiler techniques such as those described in [2]. This is illustrated in Figure 3.

This analysis identifies parallelisable data blocks within the source code. This translation process can be described as either *fully automatic* or *semi automatic* translation.

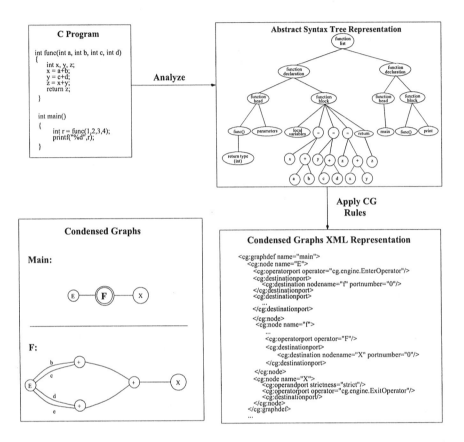

Figure 3. Example translation of sequential C code to Condensed Graphs(CG) XML representation. The C program is analyzed to produce an Abstract Syntax Tree(AST) representation. Applying CG rules to the AST results in the XML representation.

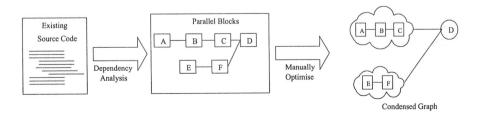

Figure 4. Manually optimising data block dependences obtained from the compiler.

For fully automatic translation, using appropriate interpretation rules, the identified data blocks are converted into a Condensed Graphs application, suitable for execution on WebCom-G.

For semi automatic translation, the uncovered data blocks are presented to the programmer, via the WebCom-G Integrated Development Environment. This facilitates the further optimisation of data blocks by the programmer, if possible. This is outlined in Figure 4.

Annotation

Annotation is a mechanism for allowing programmers to identify parallel blocks within their source code. This provides the programmer the opportunity to optimise their source code and hence the Condensed Graph obtained via the fully automatic extraction mechanism outlined previously. This mechanism may be used for high level languages as well as proprietary specification languages.

3. Automatic Parallelization

The Extraction(CG) Compiler being developed, will expose available parallelism using a combination of the Extration and Annotation mechanisms outlined in Section 2.

The compilation process depicted in Figure 2 comprises four stages: source code analysis, source code restructure, data dependency analysis using the Condensed Graph rules, and the generation of parallel code in Condensed Graph representation.

The CG compiler will attempt to fully automate the procedure of transforming traditional source code into a Condensed Graphs representation, capable of being executed in parallel. This parallelising compiler inserts all the necessary CG information into its intermediate representation.

The compiler, depicted in the Figure 2, accepts as input a source code. This input will be parsed to produce an Abstract Syntax Tree (AST)[21]. The AST represents the syntactic structure of the source code in a tree format. This tree structure will then be converted into block representation and subsequently flow graph representation. Block representation helps to identify the blocks of program structure within the source code.

The Parser module consists of Lexical Analyser and Parser. The Lexical Analyser scans the source code to identify tokens. The Parser takes the tokens produced by the analyser and produces a syntax tree corresponding to predefined Grammar rules. ANTLR[1] is used to generate the AST from higher level languages such as C, C++ and Java.

The flow graph representation outlines the program flow and identifies the data blocks that may be parallelised within the Condensed Graph representation. Control flow, Data flow and Data dependency analysis is performed on the flow graph to generate the Condensed graph representation, that will subsequently execute on WebCom-G.

4. Conclusions and Future Work

Solutions must be developed to free application programmers from the low level complexity of parallel programming in Grid environments. In this paper, the WebCom-G Programming Environment is presented. This environment supports the execution of existing applications on WebCom-G. The programmer is freed from the complexities of creating or employing complicated distributed computing systems in order to develop solutions to problems.

Different mechanisms for application execution were presented, ranging from the extraction of parallelisable tasks from scripting language files, to annotating preexisting native codes. Using compilation techniques, data blocks obtained by using data dependencies are converted into Condensed Graphs format and executed by WebCom-G.

The goal of WebCom-G is to hide the Grid, by providing a vertically integrated solution from application to hardware while maintaining interoperability with existing Grid technologies. In addition to maintaining a vertically integrated solution, the available services will be exploited to increase functionality and effect interoperability. The provision of such a Grid Operating System will remove much of the complexity from the task of the application developer.

Acknowledgments

This work is funded by Science Foundation Ireland, under the WebCom-G project.

References

[1] *ANTLR.* http://www.antlr.org.

[2] Utpal Banerjee. *Dependence Analysis.* Kluwer Academic Publishers, Boston, Massachusetts, 1997.

[3] Win Bausch, Cesare Pautasso, Reto Schaeppi, and Gustavo Alonso. *BioOpera: Cluster-aware Computing.* IEEE International Conference on Cluster Computing (CLUSTER'02), September 23 - 26, 2002, Chicago, Illinois.

[4] Bor Yuh Evan Chang. *Iktara in ConCert: Realizing a Certifirf Grid Computing Framework from a Programmers Perspective.* School of Computer Science, Carnegie Mellon University, Pittsbourghm June 2002, Technical Report: CMU-CS-02-150.

[5] Karl Czajkowski, Steven Fitzgerald, Ian Foster, and Carl Kesselman. *Grid Information Services for Distributed Resource Sharing.* Proceedings of the 10th IEEE International Symposium on High Performance Distributed Computing.

[6] D. H. J Epema, Miron Livny, R. van Dantzig ans X. Evers, and Jim Pruyne. *A World-wide Flock of Condors: Load Sharing among Workstation Clusters*. Journal on Future Generations of Computer Systems, Volume 12, 1996.

[7] Steven Fitzgerald, Ian Foster, Carl Kesselman, Gregor von Laszewski, Warren Smith, and Steven Tuecke. *A Directory Service for Configuring High-Performance Distributed Computations*. Proceedings of the 6th IEEE International Symposium on High Performance Distributed Computing.

[8] Message Passing Interface Forum. *MPI: A Message-Passing Interface Standard*. The International Journal of Supercomputer Applications and High-Performance Computing, Volume 8, 1994.

[9] I. Foster and C. Kesselman. *Globus: A Metacomputing Infrastructure Toolkit*. International Journal of Supercomputer Applications, 11(2):115-128, 1997.

[10] I. Foster and C. Kesselman. *The Grid: Blueprint for a New Computing Infrastructure*. Published by Morgan Kaufmann Publishers inc. ISBN:1-55860-475-8.

[11] Al Geist, Adam Beguelin, Jack Dongerra, Weicheng Jiang, Robert Manchek, and Vaidy Sunderam. *PVM: Parallel Virtual Machine A Users' Guide and Tutorial for Networked Parallel Computing*. MIT Press, 1994.

[12] Globus. *Globus RSL*. http://www.globus.org/gram/rsl_spec1.html.

[13] John P. Morrison. *Condensed Graphs: Unifying Availability-Driven, Coercion-Driven and Control-Driven Computing*. PhD Thesis, Eindhoven,1996.

[14] John P. Morrison, Brian Clayton, David A. Power, and Adarsh Patil. *WebCom-G: Grid Enabled Metacomputing*. The Journal of Neural, Parallel and Scientific Computation. Special issue on Grid Computing. Guest Editors: H.R. Arabnia, G. A. Gravvanis and M.P. Bekakos. April 2004.

[15] John P. Morrison, James J. Kennedy, and David A. Power. *WebCom: A Volunteer-Based Metacomputer*. The Journal of Supercomputing, Volume 18(1): 47-61, January 2001.

[16] John P. Morrison, David A. Power, and James J. Kennedy. *An Evolution of the WebCom Metacomputer*. The Journal of Mathematical Modelling and Algorithms: Special issue on Computational Science and Applications, 2003(2), pp 263-276, Editor: G. A. Gravvanis.

[17] Platform Computing: Load Sharing Facility. http://www.platform.com.

[18] Portable Batch System. http://www.openpbs.org.

[19] David A. Power, Adarsh Patil, Sunil John, and John P. Morrison. *WebCom-G*. Proceedings of the international conference on parallel and distributed processing techniques and applications (PDPTA 2003), Las Vegas, Nevada, June 23-26, 2003.

[20] Rob V. van Nieuwpoort, Jason Maassen, Rutger Hofman, Thilo Kielmann, and Henri E. Bal. *Ibis: an efficient Java-based grid programming environment*. Proceedings of the 2002 joint ACM-ISCOPE conference on Java Grande, p.18-27, November 03-05, 2002, Seattle, Washington, USA.

[21] D. A. Watt. *Programming Language Processors*. Prentice Hall International, Hemel Hempstead, UK, 1993.

GRID SOLUTION FOR E-MARKETPLACES INTEGRATED WITH LOGISTICS

L. Kacsukné Bruckner[1] and T. Kiss[2]

[1]Institute of Information Systems and Logistics, International Business School, H1021 Budapest Tárogató út 2-4, e-mail: lkacsuk@ibs-b.hu; [2]Centre for Parallel Computing, Cavendish School of Computer Science, University of Westminster, 115 New Cavendish Street, London, W1W 6UW, e-mail: kisst@wmin.ac.uk

Abstract: Electronic marketplaces are important facilitators of today's e-business activities. Besides substantial advantages offered by these exchange sites, e-marketplaces do not work up to their full potential at the moment. This paper describes both a new business model and its technical implementation using Grid technology. A new, three-sided e-commerce model is suggested that integrates buyers, sellers and logistics service providers who all participate in the same negotiation process. To solve computation intensive optimisation tasks and to integrate back-office and marketplace applications, a Grid services based marketplace implementation model is outlined.

Key words: e-business, logistics, e-marketplace, Grid service, legacy code

1.   INTRODUCTION

The evolution of business models and technological solutions advance together like intertwining spirals motivating and supporting each other. Business requirements drive information technology (IT) to find new tools and techniques that make businesses develop new needs again. Early electronic commerce – Electronic Data Interchange (EDI) - was started because telecommunication between computers facilitated a new relationship between businesses. The rise of new business needs resulted in new communication standards and protocols. Real e-commerce was born out of the opportunity offered by the World Wide Web and triggered new IT researches again. After the unrealistic hype of the 90's and the crises around 2000 e-commerce by now has entered the reality phase where efficiency drives the businesses, Internet usage adds value and increases the profitability of the companies. (Plankett Research 2004)

A main target area of seeking business efficiency is supply chain management (SCM). Today a substantial part of supply chains are managed across the Internet still they contain a surprisingly high amount of inefficiencies. (Oliver at al. 2002) Both business and technology sides should be revised to find ways of improvement. New e-commerce models might be considered and the latest information technology tools searched for to support them.

The Grid concept has been created for solving computation intensive scientific problems, but the possibility of business applications was soon discovered. The convergence between Web services and Grid computing, that was triggered by the specification of OGSA (Open Grid Services Architecture) (Foster et al., 2002), resulted in even more intensive interest from large industry players towards Grid-based solutions. OGSA defines a Grid architecture that is based on Web service standards and protocols. As Web services are becoming more and more common in business applications, a Grid architecture based on SOAP (Simple Object Access Protocol) communication and WSDL (Web Services Description Language) service descriptions is the natural model to adopt in a business environment.

This paper would like to provide a step forward both in the fields of business and technology. As an answer to SCM problems a new, three-sided e-commerce model is suggested that integrates buyers, sellers and logistics service providers in the same negotiation process. This marketplace helps trading partners to minimise their costs and increase their profit. The online optimisation requires large amounts of computation without any delay, which has focused attention on Grid technology. Following the direction set by Kacsukné (2004) and using the Grid-based e-marketplace architecture introduced by Kiss at al. (2004) this article gives a complex picture of the new e-marketplace model and its planned implementation.

2.   INTEGRATING LOGISTICS INTO E-MARKETPLACES

B2B e-marketplace models can be classified as buyer-oriented, seller-oriented and intermediary marketplaces. The first type is facilitated by a company or consortium with big buying potential aiming at optimising procurement costs and is contributed by a large number of sellers. A seller-oriented model is just the opposite while intermediary marketplaces bring together a high number of buyers and sellers. According to industries we distinguish between vertical marketplaces serving one industry and horizontal models that serve several industries. Among seller-oriented vertical marketplace providers we can find many third party logistics companies (3PL) that undertake packaging, transportation, warehousing etc. However, none of the currently used models enable optimisation that includes logistical costs as well. E-marketplaces selling goods either do not offer logistical solutions at all or offer a single solution or 2-3 possibilities in different time-cost ranges. Electronic distributors undertake the task of mediating between buyers and seller providing logistical services as well but this excludes competition from the 3PL side.

A new approach given by Kacsukné & Cselényi (2004) suggests a model that really integrates logistics services providers to goods' e-marketplaces. In this model the logistics providers are placing their offers step by step during the negotiation of buyers and sellers then each time a combined proposal showing the total costs is created by the

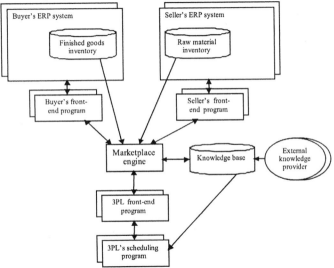

Figure 1.: Framework for an e-marketplace integrated with logistics

marketplace. The general framework of the integrated marketplace can be seen on Figure 1. In the centre there is the marketplace engine to which the entities from all the three sides – buyer, seller and 3PL – are joining with the help of front-end processors. The ratio of the number of buyers and sellers determines if the model is buyer-oriented, seller-oriented or intermediary type.

It is assumed that all participants have advanced enterprise resource planning (ERP) systems and scheduling programs that can provide the front-end processors with the relevant data within a short time.

To illustrate the computational tasks of marketplaces integrated with logistics we outline a three-sided auction algorithm involving multiple products, multiple buyers and multiple 3PLs in a single transaction:

1. The buyer issues a request for proposal (RFP) identifying the requirements
2. Sellers bid offering products.

3. The marketplace engine forwards the bids to the 3PLs who place their bids for logistics services.
4. The marketplace engine aggregates the offers from seller and 3PLs and forwards the best one to the buyer
5. The cycle is continued until the lowest accumulated cost is achieved.

We outline the optimisation algorithm of Step 4. Let us suppose that the buyer would like to purchase N different product items in a marketplace where M sellers and L logistics providers participate. The optimal proposal can be chosen by minimising the total costs i.e. the sum of the purchase price, the transportation costs and the warehousing costs for the period from the time of the actual delivery to the latest delivery as formulated in (1). We suppose that all the required amounts can be purchased, which is expressed by (2).

$$\sum_{i=1}^{N} \sum_{k=1}^{M} \delta_i^k P_i^k Q_i^k + \sum_{l=1}^{L} \sum_{i=1}^{N} \sum_{k=1}^{M} \delta_i^k \lambda_i^{kl} (K_i^{kl} + Kt_i^{kl}) Q_i^k = \min \qquad (1$$

Where:

$$Kt_i^{kl} = (ct_i + ce(P_i^k + K_i^{kl}))(LDT_i - ADT_i^{kl})$$

δ_i^k	=1, if i. product is purchased from the k. seller.
	=0 otherwise
λ_i^{kl}	=1, if i. product from k. seller is delivered by l. 3PL.
	=0 otherwise
P_i^k	unit price of the i. product asked by the k. seller
K_i^{kl}	unit cost of getting the i. product from the k. seller via the l. 3PL
Q_i^k,	quantity of the i. product purchased from the k. seller
Q_i,	required quantity of the i. product
ct_l	the technical factor of storing of the i. product for a time period
ce	capital tying up cost factor for a time period
LDT_i	the latest possible delivery time of the i. product
ADT_i^{kl}	the actual delivery time of the i. product from k. seller by l. 3PL.

$$\sum_{k=1}^{M} \delta_i^k Q_i^k = Q_i \qquad\qquad i=1....N \qquad\qquad (2)$$

This is an integer programming problem with δ_i^k and λ_i^{kl} binary variables that should be solved in each round of the auction process. This model is a grossly simplified illustration of the computational tasks because here we disregarded of the possible discounts for buying and transporting in bulk that makes the problem much more complex.

3. ROLE OF GRID COMPUTING IN E-MARKETPLACES

Besides the substantial advantages, like reduced intermediation costs, integrated processes in supply chain, shortened purchase cycle, greater transparency and lower administrative costs, e-marketplaces are still facing significant technical difficulties. Integrating legacy back-office applications and ERP systems with marketplaces is a complex, expensive, but necessary task to utilise fully the opportunities of exchanges. Also, marketplaces offer only limited functionality today because of the difficulties in integrating existing value-added services. These services may also require large computational power like the optimisation algorithm described in section 2.

The following e-marketplace model based on Grid and Web services concepts offers solutions for these problems. If both back-office and marketplace applications are implemented as Grid services they are able to communicate with each other by exchanging standard SOAP messages. Interoperability is provided by Web services standards despite any differences in hardware platforms, operating systems or programming languages applied. A Grid service based model also provides the possibility to extend the functionality of exchanges. Existing legacy applications run by participants or third party application service providers are offered as Grid services and can easily be integrated with the marketplace solution. In addition, the substantial amount of calculation that may be required can be distributed by introducing a special Grid implementation called Marketplace Support Grid (MSG) that uses the computation power offered by participants who choose this form of contribution instead of paying the registration fee.

The general architecture of MSG is illustrated on figure 2. The marketplace engine coordinates the business transactions communicating

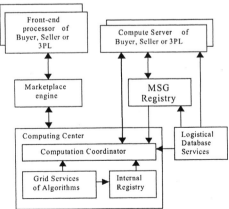

Figure 2. Marketplace Support Grid Architecture

with the front-end processors of the participants. The optimisation problems are passed to the Computation Centre. This unit consists of the

Computation Coordinator, a set of Grid services that facilitate the algorithms along with the Internal Registry where they are registered. The Computation Coordinator will run the core program distributing and invoking the relevant Grid services on the other participants' computers. All buyers, sellers and 3PLs who join the primary marketplace may take part in the MSG as well. They adopt a compute server, a special Grid service server defined by Sipos & Kacsuk (2004) that can host and execute a Grid service sent to it. These compute servers will be registered in the MSG Registry. The Computation Coordinator will allocate the Grid services of the algorithms dynamically to compute servers, send the services and get the results after invoking them. External knowledge service providers will also be registered in the MSG Registry enabling the Computation Coordinator to access them.

However, despite the significant advantages offered by Grid technology, it would be impossible to convince marketplace participants to totally reengineer their existing applications or develop completely new versions of them based on Grid services. GEMLCA (Grid Execution Management for Legacy Code Architecture) (Delaitre et al., 2004) offers a relatively easy and painless solution for this. By installing GEMLCA both by the marketplace, sellers, buyers and logistics service providers, legacy applications can be offered as Grid services without reengineering the original code.

4.   GRID EXECUTION MANAGEMENT FOR LEGACY CODE ARCHITECTURE

GEMLCA, a general architecture to deploy legacy code programs as Grid services, is developed by the research team of Centre for Parallel and Distributed Computing at the University of Westminster. GEMLCA is a client front-end Grid service that offers a number of interfaces to submit and check the status of computational jobs, and get the results back.

GEMLCA design is a three-layer architecture. The Grid Service front-end layer enables the registration of already deployed legacy code applications and provides the Grid service access point to them. The middle layer manages the legacy code program environment and job behaviour, and the inner, currently GT3 (Globus Toolkit version 3) layer offers services in order to create a Globus RSL (Resource Specification Language) file and to submit and control the job using a specific job manager.

Users only have to install GEMLCA and legacy applications can be offered as Grid services without re-engineering the code. The legacy program can be run from a Grid service client and even complex workflows can be constructed with the help of a workflow engine like the one in P-Grade (Kacsuk et al., 2001).

5. GRID SERVICES BASED E-MARKETPLACE MODEL WITH GEMLCA

The Grid services based e-marketplace model utilising the GEMLCA architecture is illustrated on figure 3.

The transformation of e-marketplaces can be done in two phases. During phase 1 marketplace operators and participants install GEMLCA that provides the capability of accessing existing legacy marketplace, back-office and third party applications through Grid service clients. The legacy programs need to be registered with the GEMLCA architecture, and using the WSDL description of the GEMLCA Grid service clients have to be generated. Following this, every communication happens by exchanging SOAP messages. GEMLCA takes care of identifying users, transferring input and output data and submitting jobs to local job managers. Phase 2 means the integration of new applications, specifically developed as Grid services, into the architecture. This requires the inclusion of local UDDI (Universal Description, Discovery, and Integration) registries for both GEMLCA and for new Grid services

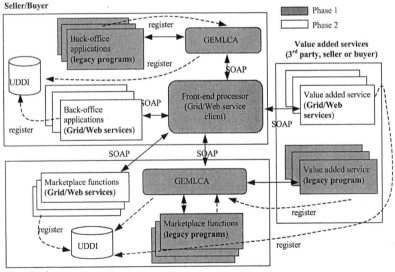

Figure 3. E-Marketplace Model Based on Grid Services

too. As all applications are accessed as Grid services and all communication happens through SOAP messages, interoperability of different solutions and the integration of back-office applications and value added services with the marketplace are provided.

Figure 4 details phase 1 solution showing file transfer and user authentication, and also demonstrates a possible architecture for the MSG.

The architecture uses GT3 security solutions to authenticate users and to delegate user Grid credentials to the Globus MMJFS (Master Managed Job Factory Service) for the allocation of resources. In order to transfer input and output parameters the client contacts an RFT (Reliable File Transfer) service instance that conducts the data exchange between the client and the GEMLCA architecture. All these functionalities are completely transparent from the user's point of view and are all managed by GEMLCA.

Local back-office applications are always executed on the company's own compute server. However, marketplace applications and value added services may require large computing power and can be distributed on the support Grid. This requires an MSG registry Grid Service, where the local compute servers register and describe their parameters. Before submitting a job GEMLCA contacts this registry, finds an appropriate compute server and submits the job there. To complete this solution the current GEMLCA architecture should be extended in order to query the MSG registry and to be able to submit computational jobs to a remote compute server.

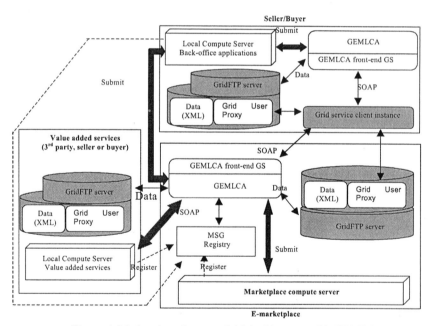

Figure 4. Marketplace Support Grid Architecture with GEMLCA

6.   SUMMARY

This paper has introduced a new type of e-marketplaces and outlined a Grid-based solution for it. The business level model is based on the contribution of buyers, sellers and logistics service providers. Optimisation algorithms involve lengthy computation. The solution suggested here exploits the advantages of Grid-services in two ways. On one hand Grid-services are used for conducting business on the marketplace enabling participants to integrate their existing business solutions easily. On the other hand partners computing resources are used to form a Marketplace Support Grid that operates with portable services. The further research work is two folded. On the business level the details of the mathematical model should be elaborated first, then the development of the distributed optimisation algorithms will be continued. On the technological level the implementation of the original GEMLCA design architecture has to be finished. Following this the necessary extensions required by e-marketplaces outlined in this paper have to be further elaborated and implemented.

7. ACKNOWLEDGEMENTS

The work presented in this paper is partly supported by EPSRC funded project, Grant no: GR/S77509/01. The authors wish to acknowledge the Support of University of Westminster, University of Miskolc and SZTAKI.

8. REFERENCES

Delaitre, T., Goyeneche, A., Kiss, T., Winter, S.C., Publishing and Executing Parallel Legacy Code using an OGSI Grid Service, To appear in Conf. Proc. of the 2004 ICCSA. May 2004, Assisi (PG), Italy

Foster, I., Keselman C., Nick, J., Tuecke, S., The Physiology of the Grid: An Open Grid Services Architecture for Distributed Systems integration, 2002, http://www.globus.org/research/papers/anatomy.pdf

Kacsuk. P., Dozsa G., Lovas, R., The GRADE Graphical Programming Environment, In the book: Parallel Program Development for Cluster Computing (Chapter 10), Editors: Kacsuk P., Cunha, J.C., and Winter, S.C., pp. 231-247, Nova Science Publishers New York, 2001.

Kacsukné Bruckner, L..: A Grid-based E- marketplaces Model Integrated with Logistics Mipro 2004, International Scientific Conference May 2004, Opatija, Croatia

Kacsukné Bruckner, L., Cselényi, J.: E- marketplaces Model Integrated with Logistics MicroCAD 2004, International Scientific Conference March 2004, Miskolc, Hungary

Kiss, T., Terstyanszky, G., Winter S.,: Electronic marketplaces based on OGSI Grid Services MicroCAD 2004, International Scientific Conference, March 2004, Miskolc

Oliver, K., Laseter, T. Chung, A., Black, D. (2002) End Game http://www.bah.de/content/downloads/logistics_endgame.pdf

Plankett Research (2004) Major Trends in E-Commerce and Internet Business. 2004, pp7.-17. Plunkett Research, Limited; Houston; http://www.plunkettresearch.com

Sipos, G. Kacsuk, P. (2004) : Connecting Condor Pools into Computational Grids by Jini, AxGrids Conference, January 2004, Nicosia, Cyprus

INCREMENTAL PLACEMENT OF NODES IN A LARGE-SCALE ADAPTIVE DISTRIBUTED MULTIMEDIA SERVER

Tibor Szkaliczki*
Computer and Automation Research Institute of the Hungarian Academy of Sciences
sztibor@sztaki.hu

László Böszörményi
University Klagenfurt, Department of Information Technology
laszlo@itec.uni-klu.ac.at

Abstract   An incremental algorithm is proposed to dynamically place the proxies of the Adaptive Distributed Multimedia Server (ADMS) developed at the University Klagenfurt. In order to enhance the performance of the server, the proposed algorithm examines the suitable network nodes for hosting proxies. The main benefit of the algorithm is the capability to process large problems within strict time constraints. The short running time of the algorithm enables the distributed server to adapt quickly to the changing network parameters and client demands.

Keywords: incremental algorithm, multimedia server, video streams, host recommendation, data collector

1.   Introduction

It is a usual task to select nodes for hosting dynamic server applications in a network. The Adaptive Distributed Multimedia Server (ADMS) of the University Klagenfurt [Tusch, 2003] is able to add and remove its components to different nodes of the network. This novel feature of the multimedia server enables the dynamic placement of the server components according to the current requests and the QoS parameters of the network. The running time of the host

---

*Partial support of the EC Centre of Excellence programme (No. ICA1-CT-2000-70025) and the Hungarian Scientific Research Fund (Grant No. OTKA 42559) is gratefully acknowledged.

recommendation algorithm becomes crucial in this case since the delivery of the data-streams can start only after the placement of the server nodes.

In this paper, we propose an incremental algorithm that is especially suitable for large-scale distributed video servers delivering stream-data to large number of clients. In this case the time-consuming algorithms aiming at the "perfect" solution are not applicable. The proposed algorithm takes the possible nodes one after the other, and it places a proxy at the examined node if it improves the solution. The simplicity of the proposed algorithm enables to find an initial solution as fast as possible and than the algorithm incrementally improves it complying with the time constraints in order to approximate the optimal placement.

2.   Related Work

Finding the optimal deployment of proxies in a network is a well known problem in the literature [Steen et al., 1999], [Qiu et al., 2001]. However, we cannot use the former results directly because of the significant differences between the ADMS proxies and the well-studied web-proxies. The placement of the web-proxies cannot be changed later or with high cost only. Moreover, the multimedia server provides huge data-streams instead of documents and images. The caching problems of the multimedia servers are not in the scope of the present paper, they are discussed in [Tusch et al., 2004].

In an earlier paper we dealt with the configuration recommend,ation algorithms for the offensive adaptation [Goldschmidt et al., 2004]. We proposed four different algorithms (greedy, particle swarm, linear programming rounding and first ideas on an incremental algorithm) and compared the results gained by running their implementations on different test networks. The particle swarm algorithm, a kind of evolutionary algorithms produced the best result while the incremental algorithm found the solution in the shortest time. The current paper explores the incremental algorithm in detail. We present the results after the definition of the problem model.

Incremental algorithms are applied to many problems in the area of the combinatorial optimisation, see as an example [Ramalingam and Reps, 1996, Zanden, 1996]. Their main step is updating the solution of a problem after a unit change is made in the input. The incremental algorithms result in significant decrease of computation time in case of many problems.

3.   The problem model

The task is to find suitable locations for proxies of the distributed multimedia server while maximising the clients' satisfaction and minimising the network load. The *clients* receive the same video in parallel. The videos are stored at the *server* nodes. The proxies get the desired video from the servers and forward the received packets to the clients without storing them. According to the present model, the proxies can reduce the bandwidth of the video and can send the same video to different clients with different bandwidths. The proxies can be located only on nodes prepared for hosting dynamic server components. The nodes that are able to host proxies are called *possible proxies*.

Technical report [Goldschmidt et al., 2004] contains the detailed description of the problem model. The network model is basically a graph where the nodes are called *areas*. An area is either a subnet (including backbone links) or a router that connects subnets. The edges of the graph are the connections between the routers and the subnets they are part of. We assume that we know the Quality of Service attributes of each area: bandwidth, delay jitter, etc.

There are three kinds of components that can be found on the nodes, namely servers, possible proxies and clients. In the problem specification, each area may contain several components with different types, such as clients, possible proxies and servers. The clients define their demands as lists that contain QoS requirements (e. g. bitrate and delay jitter) in decreasing order of preference. In the current model we assume that all clients want to see the same video immediately.

The solution of a problem is described as a possible *configuration* that provides the following information for each client: the index of the QoS demand that has been chosen to be satisfied, the possible target node that hosts the proxy for the client, the server, where the video should be collected from.

The following *cost* functions are defined to measure the quality of the solutions: the network resource needs (total allocation), the number of rejected clients, the sum of the chosen demand indices of the clients (*linear badness*), and the so called *exponential badness*, that is defined as $\sum_{c \in C} 2^{i_c}$ where C is the set of clients, and i_c is the index of the chosen demand parameter for client c.

Table 1 gives a short summary of the results published in [Goldschmidt et al., 2004] in order to compare different host recommendation algorithms. The incremental algorithm can find a solution in the shortest time. The number of rejections is also very low, but the exponential badness is higher by more than 30 percents than in case of the swarm algorithm.

algorithm	exp. badness	lin. badness	rejections	time (sec)
Greedy	800	117	8.3	296.9
Particle swarm	299	90	1.9	172.7
Linprog rounding	320	95	2.1	0.11
Incremental	400	109	1.2	0.03

Table 1. The results of the measurements for different algorithms solving networks with 50 nodes, 10 servers, 40 possible proxies and 30 clients

We enhance our model published earlier for the case when huge number of clients exist in the network. We want to serve as many clients as possible with the server, which can be much more than the number of the areas of the networks. Fortunately, the variety of the client demands is limited in practical cases regarding the case where all clients demand the same video. This enables to handle many clients without significant increase of the running time. Now, let the clients denote client groups with the same demand lists in a subnet. The problem specification can be simply modified by adding the size of the client groups to the description of the client demands. Thus, the number of client groups can be bounded by the constant multiple of the number of nodes where the constant is typically smaller than ten. The client groups may be divided into smaller groups at the output, because the clients may receive the same video in different quality even if they belong to the same client group.

4.   Incremental algorithm

According to the results presented on Table 1, the incremental algorithm proved to be promising to find a solution for large-scale networks.

A special graph is applied to store and retrieve the client-proxy-server routes that are able to satisfy the client requests. We call it FLP graph, because the idea comes from the facility location problem, a kind of optimisation problem in the area of operations research. One set of the nodes denotes the clients, the other one represents the proxy-server pairs referred to facilities. The edges between them correspond to the client-proxy-server routes. An edge is put into the graph only if the route is able to satisfy the request of the client. Using this graph, we can easily retrieve each routes for a proxy or a client.

The original algorithm is modified in order to accelerate the generation of the initial solution. The algorithm generated first the FLP graph. However, this can be time-consuming for large-scale networks. For this reason, the generation of the FLP graph is partitioned into smaller steps processing individual proxies which are inserted into the incremental algorithm.

```
1 for each proxy do
2     Calculate the QoS parameters of the routes from the proxy
3     for each server do
4         Add a facility node together with edges to the FLP graph
5         Decide on selecting the current facility
6         if the facility is selected then
7             for each client connected to the current facility do
8                 Decide on assigning the current client to the facility
9 Unselect facilities that are not connected to any client
```

The parameters of the routes between the proxy and each other nodes can be calculated in Step 2 by running the shortest path algorithm. The QoS parameters of the client-proxy-server routes can be easily determined from the results calculated in Step 2. If the QoS parameters of the route satisfy any requirements of the client, an edge is added to the FLP graph between the current client and facility. The algorithm stores the parameters of the route at the edge together with the index of the first requirement of the client that can be satisfied by the represented client-proxy-server route.

The algorithm selects facility f_i in Step 5 if there is at least one client c_j among the nodes adjacent to the facility that it is still not assigned to any facility or if client c_j is assigned to facility f_0 then the parameters of the edge between c_j and f_i are better than that between c_j and f_0, and the badness of the first satisfiable demand on the edge between c_j and f_i is not greater than that of the satisfied demand on the edge between c_j and f_0. These criteria are complemented with one more in Step 8: the demand of client c_j can be satisfied through facility f_i without overloading the network.

In order to accelerate the algorithm, only a subset of the facilities is processed instead of each possible proxy-server pair. We tested some different kinds of subsets in order to determine how the number of processed facilities can be substantially reduced without increasing the cost values. According to our experiences, a facility may be omitted from processing if there is another one where each of the QoS parameters are better. The results published in this paper are produced applying this acceleration method.

The algorithm is slightly modified in order to deal with the client groups. New procedures are needed to calculate the bandwidth requirement of the demands and to select a client group. In order to minimise the exponential badness, the algorithm tries to serve the clients belonging to the same group with equal quality, that is, the difference between the index of the satisfied demands is at most one in a client group. Each client in a group is served by the same proxy and server in the present version. This restriction can be eliminated later in order to improve the quality of the solution.

5.   Results

The implemented incremental algorithm is tested on simulated network environments. The first test network has 50 nodes, 40 possible proxies, 30 clients and 10 servers and the numbers of the components are increased proportionally in the further networks in order to find out the size of the largest problem that still can be solved, see Table 2. The test were running on a 1.2 GHz processor with 384MB memory. The algorithm successfully solves problems not greater than 500 nodes in less than 10 seconds.

Let us analyse how the cost of the solution is decreasing as the algorithm examines newer and newer facilities or proxy-server pairs. Figures 1 show the costs (exponential badnesses, numbers of rejected clients) as a function of the

nodes	servers	proxies	clients	time
50	10	40	30	0.03
100	20	80	60	0.16
200	40	160	120	0.821
300	60	240	180	2.333
400	80	320	240	5.137
500	100	400	300	9.663

Table 2. The dimensions of the test networks and the running times

time elapsed from the start of the algorithm. In the second case, the algorithm was stopped before finishing because it would be running too long.

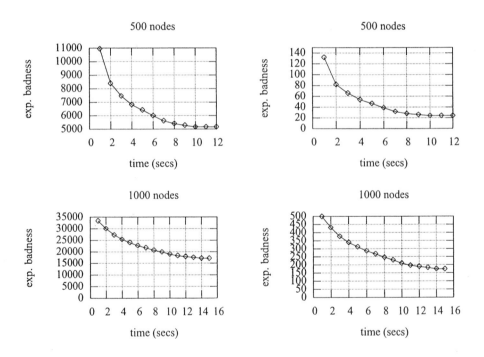

Figure 1. The badness and the number of rejections as a function of the elapsed time processing a network with 500 nodes, 100 servers, 400 possible proxies and 300 clients (above) and with 1000 nodes, 200 servers, 800 possible proxies and 600 clients (below)

As we can see, first the cost starts falling quickly and later only slight improvements are achieved. If the quick response is a crucial point, this fact makes worth realising intermediate solutions while the algorithm is running.

Thus we can instantly start to deliver media to several clients and then gradually increase both the number of the served clients and the quality of the media stream. In this way, we can give recommendation for problems even if the running time for the optimal solution would be extremely long.

We tested how the program is able to manage clients groups. The initial network consists of 50 nodes, 10 servers, 40 possible proxies and 300 clients. In this case, each client group contains only a single client. Further networks are created with 3000 and 30000 clients by increasing the size of the client groups to 10 and 100, respectively, while the size of the network and the number of server components do not change. There is no significant change in the running time as the size of the client groups increases, see Table 3.

nodes	servers	proxies	clients	exp. badn.	lin. badn.	reject.	time(sec)
50	10	40	300	5340	1141	29	0.27
50	10	40	3000	53408	11393	290	0.26
50	10	40	30000	1511544	160804	21964	0.3

Table 3.   The results for client groups with increasing sizes

At last, let us examine the quality of the solution. Using linear programming, we can find a lower bound for the cost. The algorithm accepts each of the requests in the network with 50 nodes. We find a lower bound of 7 for the number of rejections in the case of 100 nodes and the incremental algorithm generates a solution with 9 rejections. The exponential badnesses are 360 and 1152 in the two cases instead of the lower bound of 215 and 902, respectively.

6.   Conclusions and Further Work

We examined an incremental algorithm for the configuration recommendation in a large-scale adaptive distributed multimedia server with huge number of clients. The speed of the incremental algorithm, the continuous decrease of the solution cost and the introduction of client groups enabled us to solve large problems. Further development is needed to improve the quality of the solution in order to decrease the number of the rejections and to improve the quality of the delivered video.

References

[Goldschmidt et al., 2004] Goldschmidt, B., Szkaliczki, T., and Böszörményi, L (2004). Placement of Nodes in an Adaptive Distributed Multimedia Server. Technical Report TR/ITEC/04/2.06, Institute of Information Technology, Klagenfurt University, Klagenfurt, Austria. http://143.205.180.128/Publications/pubfiles/pdffiles/2004-0005-BGAT.pdf.

[Qiu et al., 2001] Qiu, L., V.N., Padmanabhan, and G.M., Voelker (2001). On the placement of web server replicas. In *INFOCOM*, pages 1587–1596.

[Ramalingam and Reps, 1996] Ramalingam, G. and Reps, Thomas W. (1996). An incremental algorithm for a generalization of the shortest-path problem. *J. Algorithms*, 21(2):267–305.

[Steen et al., 1999] Steen, M., Homburg, P., and Tannenbaum, A. S. (1999). Globe: A wide-area distributed system. *IEEE Concurrency*.

[Tusch, 2003] Tusch, R. (2003). Towards an adaptive distributed multimedia streaming server architecture based on service-oriented components. In Böszörményi, L. and Schojer, P., editors, *Modular Programming Languages, JMLC 2003*, LNCS 2789, pages 78–87. Springer.

[Tusch et al., 2004] Tusch, R., Böszörményi, L., Goldschmidt, B., Hellwagner, H., and Schojer, P. (2004). Offensive and Defensive Adaptation in Distributed Multimedia Systems. *Computer Science and Information Systems (ComSIS)*, 1(1):49–77.

[Zanden, 1996] Zanden, B. Vander (1996). An incremental algorithm for satisfying hierarchies of multiway dataflow constraints. *ACM Transactions on Programming Languages and Systems*, 18(1):30–72.

COMPONENT BASED FLIGHT SIMULATION IN DIS SYSTEMS

Krzysztof Mieloszyk, Bogdan Wiszniewski
Faculty of Electronics, Telecommunications and Informatics
Gdansk University of Technology
krzymi@due.mech.pg.gda.pl, bowisz@eti.pg.gda.pl

Abstract   Distributed interactive simulation constitutes an interesting class of information systems, which combine several areas of computer science enabling each individual simulation object to visualize dynamic states of all distributed objects participating in the simulation. Objects are unpredictable and must exchange state information in order to correctly visualize a dynamic 3D scene from their local perspectives. In the paper, a component based approach developed in the ongoing project at GUT[1], has been described; it can reduce the volume of state information being exchanged without losing messages essential for reliable execution of simulation scenarios.

Keywords: Distributed objects, remote state monitoring

Introduction

Distributed Interactive Simulation (DIS) systems form an important application class of collaborative computing environments, in which many independent and autonomous simulation objects, real objects and human operators are connected to one computational framework. In may be for example a local cluster of helicopter flight simulators in a lab with a group of real tanks operating in a remote shooting range, a city traffic simulation system where cars and traffic lights are simulated but some intersections are operated by real policemen, or a complex building on a simulated fire seen on computer screens at the command center, and real firemen on a drill. Any such system performs specific computations, which are unpredictable, have no algorithmic representation, and because of participating real objects, all events must be handled in real-time despite of the system geographical distribution.

Objects participating in a simulation exercise are sending updates on their local state to other objects in irregular intervals. If the updates were sent just in periodic samples, a network supporting any realistic DIS system with many objects would soon be overloaded. Moreover, increasing dynamics of reporting objects would imply higher sampling rate and would make the performance problems even worse. Delayed (or lost) messages would certainly make any visualization unrealistic. However, if a simulated object dynamics could be estimated with some function of time, the number of messages to be sent would be limited, since "new" states would be calculated by a receiving object instead of sending them out by the reporting object.

This paper reports on the project started at TUG in 2002 and aimed at developing a DIS system with time-critical constraints, involving simulated flying objects (helicopters) and ground vehicles (tanks) in a 3D space.

1.   DIS system architecture

Any DIS system consists of simulators (called *simulation objects*), each one designed to model a specific human operated device or vehicle. Any particular simulator may be operating in a distinct geographical location, and its underlying operating system, software and hardware are usually incompatible to other simulators, preventing direct interaction between them. In order to create a collaborative computing environment a system architecture must enable integration of such objects (called *active participants*), and also provide access for observers (called *passive participants*) with logging and monitoring capabilities. Active participants exchange information to update one another on their states as soon as they change. State updates sent by reporting objects are needed by receiving objects to model a 3D global dynamic virtual scene from their local perspectives. Passive observers usually limit their actions to on-line state tracing and logging for future replay, evaluation of active participants progress in a particular training scenario, as well as collecting data for new training scenarios. A generic architecture of a DIS system is outlined in Figure 1; it involves *communication, service,* and *interaction* layers, with distinct functionality and interfaces, marked with vertical arrows described further on.

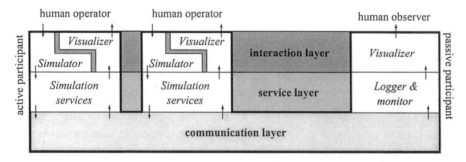

Figure 1.   Distributed interactive system architecture

Interaction layer. Human operator provides an external stimulus affecting the internal state of a simulator. According to the semantics of the latter and its current state a new state is determined, reported to the lower layer simulation services, and broadcasted via the communication layer. State updates are received at irregular intervals by simulation services of an interested participant and passed to the visualizer component, which generates (modifies) its local perspective of a global dynamic scene. Based on the view of moving objects outside the cabin and a local state indicated by flight instruments inside the cabin, a decision is made by the human operator (pilot) on the next stimulus (maneuver).

Service layer. Simulation services provided by the service layer enable reduction of the volume of state update messages being sent over the system by active participants. If the simulation object movement (state trajectory) can be described with kinesthetic parameters like acceleration, speed, position, mass, force, moment, etc., state prediction can be based on Newtonian rules of dynamics, using a technique known as *dead reckoning* [Lee2000]. States that can be calculated based on the current reported state do not have to be sent out, as the receiving participant can calculate them anyway. Further reduction of the volume of state updates can be achieved by *relevance filtering* of messages that are redundant with regard to some specific context of the scene, e.g. a reporting object is far away and its movement will result in a pixel-size change at a remote display.

Communication layer. The main job of the bottom layer shown in Figure 1 is to make the underlying network transparent to upper layers. Objects may want to join and leave the simulation at any time, require reliable sending of messages, and need time synchronization. This layer has no knowledge on the semantics of data being sent by simulation objects but has knowledge about the location of participants over the network. Two models of communication have been implemented in the project reported in this paper: one with a *dedicated server* and another with *multicast* [MKKK2003]. The former (server based) enables lossless communication and make data filtering easier, but the cost is that each message has to go through the server and a network load increases when many participants work in the same local area network. The latter is scalable, but requires implementation of dedicated transmission protocols on top of the existing unreliable UDP protocol.

2. Component interaction model

Since simulation objects have to invoke specialized services of the communication layer, rather then to communicate directly with each other. The communication layer must implement a standard, system-wide functionality.

For example, *High Level Architecture* (HLA) standard [HLA] requires delivery of such services as: *federation management* for creating, connecting, disconnecting and destroying simulation objects in the system, *time management* for controlling logical time advance and time-stamping of messages, and *declaration management* for data posting and subscribing by simulation objects.

Reduction of the volume of data being sent by objects is achieved by a *dead reckoning* technique, which basically extrapolates new position of an object using its previous position and state parameters such as velocity or acceleration. If object movements are not too complex, the amount of messages to be sent can be significantly reduced [Lee2000] However, the method developed in the reported project utilizes a notion of a semantics driven approach to message filtering, based on maneuver detection, allowing for further reduction of the space of states to be reported. This has been made possible by introducing operational limits characterizing real (physical) objects (vehicles) [OW2003]. We will refer to this method briefly when presenting below another important concept introduced in the reported project, which is *component based simulation*.

In order to build and run a simulation system, the reported project required simulators of various physical objects of interest. They had to be realistic in the sense of their physical models, but allowing for easy configuration and scalability of simulated vehicles. This has been achieved by adopting the concept of a physical component shown in Figure 2a.

A component has its local state $\vec{S}$, set initially to some predefined value. Upon the external stimulus $\vec{x}$ coming from the operator or other component its new (resultant) state $\vec{S}'$ is calculated as $\vec{S}' = G(\vec{S}, \vec{x})$, where G represents a state trajectory of the simulated component, given explicitly by a state function or implicitly by a state equation. Subvector $F(\vec{S})$ of the resultant state is reported outside to other components (locally) or other simulators (externally), where F is a filtering function, selecting state vector elements relevant to other components or simulators.

With such a generic representation a component may range from the body with a mass, airfoil objects, like a wing, rotor or propeller, through various types of engines generating power and momentum, up to undercarriage interacting with a ground.

Simulation object

The main idea behind the component based approach is to divide a simulated object into most significant units, and then to simulate each one separately. This approach allows for *flexibility*, since simulators can be readily reconfigured by changing parameters of a particular component (or by replac-

a)

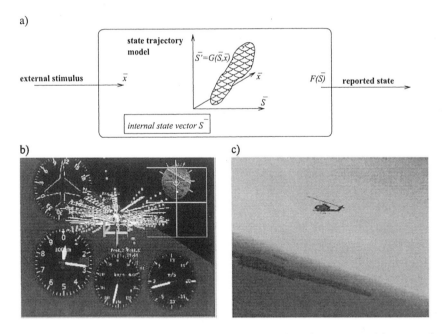

b)   c)

Figure 2.   Simulation object: (a) generic component (b) view of components (c) remote view

ing one with another), as well as *parallelization*, since components may run on clusters if more detailed calculations are required.

With the external stimulus, the user can influence behavior of the component work by changing some of its parameters. Reported state vector $F(\vec{S})$ can affect the state of other components of the simulation object. Based on all states, control parameters and the semantics of a component, it is possible to calculate the external state vector as an influence of the component on simulated object. After combining all state vectors reported by components of the simulation object, it is possible to define its resultant behavior.

Consider for example two cooperating components, an engine and a propeller. In order to simulate correctly each component, local state vectors $\vec{S}$ of an engine and a propeller have over 10 elements, and over 15 elements respectively. However, interaction between them can be modeled with just a 2-element vector consisting of a rotation velocity and torque. Similarly, a two element state vector is sufficient to represent cooperation between a helicopter rotor and an engine, despite that simulation of a rotor requires over 25-element state vectors.

The general modeling technique is to describe a simulation object with a graph, of which each single node corresponds to the respective component. For each pair of nodes which can affect one another an arc is drawn and the corresponding reported state vector $F(\vec{S})$ associated. The size of reported state vectors attributed to individual arcs determine the real volume of data that have to be exchanged between components during simulation. For simulation objects considered in the project, namely ground vehicles, single and twin rotor helicopters, propeller and jet planes, and which may consist of the components described below the size of reported state vectors $F(\vec{S})$ never exceeded two. A sample view of cooperating components of a simulated single rotor helicopter is shown in Figure 2b

Wing. A wing has parameters which describe its dimension, fixing point to the fuselage and the airfoil sections with characteristics combining lift and drag with angle of attack. State of the wing can be affected by the arrangement of ailerons and flaps, and its possible rotation along the longitudinal axis. In this way it is possible to model both lifting and control surfaces of the wing. Additionally, by taking into consideration linear speed of the air stream or angular speed of the wing, the resultant moment and force applied to the simulated object can also be calculated.

Rotor. A helicopter rotor is the most complex component in the project, as it is modeled with several rotating wings (blades). Its state vector elements include dimension of blades, their number, elasticity, induced speed of air flow, airfoil section characteristics, blade fluctuations and angular speed. By changing parameters affecting the collective pitch and periodic pitch, the user (pilot) can control the rotor in the same way as in a real helicopter [SN2002]. Reported state vector $F(\vec{S})$ consists of the resultant forces and moments calculated at over a dozen points evenly distributed over a rotor disk. It is also necessary to consider torque, which is required to determine correctly the state of the entire power transmission system.

Propeller. This component is a simplified version of a helicopter rotor, based on the same semantics and parameters. Elasticity and fluctuations of blades are neglected in calculating of $F(\vec{S})$, but the parameter describing the collective pitch setting is added. The internal state vector of a propeller is the same as in the rotor component.

Engine. This component supports the semantics of both, a jet turbine and a piston engine. Including the internal state vector describing angular speed, working temperature and the maximum power, the user can control its behavior by setting up a throttle. Calculation of the reported state vector $F(\vec{S})$ requires gathering torque values of all attached components, like a propeller or rotor, to calculate the resulting angular speed for the entire power transmission unit taking into account its inertia.

Undercarriage. It is the only component that allows the simulated object to interact with a ground. The internal state vector describes the radius of a tire, shock-absorber lead, and its elasticity, as well as speed of the entire plane, and the relative location of the undercarriage with regard to the plane (helicopter) body. This component has its semantics, defined by a characteristic describing interaction patterns between the tire and the absorber during the contact with a ground. By changing the angle of turn of the wheel and the braking factor, it is possible to control the traction over the runway. As with other components, the reported state vector $F(\vec{S})$ describes the moment and the reaction force of the ground applied through the undercarriage to the simulated object body.

Remote object interaction

As mentioned before any simulation object in a DIS system sends out updates on its state changes to enable other (remote) objects to calculate its position in global scene from the local perspective of each one. The volume of messages is reduced by adopting a dead reckoning scheme, allowing calculation of some "future" states based on current states. While dead reckoning applies mostly to calculating trajectories of moving objects, further reduction of the volume of information being sent is possible based on specific relationships between various elements of the material object state vector. A sample view of a remote object's state (a helicopter) from the local perspective of another object (also a helicopter) is shown in Figure 2c

Active participants. State vector $F(\vec{S})$ reported by each component locally may allow a certain degree of redundancy, depending on the specific internal details of the simulation object. However, the reported state (update) sent out to remote objects must use a state vector in a standard form. In the current implementation it consists of position $\vec{L}$, orientation $\vec{O}$, linear velocity $\vec{v}$, linear acceleration $\vec{a}$, angular velocity $\vec{\omega}$, angular acceleration $\vec{\gamma}$, resultant force $\vec{F}$, and resultant moment $\vec{M}$. In a properly initiated simulation system, where each receiver (observer) has once got full information about each participant, for objects associated with decision events (maneuvers initiated by their human operators) only changes in their acceleration are needed [OW2003].

Passive participants. State prediction is less critical for passive participants, as they do not interact (in the sense of providing a stimulus) with other objects. They do not have any physical interpretation and there is no need to inform users about their existence in a system. They may be independent 3D observers, like a hot-air balloon, or a 2D radar screen, or a map with points moving on it. Their only functionality is monitoring and/or logging the traffic of state update messages. In a DIS system implemented in the project a logger has been introduced. Based on the recorded log entries it can create simulation scenarios, which can be next edited, modified and replayed in the system. In that particular case the logger may temporarily become an active participant.

Human operator

In order to implement any realistic DIS scenario involving "material" objects two problems must be solved. One is state predictability, important from the point of view of the volume of state update messages, and another is object ability to perform maneuvers within specific limits imposed by its operational characteristics. Each object having a mass and characterized with kinesthetic parameters behaves according to the Newtonian laws of dynamics. Classes of behavior that such a material object may exhibit are described by basic equations combining these parameters (function $G(\vec{S})$. Such a form of object representation, although true from the point of view of physics is far too detailed from the point of view of simulating exercises with real flying objects controlled by humans. It has been argued [OW2003] that by introducing the notion of a *maneuver* and *operational characteristics* of simulation objects, the space of possible states to be considered can be significantly reduced. In consequence, there are less states to predict and the flow of state update messages can be reduced further.

State predictability.   The "logic" of flight may be described with a simple automaton involving just five states representing human operator (pilot). The basic state of a flying object is *neutral*, i.e. it remains still or is in a uniform straight line motion. According to the first Newton's law of dynamics both linear and angular accelerations are zero, while the linear velocity is constant. An object in a neutral state may start *entering* a new maneuver and keep doing it as long as its linear or angular acceleration vary. This may eventually lead to a stable state, which is the actual maneuver; in that case both linear and angular acceleration vectors of the object are constant and at least one of them must be non-zero. Any subsequent increase or decrease of any of these acceleration vectors implies further *entering* or *exiting* a maneuver. Exiting a maneuver may end up with entering another maneuver or returning to a neutral state. There is also a *crash* state, when at least one of the object parameters exceeds its allowed limits, e.g. exceeding a structural speed of the airplane ends-up with its disintegration. It found out in the project, practically each state transition of the automaton described above can be detected just by tracing changes of angular or linear acceleration.

Operational characteristics.   All components described before has realistic operational limits, usually listed in the user's manual of the simulated object. The mass may vary, but stay between some minimum (empty) and maximum (loaded) values. There are several speeds characterizing a flying object, e.g.

for planes it is the minimum (stall) speed for each possible configuration (flaps up or down, landing gear up or down), maximum maneuvering speed to use in maneuvers or turbulent air, and maximum structural speed not to be exceeded even in a still air. Resultant lift and drag forces for the wing are the function of the airflow speed and angle of attack, which may change up to the critical (stall) angle, specific to a given profile. Finally thrust is a function of engine RPMs, which may change within a strictly defined range of $[min, max]$ values. Based on these parameters, and a maneuver "semantics" described before, it is possible to calculate (predict) most of the in-flight states intended by the human operator, excluding only random and drastic state changes such as mid-air collision or self-inflicted explosion.

3. Summary

In the current experimental DIS application three classes of simulation objects have been implemented using components described in the paper: a tank, a light propeller airplane, and two kinds of helicopters, with single or twin rotors. The notion of a generic component introduced in Figure 2a proved to be very useful. Current development is aimed at expanding the concept of components on vessels, which besides a propeller-like component and engine, require a body model, simple enough to avoid complex computations but precise to describe interactions between the hull and surrounding water.

Notes

1. Funded by the State Committee for Scientific Research (KBN) under grant T-11C-004-22

References

[SN2002] Seddon J. and Newman S. (2002). *Basic Helicopter Aerodynamics* Masterson Book Services Ltd.

[HLA] DoD. *High Level Architecture interface specification.* IEEE P1516.1, Version 1.3. http://hla.dmso.mil.

[Lee2000] Lee B.S., Cai W., Tirner S.J., and Chen L. (2000). Adaptive dead reckoning algorithms for distributed interactive simulation. *I. J. of Simulation*, 1(1-2):21–34.

[MKKK2003] Mieloszyk K., Kozlowski S., Kuklinski R., and Kwoska A. (2003). Architectural design document of a distributed interactive simulation system KBN-DIS (in Polish). Technical Report 17, Faculty of ETI, GUT.

[OW2003] Orlowski T. and Wiszniewski B. (2003). Stepwise development of distributed interactive simulation systems. In *Proc. Int. Conf. Parallel and Applied Mathematics, PPAM03*, LNCS, Springer Verlag, to appear.

VI

ALGORITHMS

MANAGEMENT OF COMMUNICATION ENVIRONMENTS FOR MINIMALLY SYNCHRONOUS PARALLEL ML

Frédéric Loulergue
Laboratory of Algorithms, Complexity and Logic, Créteil, France
loulergue@univ-paris12.fr

Abstract   Minimally Synchronous Parallel ML is a functional parallel language whose execution time can then be estimated and dead-locks and indeterminism are avoided. Programs are written as usual ML programs but using a small set of additional functions. Provided functions are used to access the parameters of the parallel machine and to create and operate on a parallel data structure. It follows the cost model of the Message Passing Machine model (MPM).

In the current implementation, the asynchrony is limited by a parameter called the asynchrony depth. When processes reach this depth a global synchronization occurs. This is necessary to avoid memory leak. In this paper we propose another mechanism to avoid such synchronization barriers.

1.   Introduction

Bulk Synchronous Parallel (BSP) computing, and the Coarse-Grained Multicomputer model, CGM, which can be seen as a special case of the BSP model, have been used for a large variety of domains [4], and are currently widely used in the research on parallel algorithms. The main advantages of the BSP model are: deadlocks avoidance, indeterminism can be either avoided or restricted to very specific cases ; portability and performance predictability.

The global synchronizations of the BSP model make many practical MPI [18] parallel programs hardly expressible using the BSPlib library. This is why some authors proposed [16] the BSP without barrier and the Message Passing Machine (MPM) model. We decided to investigate the semantics of a new functional parallel language, without synchronization barriers, called Minimally Synchronous Parallel ML (MSPML) [14]. As a first phase we aimed at having (almost) the same source language and high level semantics (programmer's view) than Bulk Synchronous Parallel ML [12], a functional language for Bulk Synchronous Parallelism (in particular to be able to use with MSPML work done on proof of parallel BSML programs with the Coq proof assistant), but with a different (and more efficient for unbalanced programs) low-level semantics and implementation.

Due to the asynchronous nature of MSPML, storage of values, which may be requested by processors in the future, is needed in *communication environments*. For a realistic implementation the size of these communications environments should be of course bounded. This makes the emptying of the communications environments necessary when they are full. This paper presents two solutions for this problem.

We first present informally MSPML (section 2). Then (section 3) we give the mechanism to empty the communication environments. We end with related work, conclusions and future work (sections 4 and 5).

2.   Minimally Synchronous Parallel ML

Bulk Synchronous Parallel (BSP) computing is a parallel programming model introduced by Valiant [17] to offer a high degree of abstraction in the same way as PRAM models and yet allow portable and predictable performance on a wide variety of architectures. A BSP computer is a homogeneous distributed memory machine with a global synchronization unit which executes collective requests for a *synchronization barrier*.

The BSP execution model represents a parallel computation on p processors as an alternating sequence of computation *super-steps* and communications super-steps with global synchronization. BSPWB, for *BSP Without Barrier*, is a model directly inspired by the BSP model. It proposes to replace the notion of super-step by the notion of m-step defined as: at each m-step, each process performs a sequential computation phase then a communication phase. During this communication phase the processes exchange the data they need for the next m-step. The parallel machine in this model is characterized by three parameters (expressed as multiples of the processors speed): the number of processes p, the latency L of the network, the time g which is taken to one word to be exchanged between two processes. This model could be applied to MSPML but it will be not accurate enough because the bounds used in the cost model are too coarse.

A better bound is given by the Message Passing Machine (MPM) model [16]. The parameters of the Message Passing Machine are the same than those of the BSPWB model but the MPM model takes into account that a process only synchronizes with each of its incoming partners and is therefore more accurate (the cost model is omitted here). The MPM model is used as the execution and cost model for our Minimally Synchronous Parallel ML language.

There is no implementation of a full Minimally Synchronous Parallel ML (MSPML) language but rather a partial implementation as a library for the functional programming language Objective Caml [11]. The so-called MSPML library is based on the following elements:

$$
\begin{array}{rcl}
\mathbf{p} & : & \text{unit} \rightarrow \text{int} \qquad\qquad \mathbf{g} : \text{unit} \rightarrow \text{float} \qquad\qquad \mathbf{l} : \text{unit} \rightarrow \text{float} \\
\mathbf{mkpar} & : & (\text{int} \rightarrow \alpha) \rightarrow \alpha \, \mathbf{par} \\
\mathbf{apply} & : & (\alpha \rightarrow \beta) \, \mathbf{par} \rightarrow \alpha \, \mathbf{par} \rightarrow \beta \, \mathbf{par} \\
\mathbf{get} & : & \alpha \, \mathbf{par} \rightarrow \text{int} \, \mathbf{par} \rightarrow \alpha \, \mathbf{par}
\end{array}
$$

It gives access to the parameters of the underling architecture which is considered as a Message Passing Machine (MPM). In particular, it offers the function **p** such that the value of **p**() is p, the static number of processes of the parallel machine. The value of this variable does not change during execution. There is also an abstract polymorphic type α **par** which represents the type of p-wide parallel vectors of objects of type α, one per process. The nesting of **par** types is prohibited. This can be ensured by a type system [5].

The parallel constructs of MSPML operate on parallel vectors. A MSPML program can be seen as a sequential program on this parallel data structure and is thus very different from the SPMD paradigm (of course the implementation of the library is done in SPMD style). Those parallel vectors are created by **mkpar**, so that (**mkpar** f) stores (f i) on process i for i between 0 and $(p-1)$. We usually write **fun** pid $\rightarrow$ e for f to show that the expression e may be different on each process. This expression e is said to be *local*. The expression (**mkpar** f) is a parallel object and it is said to be *global*. For example the expression **mkpar(fun** pid $\rightarrow$ pid) will be evaluated to the parallel vector $\langle 0, \ldots, p-1 \rangle$.

In the MPM model, an algorithm is expressed as a combination of asynchronous local computations and phases of communication. Asynchronous phases are programmed with **mkpar** and with **apply**.

It is such as **apply** (**mkpar** f) (**mkpar** e) stores (f i) (e i) on process i.

The communication phases are expressed by **get** and **mget**. The semantics of **get** is given by the following equation where % is the modulo:

$$
\mathbf{get} \langle v_0, \ldots, v_{p-1} \rangle \langle i_0, \ldots, i_{p-1} \rangle \;=\; \langle v_{i_0 \% p}, \ldots, v_{i_{(p-1)} \% p} \rangle
$$

The **mget** function is a generalization which allows to request data from several processes during the same m-step and to deliver different messages to different processes. It is omitted here for the sake of conciseness (as well as the global conditional).

A MSPML program is correct only if each process performs the same overall number of m-steps, thus the same number of calls to **get** (or **mget**). Incorrect programs could be written when nested parallelism is used. This is why it is currently forbidden (a type system can enforce this restriction [5]).

Some useful functions can be defined using the primitives. This set of functions constitutes the standard MSPML library (http://mspml.free.fr). For example, the direct broadcast function which realizes a broadcast can be written:

let bcast root vv = **get** vv (replicate root)

The semantics of bcast is: bcast $\langle v_0, \ldots, v_{p-1} \rangle\, r = \langle v_{r\%p}, \ldots, v_{r\%p} \rangle$.

3.   Management of Communication Environments

To explain how the communication environments could be emptied, the low-level semantics of MSPML should be presented.

During the execution of and MSPML program, at each process i the system has a variable $\mathbf{mstep}_i$ containing the number of the current m-step. Each time the expression **get** vv vi is evaluated, at a given process i:

1 $\mathbf{mstep}_i$ is increased by one.

2 the value this process holds in parallel vector vv is stored together with the value of $\mathbf{mstep}_i$ in the communication environment. A communication environment can be seen as an association list which relates m-step numbers with values.

3 the value j this process holds in parallel vector vi is the process number from which the process i wants to receive a value. Thus process i sends a request to process j: it asks for the value at m-step $\mathbf{mstep}_i$. When process j receives the request (threads are dedicated to handle requests, so the work of process j is not interrupted by the request), there are two cases:

   ■ $\mathbf{mstep}_j \geq \mathbf{mstep}_i$: it means that process j has already reached the same m-step than process i. Thus process j looks in its communication environment for the value associated with m-step $\mathbf{mstep}_i$ and sends it to process i

   ■ $\mathbf{mstep}_j < \mathbf{mstep}_i$: nothing can be done until process j reaches the same m-step than process i.

If $i = j$ the step 2 is of course not performed.

In a real implementation of MSPML, the size of the communication environment is of course limited. It is necessary to provide the runtime system a parameter called the asynchrony depth. This value, called **mstepmax**, is the size of the communication environment in terms of number of values it can store (number of m-steps). The implementation of communication environments are arrays **com_env** of size **mstepmax**, each element of the array being a kind of pointer to the serialized value stored at the m-step whose number is the array index.

A problem arises when the communication environments are full. When the array at one process is filled then the process must wait because it cannot proceed the next m-step. When all the communication environments are full, a global synchronization occurs and the arrays are emptied. The m-step counter is also reset to its initial value.

The advantage of this method is its simplicity. Nevertheless it could be inefficient in terms of memory but also in terms of execution time since a global synchronization is needed. Note that it is not only due to the communication cost of the synchronization barrier which is $g \times (p-1) + L$ (please see definitions in section 2) for each process but also to the fact that a globally balanced program but always locally imbalanced (which means that the communication steps never occur at the same time) could lose a lot of efficiency. Thus another mechanism could be proposed.

In order to avoid the waste of memory, each process should free the useless values stored in its communication environment. These useless values are those whose associated m-step (the index in the array) is lower than the m-step counter of each process, or to say it differently lower than the smallest m-step counter.

Of course this information cannot be updated at each m-step without performing a global synchronization, but it can be updated when a communication occur between two processes. These processes could exchange their knowledge of the current state of the other processes. To do so, each process has in addition to its **com_env** array of size **mstepmax** and to its m-step counter **mstep**: a value **mstepmin**, the smallest known m-step counter.

The **com_env** array is now a kind of queue. If $mstep - mstepmin \leq mstepmax$ then there is still enough room to add a value in the communication environment at index $mstep\%mstepmax$. The problem now is to update the value **mstepmin**.

This can be done using an array **msteps** of size p the last known m-step counters, the value of **msteps** at index i at process i being unused (if used it should be the value **mstep**). Without changing the data exchanged for performing a **get**, each time a process i requests a value from a process j, it sends its **mstep** value. This value is put in the array **msteps** of process j at index i. When the process j answers, i knows that j has at least reached the same m-step as itself and it can update its array **msteps** at index j.

The new value of **mstepmin**, which is the minimum of the values of the array **msteps**, could be computed only when needed, ie when the array **com_env** is full, or could be computed each time a value is changed in the array **msteps**. In the former case there may be a waste of memory, but in the latter case there is a small overhead for the computation of the new value.

As an example we could have a MSPML program in which we evaluate (bcast 0 vec) on a 3-processors machine. At the beginning each processor has the following **msteps** array: | -1 | -1 | -1 | (here we use at process i the value at index i). After the first get is done, the **msteps** arrays are:

Processor: 0   1   2

msteps: | 0 | 0 | 0 | | 0 | 0 | -1 | | 0 | -1 | 0 |

In fact, at the first m-step, process 0 has no communication request to do, so it may reach the m-step number 1 before the communications are done with the two other processes. So at process 0, the **msteps** array is more likely to be: | 1 | 0 | 0 |. In both cases the first cell of the **com_env** array at process 0 could be freed.

To increase the updating of the **mstepmin** value, we can change the data exchanged during a **get**. When a process j answers to a request from a process i it could send the answer plus its **mstep** value to process i which updates its array **msteps** at index j.

In the previous example, assuming process 0 reached m-step number 1 before the communications are done with the two other processes, we would have:

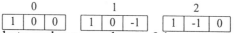

It is also possible to exchange a subpart of the arrays **msteps** during a **get** to improve the updating of **mstepmin**. To do so we can keep a fixed number of process identifiers for which the information has the most recently been updated. In the previous example, assuming we keep only one identifier of the most recently updated process and that the request from process 1 arrives at process 0 before the request from process 2 we would have **msteps**[1] $= 0$ at process 2. With this solution the first cell of the **com_env** environment at process 2 could be freed also after the first m-step.

Unfortunately these various protocols have a flaw: if one processor does not communicate at all with the remaining of the parallel machine, its **mstepmin** value will never be updated and this process will be blocked as soon as its communication environment will be full. The solution to avoid deadlock is that each time a process is blocked because of a full communication environment, then it will request, after some delay, the value of **mstep** from one or several other processes. This could be from only one processor at random, or from all the processes. The former case decrease the chance to obtain a new value for **mstepmin** but the latter is of course more costly.

We performed some experiments corresponding to the various versions presented in the examples [13]. Even when a reasonable subpart of **msteps** is exchanged, the overhead is very small. Thus usually this would be more interesting to use this protocol than to empty the communication environments after a global synchronization barrier.

4.   Comparison to Related Work

Caml-flight, a functional parallel language [3], relies on the wave mechanism. A **sync** primitive is used to indicated which processes could exchange messages using a **get** primitive which is very different from ours: this primitive asks the remote evaluation of an expression given as argument. This mechanism is more complex than ours and there is no pure functional high level semantics for Caml-flight. Moreover Caml-flight programs are SPMD programs which are more difficult to write and read. The environments used could store $p - 1$ values at each step. An asynchrony depth is also used in Caml-Flight but it should usually be much smaller than in MSPML.

There are several works on extension of the BSPlib library or libraries to avoid synchronization barrier (for example [10]) which rely on different kind of messages counting. To our knowledge the only extension to the BSPlib standard which offers zero-cost synchronization barriers and which is available for downloading is the PUB library [2]. The **bsp_oblsync** function takes as argument the number of messages which should be received before the superstep could end. This is of course less expensive than a synchronization barrier but it is also less flexible (the number of messages have to be known). With this oblivious synchronization, two processes could be at different super-steps. Two kind of communications are possible: to send a value (either in message-passing style or in direct remote memory access, or DRMA, style) or to request a value (in DRMA style). In the former case, the process which done more super-steps could send a value (using **bsp_put** or **bsp_send**) to the other process. This message is then stored in a queue at the destination. In the latter case the PUB documentation indicates that a **bsp_get** produces "a communication" both at the process which requests the value and the process which receives the request. Thus it is impossible in this case that the two processes are not in the same super-step. MSPML being a functional language, this kind of put-like communication is not possible. But the get communication of MSPML is more flexible than PUB's one.

The careful management of memory is also very important in distributed languages where references to remote values or objects can exist. There are many distributed garbage collection techniques [9, 15]. They could be hardly compared to our mechanism since there are no such references in MSPML. The management of the communication environments is completely independent from the (local) garbage collection of Objective Caml: the values put by a **get** operation are *copied* in the communication environments making safe the collection, at any time, of these values by the GC.

5.   Conclusions and Future Work

There are several ways to manage the communication environments of Minimally Synchronous Parallel ML. In most cases a small additional exchange of information during each communication provide the best overall solution, both in term of memory usage and time.

We will prove the correctness of the presented mechanism using Abstract State Machines [7] by modeling the **get** operation with communicating evolving algebras [6]. The properties will be expressed using First Order Timed Logic [1] and the verification will be automated using model checking tools. We also will perform more experiments, especially with applications rather than examples. In particular we will further investigate the implementation of the Diffusion algorithmic skeleton [8, 14] using MSPML and applications implemented using this algorithmic skeleton.

References

[1] D. Beauquier and A. Slissenko. A first order logic for specification of timed algorithms: basic properties and a decidable class. *Annals of Pure and Applied Logic*, 113, 2002.

[2] O. Bonorden, B. Juurlink, I. von Otte, and O. Rieping. The Paderborn University BSP (PUB) library. *Parallel Computing*, 29(2):187–207, 2003.

[3] E. Chailloux and C. Foisy. A Portable Implementation for Objective Caml Flight. *Parallel Processing Letters*, 13(3):425–436, 2003.

[4] F. Dehne. Special issue on coarse-grained parallel algorithms. *Algorithmica*, 14, 1999.

[5] F. Gava and F. Loulergue. A Polymorphic Type System for Bulk Synchronous Parallel ML. In *PaCT 2003*, number 2763 in LNCS, pp. 215–229. Springer, 2003.

[6] P. Glavan and D. Rosenzweig. Communicating Evolving Algebras. In *Computer Science Logic*, number 702 in LNCS, pp. 182–215. Springer, 1993.

[7] Y. Gurevich. Evolving Algebras 1993: Lipari Guide. In *Specification and Validation Methods*, pp. 9–36. Oxford University Press, 1995.

[8] Z. Hu, H. Iwasaki, and M. Takeichi. An accumulative parallel skeleton for all. In *European Symposium on Programming*, number 2305 in LNCS, pp. 83–97. Springer, 2002.

[9] R. Jones. *Garbage Collection: algorithms for automatic dynamic memory management* . Wiley, 1999.

[10] Jin-Soo Kim, Soonhoi Ha, and Chu Shik Jhon. Relaxed barrier synchronization for the BSP model of computation on message-passing architectures. *Information Processing Letters*, 66(5):247–253, 1998.

[11] Xavier Leroy. The Objective Caml System 3.07, 2003. web pp. at www.ocaml.org.

[12] F. Loulergue. Implementation of a Functional Bulk Synchronous Parallel Programming Library. In *14th IASTED PDCS Conference*, pp. 452–457. ACTA Press, 2002.

[13] F. Loulergue. Management of Communication Environments for Minimally Synchronous Parallel ML. Technical Report 2004-06, University of Paris 12, LACL, 2004.

[14] F. Loulergue, F. Gava, M. Arapinis, and F. Dabrowski. Semantics and Implementation of Minimally Synchronous Parallel ML. *International Journal of Computer & Information Science*, 2004. to appear.

[15] David Plainfossé and Marc Shapiro. A survey of distributed garbage collection techniques. In *Proc. Int. Workshop on Memory Management*, 1995.

[16] J. L. Roda, C. Rodríguez, D. G. Morales, and F. Almeida. Predicting the execution time of message passing models. *Concurrency: Practice and Experience*, 11(9):461–477, 1999.

[17] D. B. Skillicorn, J. M. D. Hill, and W. F. McColl. Questions and Answers about BSP. *Scientific Programming*, 6(3):249–274, 1997.

[18] M. Snir and W. Gropp. *MPI the Complete Reference*. MIT Press, 1998.

ANALYSIS OF THE MULTI-PHASE COPYING GARBAGE COLLECTION ALGORITHM

Norbert Podhorszki
MTA SZTAKI
H-1518 Budapest, P.O.Box 63
pnorbert@sztaki.hu

Abstract   The multi-phase copying garbage collection was designed to avoid the need for large amount of reserved memory usually required for the copying types of garbage collection algorithms. The collection is performed in multiple phases using the available free memory. The number of phases depends on the size of the reserved memory and the ratio of the garbage and accessible objects.

Keywords: Garbage collection, logic programming.

Introduction

In the execution of logic programming languages, a logic variable can have only one value during its existence, after its instantiation it cannot be changed. Therefore, new values cannot be stored in the same memory area. Thus, the memory consumption speed is very high and much smaller problems can be solved with declarative languages than with procedural ones. Garbage collection is a very important procedure in logic programming systems to look for memory cells that are allocated but not used (referenced) any more. Since the late 50's many garbage collection algorithms have been proposed, see classifications of them in [1][6]. The classical copying garbage collection [2] method provides a very fast one-phase collection algorithm but its main disadvantage is that the half of the memory is reserved for the algorithm. During the execution of an application, in every moment, the number of all accessible objects on a processing element must be less than the available memory for storing them. Otherwise, the system fails whether garbage collector is implemented or not. If the classical copying collector allocates the half of the memory for own use, applications may not be executed. To decrease the size of the reserved area, a multi-phase copying garbage collection (MC-GC) algorithm was presented in [4]. It has been implemented in LOGFLOW [3], a fine-grained dataflow system for executing Prolog programs on distributed systems. In this paper, the

MC-GC algorithm is analysed giving its cost and the number of phases as a function of the size of the reserved area and the ratio of garbage and accessible memory areas. A short description of the multi-phase copying garbage collection algorithm can be found in Section 1. The costs and the number of phases of the algorithm is analysed in Section 2.

1.   Multi-Phase Copying Garbage Collection Algorithm

The MC-GC algorithm splits the memory area to be collected into two parts, the Copy and the Counting area, see Figure 1. The size of the Copy area is chosen as large as possible but ensuring that all accessible objects can be moved into the available Free area. The Free area is the reserved memory area at the beginning and by not knowing the number of accessible objects in the memory, the size of the Copy area equals to the size of the Free area. In the first phase, see Figure 2, when traversing the references, objects stored in the Copy area are moved to the Free area, while objects in the Counting area are just marked (counted). At the end of the phase, the moved objects are moved to their final place at the beginning of the memory (the references are already set to this final place at the traversal).

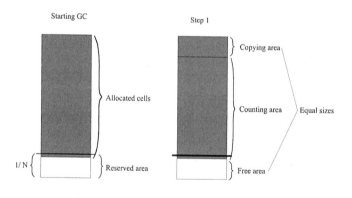

Figure 1.   MC-GC algorithm, starting

In the forthcoming phases, see Figure 3, the Counting area of the previous phase should be collected. Knowing now the number of objects in this area, the Copy area can be chosen larger than the available Free memory (which has become also larger because garbage occupying the previous Copy area are freed now). In other aspects, the algorithm is the same in all phases. The algorithm repeats the phases until the whole memory is collected.

The main advantage of MC-GC is the efficiency: it provides a sufficiently fast collector, all garbage is thrown away and a continuous memory can be used by the application without the overhead of any special memory management.

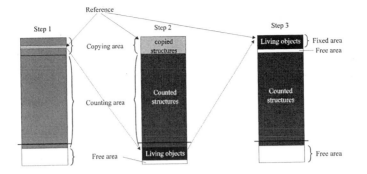

Figure 2. MC-GC algorithm, phase 1. The dashed arrows at Reference indicate the real movement of an object while the solid arrows indicate the settings of its references

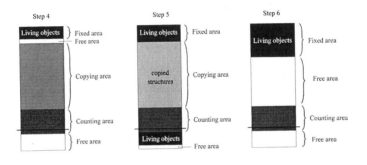

Figure 3. MC-GC algorithm, further phases

2. Analysis of the algorithm

Let us denote

O_A	number of accessible objects in the memory
O_G	number of inaccessible objects (i.e. garbage)
R	number of references all together, where
	R_S is the number of references to different objects +
	R_M is the number of other references
C_{copy}	the cost of copying an object in the memory
C_{update}	the cost for updating a reference
C_{check}	the cost of checking/traversing the reference

The C_{check} is the cost of reading the value of a reference and reading the memory of the object that is referenced. The C_{update} is the additional cost of updating the reference, that is, writing the new address into the reference.

The original copying garbage collection algorithm traverses all references once and moves the accessed objects once in the memory while updating the reference to it as well. That is, the algorithm's cost function is:

$$C_{CopyingGC} = R_S * (C_{copy} + C_{update} + C_{check}) + R_M * (C_{update} + C_{check})$$
$$= R_S * C_{copy} + R * C_{update} + R * C_{check} \tag{1}$$

To determine the cost of the MC-GC algorithm, let us denote

$Copy_N$	the copying area of the memory in phase N
$Count_N$	the counting area of the memory in phase N
$R\vert_{Copy_N}$	number of references that point into the area which becomes the copying area in the Nth phase of the algorithm
$R_S\vert_{Copy_N}$	number of references to different objects (from $R\vert_{Copy_N}$)
$R_S\vert_{Count_N}$	number of references to different objects in counting area of phase N
C_{count}	cost of counting (updating a counter)
$C_{BlockCopy_N}$	cost of copying one large memory block of phase N

When a reference is accessed in MC-GC, one of the following operations is performed: the referenced object is in the copying area and is moved thus, the reference is updated (cost C_{update}); the referenced object is in the counting area and thus, the reference is counted (cost C_{count}); the referenced object has been already moved in previous phases and thus, nothing is done to the reference. In all of the three cases, however, the reference has been checked / traversed, so this operation has also some cost (C_{check}).

First, let us determine the steps of the algorithm in phase k. Objects in the $Copy_k$ area are copied into the free area ($R_S\vert_{Copy_k} * C_{copy}$). All references pointing into $Copy_k$ are updated ($R\vert_{Copy_k} * C_{update}$) and all references pointing into $Count_k$ are counted (but one object only once) ($R_S\vert_{Count_k} * C_{count}$). Additionally, all references are checked. At the end of the phase, the contiguous area of the copied objects is moved with one block copy to the final place of the objects ($C_{BlockCopy_k}$):

$$C_{phase_k} = R_S\vert_{Copy_k} * C_{copy} + R\vert_{Copy_k} * C_{update} + R * C_{check} +$$
$$+ R_S\vert_{Count_k} * C_{count} + C_{BlockCopy_k} \tag{2}$$

For simplicity, let us consider that the costs of block copies are identical, i.e. $C_{BlockCopy1} = ... = C_{BlockCopyN}$. The cost of the MC-GC algorithm is the sum of all phases, from 1 to N:

$$C_{MCGC} = C_{phase_1} + ... + C_{phase_N} =$$
$$= (R_S\vert_{Copy_1} + ... + R_S\vert_{Copy_N}) * C_{copy} + (R\vert_{Copy_1} + ... + R\vert_{Copy_N}) * C_{update} +$$
$$+ N * R * C_{check} + (R_S\vert_{Count_1} + ... + R_S\vert_{Count_N}) * C_{count} + N * C_{BlockCopy}$$
$$\tag{3}$$

The copying areas ($Copy_1...Copy_N$) cover the whole memory exactly once thus, $R_S\vert_{Copy_1} + ... + R_S\vert_{Copy_N} = R_S$ and $R\vert_{Copy_1} + ... + R\vert_{Copy_N} = R$.

Without knowing the sizes of each counting area, the value of $R_S|_{Count_1} + \ldots + R_S|_{Count_N}$ cannot be calculated. An upper estimate is given in [5]: $(N - 1)/2 * R_S$. Thus, the cost of the algorithm is

$$
\begin{aligned}
C_{MCGC} = {} & R_S * C_{copy} + R * C_{update} + N * R * C_{check} + \\
& + (N - 1)/2 * R_S * C_{count} + N * C_{BlockCopy}
\end{aligned}
\tag{4}
$$

The final equation shows, that each object is copied once and all references are updated once as in the original copying garbage collection algorithm. However, the references have to be checked once in each phase, i.e. N times if there are N phases. Additional costs to the original algorithm are the counting of references and the N memory block copies. The number of phases is analysed in the next section.

Number of phases in the MC-GC algorithm

Intuitively, it can be seen that the number of phases in this algorithm depends on the size of the reserved area and the ratio of the accessible and garbage cells. Therefore, we are looking for an equation where the number of phases is expressed as a function of these two parameters. The MC-GC algorithm performs N phases of collections until the Copy∪Count area becomes empty. To determine the number of phases in the algorithm, we focus on the size of Copy∪Count area and try to determine, when it becomes zero.

Note, that the first phase of the algorithm is different from other phases in that the size of the Copy area equals to the Free area while in other phases it can become larger than the actual size of the Free area. It is ensured that the number of the accessible cells in the Copy area equals to the size of the Free area but the Copy area contains garbage cells as well. Therefore, we need to consider the first and other phases separately in the deduction. Let us denote

M	number of all cells (size of the memory)
F_N	number of free cells in phase N (i.e. size of the Free area)
A_N	number of accessible cells in area $Copy_N$ in phase N
G_N	number of garbage cells in area $Copy_N$ in phase N
	i.e. size of $Copy_N = A_N + G_N$
C_N	number of cells in $Copy_N * Count_N$ area in phase N

The size of the $Copy1 \cup Count1$ area is the whole memory without the free area: $C_1 = M - F1$. When the first phase is finished, the accessible cells of $Copy_1$ (A_1) are moved into their final place. The size of the free area (F_2) in the next phase is determined by the algorithm somehow and thus, the $Copy_2 \cup Count2$ area is the whole memory except the moved cells (A_1) and the current Free area (F_2). From the second phase, in each step, the $Copy_N \cup Count_N$ area is the whole memory except all the moved cells ($A_1 + \ldots + A_{N-1}$) and the current Free area (F_N):

$$C_1 = M - F_1 \quad \text{and} \quad C_N = M - A_1 - ... - A_{N-1} - F_N, N \geq 2 \quad (5)$$

At each phase (except the first one) the algorithm chooses as large Copy area as possible, that is, it ensures that the accessible cells in the $Copy_N$ area (A_N) is less or equal to the size of the free area (F_N). The equality or inequality depends on the quality of the counting in the previous phase only. Let us suppose that the equality holds: $A_N = F_N, N \geq 2$. Thus we get, that the size of the $Copy_N \cup Count_N$ area is

$$C_N = M - A_1 - \sum_{k=2}^{N} F_k \quad, N \geq 2 \quad (6)$$

We can see from the above equation that the size of the working area depends from the sizes of the free areas of all phases. Let us turn now to the determination of the size of the free area in each step. At start, the size of the copying area ($Copy_1$) is chosen to be equal to the size of the reserved free area (F_1), that is F_1 equals to the number of the accessible cells (A_1) plus the garbage cells (G_1) in $Copy_1$: $F_1 = A_1 + G_1$. The free area ($Free_2$) in the second phase is the previous free area ($Free_1$) plus what becomes free from the $Copy_1$ area. The latter one equals to the number of garbage cells of $Copy_1$ (G_1). The same holds for the free areas in all further phases. Thus,

$$F_1 = A_1 + G_1 \text{ and } F_N = F_{N-1} + G_{N-1} = F_1 + G_1 + G_2 + ... + G_{N-1}, N \geq 2 \quad (7)$$

Let us consider the ratio of the garbage and accessible cells in the memory to be able to reason further. Let us denote

r the ratio of garbage and accessible cells in the memory;
                        $r \in [0, 1), r = 0$ means that there is no garbage at all,
                        $r = 1$ would mean that there are no accessible cells.

Note that the case of $r = 1$ is excluded because there will be a division by $1/r$ in the following equations. The case of $r = 1$ means that there is only garbage in the memory and no accessible cells. This is the best case for the algorithm and the number of phases is always 2 independently from the size of the memory and the reserved area (without actually copying a single cell or updating a single reference).

Let us suppose that the accessible cells and the garbage cells are spread in the memory homogenously, that is, for all part of memory, the ratio of garbage and accessible cells is r. We need to express G_N and F_N as a function of F_1 and r and thus be able to express C_N as a function of F_1 and the ratio r.

At the beginning, the size of $Copy_1$ area equals to the size of the $Free_1$ area, $F_1 = A_1 + G_1$. The ratio of garbage (G_1) and accessible cells (A_1) in

$Copy_1$ area is r by our assumption. Thus, $G_1 = r * F1$. From the second phase, the size of accessible cells in the $Copy_N$ area (A_N) equals to the size of the $Free_N$ area (F_N). The ratio of A_N and G_N is again r by our assumption. Thus,

$$\frac{G_N}{A_N} = \frac{r}{1-r} \Rightarrow G_N = \frac{r}{1-r} F_N \quad r \in [0,1), N \geq 2 \tag{8}$$

The size of the garbage in each phase is now expressed as a function of F_N. We need to express F_N as a function of F_1 to finish our reasoning. By equations 7 and 8 and by recursion on F_N:

$$F_2 = F_1 + G_1 = (1+r) * F_1$$

$$F_N = F_{N-1} - G_{N-1} = F_{N-1} + \frac{r}{1-r} F_{N-1} = \frac{1}{1-r} F_{N-1} \quad , N \geq 3 \tag{9}$$

$$F_N = \frac{1+r}{(1-r)^{N-2}} * F_1, \quad , N \geq 2$$

Finally, we express C_N as the function of F_1 and the ratio of the garbage and accessible cells, that is, equation 6 can be expressed as (expressing A_1 as $(1-r) * F_1$)

$$C_N = M - (1-r) * F_1 - \sum_{k=2}^{N} \frac{1+r}{(1-r)^{k-2}} F_1$$

$$C_N = M - \left((1-r) + \frac{1+r}{(1-r)^{N-2}} * \sum_{k=0}^{N-2} (1-r)^k \right) * F_1 \quad N \geq 2 \tag{10}$$

$$C_N = M - \frac{1+r-(1-r)^{N-1}}{r(1-r)^{N-2}} * F_1$$

Corollary.   For a given size of the reserved area (F1) and a given ratio of garbage and accessible cells (r) in the memory, the MC-GC algorithm performs N phases of collection if and only if $C_{N+1} \leq 0$ and $C_N > 0$.

The worst case for copying garbage collection algorithms is that when there is no garbage, that is, all objects (cells) in the memory are accessible and should be kept. In the equations above, the worst case means that $r = 0$. From equation 9, $F_N = F_1$ and thus from equation 10, $C_N = M - N * F1$. As a consequence, to ensure that at most N phases of collections are performed by MC-GC independently from the amount of garbage, the size of the reserved area should be $1/N + 1$ part of the available memory size. If we reserve half of the memory we get the original copying collection algorithm, performing the garbage collection in one single phase. If we reserve $1/3$ part of memory, at most two phases are performed.

In the general case, the equation 10 is too complex to see immediately, how many phases are performed for a given r and F_1. If half of the memory contains garbage ($r = 0.5$), $1/5$ of the memory is enough to reserve to have at most two phases. Very frequently, the ratio of garbage is even higher (80-90%) and according to the equation 10% reserved memory is enough to have at most two phases. In practice, with 10% reserved memory the number of phases varies between 2 and 4, according to the actual garbage ratio. In the LOGFLOW system, the MC-GC algorithm performs well, resulting 10-15% slowdown in the execution in the worst case and usually between 2-5%.

3. Conclusion

The Multi-Phase Copying Garbage Collection algorithm belongs to the copying type of garbage collection techniques. However, it does not need the half of the memory as a reserved area. Knowing the ratio of the garbage and accessible objects in a system, and by setting a limit on the number of phases and the cost of the algorithm, the size of the required reserved area can be computed. The algorithm can be used in systems where the order of objects in memory is not important and the whole memory is equally accessible. A modification of the algorithm for virtual memory using memory pages can be found in [5].

References

[1] J. Cohen: Garbage Collection of Linked Data Structures. *Computing Surveys*, Vol. 13, No. 3, September 1981.

[2] R. Fenichel, J. Yochelson: A LISP garbage collector for virtual memory computer systems. *Communications of ACM*, Vol. 12, No. 11, 611-612, Nov. 1969.

[3] P. Kacsuk: Execution models for a Massively Parallel Prolog Implementation. *Journal of Computers and Artifical Intelligence*. Slovak Academy of Sciences, Vol. 17, No. 4, 1998, pp. 337-364 (part 1) and Vol. 18, No. 2, 1999, pp. 113-138 (part 2)

[4] N. Podhorszki: Multi-Phase Copying Garbage Collection in LOGFLOW. In: Parallelism and Implementation of Logic and Constraint Logic Programming, Ines de Castro Dutra et al. (eds.), pp. 229-252. Nova Science Publishers, ISBN 1-56072-673-3, 1999.

[5] N. Podhorszki: Performance Issues of Message-Passing Parallel Systems. PhD Thesis, ELTE University of Budapest, 2004.

[6] P. R. Wilson: Uniprocessor Garbage Collection Techniques. Proc. of the 1992 Intl. Workshop on Memory Management, St. Malo, France, Yves Bekkers and Jacques Cohen, eds.). Springer-Verlag, LNCS 637, 1992.

A CONCURRENT IMPLEMENTATION OF SIMULATED ANNEALING AND ITS APPLICATION TO THE VRPTW OPTIMIZATION PROBLEM

Agnieszka Debudaj-Grabysz[1] and Zbigniew J. Czech[2]

[1]*Silesia University of Technology, Gliwice, Poland;* [2]*Silesia University of Technology, Gliwice, and University of Silesia, Sosnowiec, Poland*

Abstract: It is known, that concurrent computing can be applied to heuristic methods (e.g. simulated annealing) for combinatorial optimization to shorten time of computation. This paper presents a communication scheme for message passing environment, tested on the known optimization problem – VRPTW. Application of the scheme allows speed-up without worsening quality of solutions – for one of Solomon's benchmarking tests the new best solution was found.

Key words: simulated annealing, message passing, VRPTW, parallel processing, communication.

1.   INTRODUCTION

Desire to reduce time to get a solution is the reason to develop concurrent versions of existing sequential algorithms. This paper describes an attempt to parallelize the simulated annealing (SA) – a heuristic method of optimization. Heuristic methods are applied when the universe of possible solutions of the problem is so large, that it cannot be scanned in finite – or at least acceptable – time. Vehicle routing problem with time windows (VRPTW) is an example of such problems. To get a practical feeling of the subject, one can imagine a factory dealing with distribution of its own products according to incoming orders. Optimization of routing makes the distribution cost efficient, whereas parallelization accelerates the preparation of routes description. Thus, practically, vehicles can depart earlier or, alternatively, last orders could be accepted later.

The SA bibliography focuses on sequential version of the algorithm (e.g. Aarts and Korst, 1989; Salamon, Sibani and Frost, 2002), however, parallel versions are investigated too. Aarts and Korst (1989) as well as Azencott (1992) give directional recommendations as for parallelization of SA. This research refers to a known approach of parallelization of the simulated annealing, named multiple trial method (Aarts and Korst, 1989; Roussel-Ragot and Dreyfus, 1992), but introduces modifications to the known approach, with synchronization limited to solution acceptance events as the most prominent one. Simplicity of the statement could be misleading: the implementation has to overcome many practical problems with communication in order to efficiently speed up computation. For example:

- Polling is applied to detect moments when data are sent, because message passing – more precisely: Message Passing Interface (Gropp et al., 1996, Gropp and Lusk, 1996) – was selected as the communication model in the work.
- Original tuning of the algorithm was conducted. Without that tuning no speed-up was observed, especially in case of more then two processors.

As for the problem domain, VRPTW – formally formulated by Solomon, (1987), who proposed also a suite of tests for benchmarking, has a rich bibliography too, with papers of Larsen (1999) and Tan, Lee and Zhu (1999) as ones of the newest examples. There is, however, only one paper known to the authors, namely by Czech and Czarnas (2002), devoted to a parallel version of SA applied to VRPTW. In contrast to the motivation of our research, i.e. speed-up, Czech and Czarnas (2002) take advantage of the parallel algorithm to achieve higher accuracy of solutions of some Solomon instances of VRPTW.

The plan of the paper is as follows: section 2 briefs theoretical basis of the sequential and parallel SA algorithm. Section 3 describes applied message passing with synchronization at solution finding events and algorithm tuning. Section 4 collects results of experiments. The paper is concluded by brief description of possible further modifications.

2.   SIMULATED ANNEALING

In the simulated annealing one searches the optimal state, i.e. the state attributed by either minimal or maximal value of the *cost function*. It is achieved by comparing the current solution with a random solution from a specific *neighborhood*. With some probability, worse solutions could be accepted as well, which prevents convergence to local optima. The probability decreases over the process of annealing, in sync with the parameter called – by analogy to the real process – *temperature*. Ideally, the annealing should last infinitely long and temperature should decrease infinitesimally slowly. An outline of the SA algorithm is presented in Figure 1.

```
S := GetInitialSolution();
T := InitialTemperature;
for i := 1 to NumberOfTemperatureReduction do
  for j := 1 to EpochLength do
    S' := GetSolutionFromNeighborhood();
    ΔC := CostFunction(S') - CostFunction(S);
    if  ΔC<0 or AcceptWithProbabilityP(ΔC)
      S := S'
    end if
  end for;
  T := λT
end for
```

Figure 1. SA algorithm

A single execution of the inner loop step is called a *trial*.

In multiple trial parallelism (Aarts and Korst, 1989) trials run concurrently on separate processors. A more detailed description of this strategy is given by Azencott (1992). By assumption, there are p processors available and working in parallel. At time i the process of annealing is characterized by a configuration belonging to the universe of solutions. At $i+1$, every processor generates a solution. The new one, common for all configurations, is randomly selected from accepted solutions. If no solution is accepted, then the configuration from time i is not changed.

3. COMMUNICATION SCHEME OF CONCURRENT SIMULATED ANNEALING

The master-slave communication scheme proposed by Roussel-Ragot and Dreyfus (1992) is the starting point of this research. It refers to shared memory model, so it can be assumed that time to exchange information among processors is neglectable – the assumption is not necessarily true in case of message passing environment. Because timing of events requiring information to be sent is not known in advance, polling is used to define timing of information arrival: in every step of the algorithm, processors check whether there is a message to be received. This is the main modification of the Roussel-Ragot and Dreyfus scheme applied, resulting from the assumption that time to check, if there is a message to receive is substantially shorter than time to send and receive a message. Among other modifications, let us mention that there is no master processor: an accepted solution is broadcast to all processors.

Two strategies to organize asynchronous communication in distributed systems are defined in literature (Fujimoto, 2000). The first strategy, so called optimistic, assumes that processors work totally asynchronously, however it must be possible for them to step back to whatever point. This is due to the fact that independent processors can get information on a solution that has been found with some delay.

In this research the focus is put on the second, conservative strategy. It assumes that when an event occurs which requires information to be sent, the sending processor does not undertake any further actions without acknowledgement from remaining processors that they have received the information. In our paper the proposed model of communication, conforming to the conservative strategy, is named as *model with synchronization at solution acceptance events*. The model is not purely asynchronous, but during a sequence of steps when no solution is found it allows asynchronous work.

3.1   Implementation of communication with synchronization at solution acceptance events

The scheme of communication assumes that when a processor finds a new solution, all processors must be synchronized to align their configurations:

1. Processors work asynchronously.
2. The processor which finds a solution broadcasts a synchronization request.
3. The processor requesting synchronization stops after the broadcast.
4. The processor which gets the request takes part in synchronization.
5. During synchronization processors exchange their data, i.e. each processor receives information on what all other processors have accepted and how many trials each of them have done. After this, processors select solution individually, according to the same criteria:
   - if only one solution is accepted it is automatically selected
   - if more than one solution is accepted, then the one generated at the processor with the lowest rank (order number) is selected; it is analogous to a random selection

– an effective number of investigated moves L_b^* between two synchronization points is calculated according to the following formula:

$$L_b^* = (sum\_of\_trials - p) + \frac{p+1}{p-r+1}$$

where *sum_of_trials* is the total number of trials, r is the number of rejected moves, p is the number of processors.
6. Following synchronization and agreement on a new solution, processors continue work asynchronously.

3.2 Tuning of the algorithm

To analyze the process of passing the messages, the program Jumpshot-3 was used (Chan, Gropp and Lusk, 2000). It is a visualization tool to trace data written in *scalable log format* (SLOG), generated by parallel program during its execution. Jumpshot displays Gantt charts visualizing MPI functions together with arrows that indicate messages. In Figure 2:
- Processor 0 (top one in the picture) accepts the solution and sends synchronization request (SEND instruction) to the processor 1 (bottom one).
- Processor 1 checks, if there is a message that can be received (IPROBE instruction).
- Processors agree on solutions (two ALLREDUCE instruction).
- Processor 0 broadcasts the data (BCAST instruction).
- Additionally, two IPROBE instructions delimit the computation phase.
  Looking at the picture, it is clear that duration of the communication is too long compared to the duration of the computation phase. So the following improvements were implemented:
- The long message was split into two.
- Data structure was reorganized: table of structures gave way to a structure of tables.
- Two ALLREDUCE instructions were merged.
  The resulting efficiency gain is clearly visible in Figure 3.

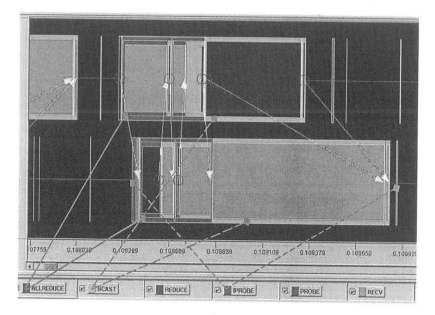

Figure 2. Communication before improvement

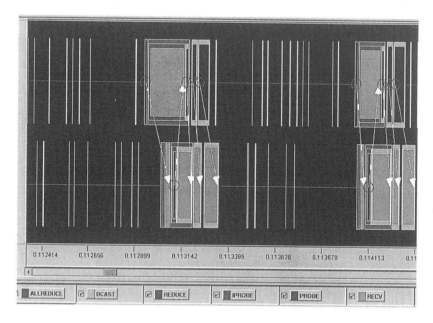

Figure 3. Communication after improvement

4. EXPERIMENTAL RESULTS

4.1 VRPTW

It is assumed that there is a warehouse, centrally located to n customers (cities). There is a road d_{ij} between each pair of customers $(i,j = 1, 2, ..., n)$ and between each customer and the warehouse $(i = 0)$. The objective is to supply goods to all customers at minimum cost vehicle routes (i.e. total travel distance should be minimized). Each customer has its own demand q_i and associated time window $[e_i, f_i]$, where e_i and f_i determine the earliest and the latest time to start servicing. Each customer should be visited only once. Each route must start and terminate at the warehouse, and should preserve maximum vehicle capacity Q. The warehouse also has its own time window, i. e. each route must start and terminate within this window. The solution with least number of route legs (the first goal of optimization) is better then a solution with smallest total distance traveled (the second goal of optimization).

The sequential algorithm by Czarnas (2002) was the basis for parallelization. The main parameters of annealing for the *reduction of the number of route legs phase* (phase 1) and the *reduction of the route length phase* (phase 2) have been assumed as follows:

- *Cooling schedule* – temperature decreases according to the formula: $T_{i+1} = \lambda T_i$, where cooling ratio λ is 0.85 in the phase 1 and 0.98 in the phase 2.
- *Epoch length* – the number of trials executed at each temperature – is 10 n^2, (n means the number of customers).
- *Termination conditions:* SA stops after 40 temperature reductions in phase 1 and 200 temperature reductions in phase 2.

5. IMPLEMENTATION

Experiments were carried out on UltraSPARC Sun Enterprise installed at the Silesia University of Technology Computer Center.

A test means a series of concurrent computations, carried out on an increasing number of processors to observe the computation time and qualitative parameters. The numerical data were obtained by running the program a number of times (up to 100) for the same set of parameters. Tests belong to two of Solomon's benchmarking problem sets (RC1 – narrow time windows and RC2 – wide time window) with 100 customers. The measured time is the real time of the execution, reported by time command of UNIX system. Processes had the highest priority to simulate the situation of exclusive access to a multi-user machine.

The relationship between speed-up and number of processors is graphically shown in Figure 4. Formally, speed-up denotes a quotient of the computation time on one processor and computation time on p processors. Data illustrating lowest and highest speed-up for both sets are shown.

As for quality of results it should be noted that the algorithm gives very good solutions, usually best known. Specifically, **for the set RC202 the new best solution was found** with total distance of 1365.64.

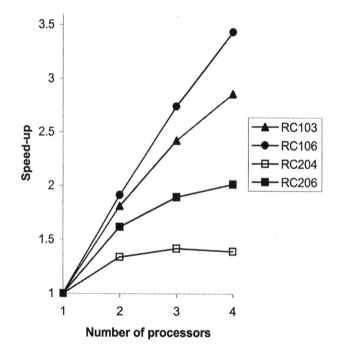

Figure 4. Relationship between speed-up and number of engaged processors for sets RC1 and RC2

6.   CONCLUSIONS

- The development of a communication model and its implementation for a concurrent version of multiple trial simulated annealing in message passing environment was proposed.
- Testing on VRPTW shows speed-up increases with number of processors for majority of benchmark tests (the saturation as in case of RC204 was

observed only for two tests). At the same time there in no clear relationship between the average cost and the number of processors, however, often the cost is better than in case of single processor (more detailed data available on request).

- Further possible improvements are:
  - Broadcasting only sequence of moves instead of sending the whole solution
  - Application of optimistic strategy to asynchronous communication
  - Clustering as described by Aarts (1986).

REFERENCES

Aarts, E.H.L, and Korst, J., 1989, *Simulated Annealing and Boltzman Machines*, John Wiley & Sons.

Aarts, E.H.L., 1986, Parallel implementation of the statistical cooling algorithm. *INTEGRATION, the VLSI journal*.

Azencott, R., ed., 1992, *Simulated Annealing. Parallelization Techniques*, John Wiley & Sons.

Chan, A., Gropp, W., and Lusk, E., 2000, A tour of Jumpshot-3, ftp:// ftp.mcs.anl.gov/pub/mpi/nt /binaries.

Czarnas, P, 2001, *Traveling Salesman Problem With Time Windows. Solution by Simulated Annealing*, MSc thesis (in Polish), Uniwersytet Wrocławski, Wrocław.

Czech, Z.J., and Czarnas, P., 2002, Parallel simulated annealing for the vehicle routing problem with time windows, 10th Euromicro Workshop on Parallel, Distributed and Network-based Processing, Canary Islands - Spain, (January 9-11, 2002).

Fujimoto, R.M., 2000, *Parallel and Distributed Simulation Systems*, A Wiley-Interscience Publication.

Gropp, W., Lusk, E., Doss, N., and Skjellum A., 1996, A high-performance, portable implementation of the MPI message passing interface standard, *Parallel Computing* **22**(6):789-828.

Gropp, W., and Lusk, E., 1996, *User's Guide for mpich, a Portable Implementation of MPI*, ANL-96/6, Mathematics and Computer Science Division, Argonne National Laboratory.

Larsen, J., 1999, Vehicle routing with time windows – finding optimal solutions efficiently, http://citeseer.nj.nec.com/larsen99vehicle.html, (September 15, 1999).

Roussel-Ragot, P., and Dreyfus, G., 1992, Parallel annealing by multiple trials: an experimental study on a transputer network, in Azencott (1992), pp. 91–108.

Solomon, M., 1987, Algorithms for the vehicle routing and scheduling problem with time windows constraints, *Oper. Res.* **35**:254–265.

Salamon, P., Sibani, P., and Frost, R., 2002, *Facts, Conjectures and Improvements for Simulated Annealing*, SIAM.

Tan, K.C., Lee, L.H., and Zhu, K.Q., 1999, Heuristic methods for vehicle routing problem with time widows, 1999.

Author Index

Aichinger, Bernhard, 73
Alves, Albano, 63
Böszörményi, Lászlo, 155
Belloum, Adam, 21
Bencsura, Ákos, 121
Borkowski, J., 113
Brunst, Holger, 93
Czech, Zbigniew J., 201
Debudaj-Grabysz, Agnieszka, 201
Delaitre, Thierry, 129
Exposto, José, 63
Gansterer, Wilfried N., 39
Gourgoulis, A., 129
Goyeneche, A., 129
Heinzlreiter, Paul, 29
Hertzberger, L.O., 21
John, Sunil, 147
Juhasz, Zoltan, 13
Kacsuk, Peter, 13
Kacsukné Bruckner, Livia, 155
Kiss, Tamás, 129, 155
Kobler, Rene, 73
Kopanski, D., 113
Korkhov, Vladimir, 21
Kovács, József, 103
Kranzlmüller, Dieter, 73, 93
Lagzi, István, 137

Lendvay, György, 121
Loulergue, Frédéric, 185
Lovas, Róbert, 83, 137
Macías, Elsa M., 55
Maselino, P., 129
Mieloszyk, Krzysztof, 173
Morrison, John P., 147
Nagel, Wolfgang E., 93
Pina, António, 63
Podhorszki, Norbert, 193
Pota, Szabolcs, 13
Power, David A., 147
Rosmanith, Herbert, 3
Rufino, José, 63
Schaubschläger, Christian, 73
Sipos, Gergely, 13
Sunderam, Vaidy, 55
Suárez, Alvaro, 55
Szkaliczki, Tibor, 155
Terstyanszky, Gábor, 129
Tsujita, Yuichi, 47
Tudruj, Marek, 113
Turányi, Tamás, 137
Vécsei, Bertalan, 83
Volkert, Jens, 29, 73, 3
Weingarten, N., 129
Winter, S. C., 129
Wiszniewski, Bogdan, 173